Ipanema Turtles

A South American Adventure by Bike

Laura Mottram

Ipanema Turtles

First published 2014

ISBN-13: 978-1499386837
ISBN-10: 1499386834

Cover design © Nicky Borowiec

Contact details for the author can be found at
www.pedallingabout.com

For Paddy
The best partner I could ever wish for in the adventure that is life.

Contents

Our route around South America

1. Leaving Ipanema

Looking up into the maze of streets, I couldn't work out where the rickety collection of shacks that wrapped around the hillside ended. From the road where I stood, dusty footpaths wound up the steep slope, past grey block buildings with roofs that looked ready to take off with the coastal wind. I wondered what would happen if you were to brush against one of the thick power cables hanging at head height across the path, but I had no intention of going up there to find out. Stood at the entrance to one of Rio de Janeiro's notorious *favelas*, I already felt beyond my comfort zone and my father's parting words rattled around my head: "Watch out for bandits."

I had been in Brazil's iconic city for a few days, listening to frequent warnings from people who had me convinced criminals were waiting at every corner to attack me. Each time Paddy and I said we planned to cycle around South America, people would shake their heads and say "No, no, no. Brazil is too dangerous," or "You are crazy, it can't be done." I'd grown used to comments like these in London from people who had never been to the continent, but had expected being in Rio would reassure me this wasn't a stupid idea.

Each morning over breakfast we would watch on the news as armed police launched raids of *favelas* in search of local drug barons. There was a different operation each day, whether to entertain the viewers or simply because there were so many 'bad people' out there, we didn't know. Our hostel was in the tourist area of Ipanema, a part of town we'd chosen because of its relative safety in a city with one of the world's worst reputations for crime. In recent decades Rio had been plagued by violent gun crime, assassinations and drug-trafficking, and nearly 50,000 people had died from crime-related violence between 1978 and 2000. Even in the safer suburbs like Ipanema, residents lived behind gates with security guards and fierce dogs. "Don't go on the beach after dark." "Don't carry valuables." The endless advice on security had me fearing an attack at any minute.

My nerves were already in tatters as we wobbled away from the hostel on our shiny new bikes loaded with kit. Unaccustomed to steering with so much weight, I took it slowly as we rode along the cycle path that frames the long white Ipanema Beach. Joggers pounded the sand as I swerved around cleaners sweeping up after *caipirinha*-drinking revellers. I didn't know if we would manage to cycle all the way around South America back to this point. At that moment, I was highly doubtful we would make it out of the city.

What I hadn't realised was the first test would arise just one kilometre further on from Ipanema, under the *favela* where I now stood. The road which hugged the Atlantic Ocean, heading out of the city, had seemed the best route to leave Rio by as it would be hard to get lost along it. But instead we found the traffic heading directly towards us on a rush-hour contraflow. Undeterred, we pushed the bikes along the pavement until we found ourselves on the road, squeezed between oncoming traffic and a wall slimy with waste from the *favela*.

It was at this point that I found myself looking up and wondering how many bad guys were watching us, hatching a plan to attack. If they came there would be nowhere to escape; we were hemmed in by traffic, the ocean and the haphazard collection of huts. I broke into a jog and pushed harder. Our cycle adventure around South America had begun.

I first met Paddy in the drill hall of the University of London Officer Training Corps, a branch of the Territorial Army aimed at giving students a glimpse of life in the British Army. Two weeks earlier I had arrived in London from my hometown of Manchester, to start a degree in War Studies at Kings College London. I had absolutely no intention of signing up to the army, but I was swayed to join the ULOTC by the promise they would teach me skiing and skydiving, and pay me for the privilege, which meant fewer shifts in the wine bar where I had already found a job.

It was October 2001. The terrorist attacks on the World Trade Centre had happened only a few weeks earlier and the ULOTC was going about business as it knew it – there were no thoughts of war within this unit. All that was required of us was one night's training a week, when we learnt the theories of infantry attacks, plus one weekend a month spent in 'the field', where we would wear combats, sleep outside in the cold and run around the English countryside shooting blank rounds at each other. Afterwards, we would celebrate surviving the training exercise with a night in the pub, where people would compete to drink as much as possible without passing out.

The unit was good to its promise on adventure training, which is how one Saturday afternoon, Paddy and I ended up throwing ourselves out of a plane from 1,000 metres on a solo static line parachute jump. Paddy had joined the ULOTC in his second year at University College London, where he was studying Geology. There was no romantic connection between us at that stage but we kept in touch after the ULOTC, meeting for drinks and swapping stories of our latest failed relationships until, nearly six years after we first met, we got together as a couple.

Our timing wasn't great. I had just accepted a temporary position with a disability charity based in the Kenyan capital, Nairobi. Since university I had been building a career in fundraising and marketing within the charity sector, and I hoped this six-month role might lead to something permanent working in international development. I loved working in Kenya and tried to convince Paddy to join me, but his financial analysis job in the City of London wasn't something that could be done in chaotic Nairobi. So instead I returned to a job for a campaigning organisation working on southern Africa, on the proviso that we would look to go abroad together in the future.

While I was in Kenya, Paddy had completed a bike ride with two friends along the length of the UK, from Land's End in Cornwall to John O'Groats in Scotland. In spite of the hills and some atrocious weather riding through Devon, he fell in love with travelling by bike and set about convincing me of the virtues of long distance cycle touring. Over the next few summers our bikes carried us from London to Amsterdam, up to Hamburg and into Denmark, as we followed the North Sea Cycle Route along the coastline. We commuted to work on our bikes and spent our weekends exploring the English countryside, stopping in pubs to refuel on ploughman's lunches and dreaming of a 'real' challenge.

Our different jobs meant finding somewhere we could both work abroad was virtually impossible, and our thoughts drifted to travelling instead. Neither of us were interested in backpacking. I had spent my gap year before university carting a rucksack from buses to hostels around Africa and Australia, and I wanted an opportunity to see more than the normal tourist trail. Our recent bike trips around Europe made us think that a cycle tour would be perfect for that.

A bike is by far the best mode of transport. You pedal fast enough to get between places at a reasonable pace, but you travel at a speed that allows you to see and understand the areas you pass through. On the trip around South America we would often see sleeping backpackers zoom past in air-conditioned buses, unknowingly missing a fantastic food stall or an impromptu football match with locals. Travelling by bike is about far more than ticking off the tourist highlights, it allows you to meet people and discover places not mentioned in any guidebook.

After much deliberation, we decided to explore South America as neither of us had been there before or knew much about it. Poring over maps, we had been amazed to find three tiny countries at the top of the continent that we had never heard of – there would be plenty to discover. It would be challenging too; our route would take us over the world's second highest mountain range, through the driest desert and the largest rainforest.

From looking at other cyclist's blogs, it seemed that nearly everybody who rode through South America came down the western coast of the continent, many on the popular route from Alaska down to Ushuaia at the tip of Argentina. However, we intended to start from Rio de Janeiro's Ipanema Beach on the east coast of Brazil and continue around the continent in a clockwise loop, back to the very spot where we began. Our route would take us through every one of South America's 13 countries, giving us a glimpse into life on the continent and taking us off the beaten track.

We had chosen to start in Rio de Janeiro because, with its imposing Cristo Redentor statue looking down on the city, it felt like it represented the gateway to Brazil and South America. Plus, there were the practical reasons of direct flights from London, as well as gentler terrain on the eastern coast where we could break in our saddles and legs before we arrived at the Andes Mountains.

Our bikes were Thorn Nomads: specialised steel frames made in the UK for bike touring. They were heavy but robust, and the internal gear system meant we were likely to have fewer mechanical failures. Instead of a derailleur we were using a Rohloff hub, which from the outside made the bike look like it was single speed, with a chain that ran around one front and one back cog. However, inside there were 12 gears sitting in oil that kept the system running smoothly. This was important as neither of us had much mechanical nous. In the UK we'd been known to jump on a train home when a simple problem struck and hand them to a bike shop to repair; this wouldn't be an option in South America.

In fact, this trip would be unlike any other we'd done before. To keep costs down, we planned to camp whenever possible and would be cooking our meals on a single, multi-fuel stove. Our bags would contain all the equipment for life on the road, including sleeping bags, roll mats, kitchen kit and clothes for all temperature extremes. Trying to fit everything into four small pannier bags that hung off the front and back racks would be a complex puzzle.

We spent two years saving for the trip, putting a percentage of our monthly salaries into an account that slowly increased to the amount we thought we needed to make it around South America. At Christmas and birthdays, we asked for much needed items from each other and family, who not seeing the attraction of a head torch or a Spork would hand over their gifts apologetically, while we excitedly ripped open the parcel. We were working to a rough budget of £25 per day to cover food, accommodation and other items for the two of us. This wasn't a meagre amount by any stretch, meaning that if we couldn't find somewhere to camp we could afford to stay in basic accommodation every now and then, especially in countries like Bolivia where costs were much lower.

Our plan was to leave Rio de Janeiro in May 2011 and return by July 2012, to make it home for the 2012 Olympic Games in London. By our calculations we needed to cover an average of 80 kilometres per day, allowing us up to ten days off a month. It wasn't a tight schedule, there was room for minor delays, but we had a date to aim for. We felt that this was important as we knew that, tempted by beautiful beaches and vibrant cities, we would be prone to procrastination. Most significantly, however, it meant from the beginning we both had a goal to work towards.

Obviously, neither of us wanted the trip to jeopardise our relationship, and we agreed we wouldn't push each other to do something the other didn't want – if one of us wanted to stop, either for the day or for good, then we would stop.

If something went wrong or we didn't like it we could always come home, but this fact didn't seem to placate our family and friends. When we told our parents about our plans, my mum's response was deathly silence.

"Do you not think it's a good idea?" I asked.

"Well," she replied, as if we were ten years old, "If you want to play out on your bikes, it's up to you."

Paddy and I were both 29 and had been together for over three years. I think our families were anticipating wedding bells and babies rather than a cycle trip around South America, but we weren't quite ready for that. Although, part of me did wonder if (as long as we didn't split up) we might get engaged on the trip. I thought perhaps Paddy might propose if we made it back to Ipanema Beach, but that was a very long way away and far from the front of my thoughts.

Most of the negative comments we received (all from people who had never been to the continent) were about how dangerous South America was. Obviously, we were destined to be mugged, kidnapped or murdered, if we weren't knocked off our bikes first. If, miraculously, we did make it back to London, it would be impossible for us to get jobs again – the long break would be detrimental to our careers, apparently. We, however, didn't see it that way.

If we stayed in our jobs we knew we would spend the next year exactly like the last; we weren't due promotions and little would change in our financial position or weekly routine. We worked for money's sake, to earn enough to buy stuff we didn't really need and to go out with friends, drink too much and end up nursing hangovers. Each Monday morning the weekly cycle started again, and we would spend the next five days in stuffy offices watching the clock slowly tick down towards the weekend. It was not my idea of living life.

Throughout the trip we were asked countless times why we were riding our bikes around South America. Our stock answer was that it beat working, which always provoked a laugh. But really, we thought, given the opportunity to escape the rat race and explore by bike, "Why wouldn't you?"

2. Brazil

People were hurrying around, jostling for position and pointing long lenses in all directions. A group of priests was squeezed together, creating an allusion of being embraced by the outstretched arms above. Their robed photographer lay on the floor, contorted at strange angles and bellowing instructions as he framed the shot. His desire to get the perfect picture meant impatient tourists stepped over him as he worked. Satisfied, he finished and the priests were unceremoniously elbowed away by sightseers keen for their own snapshot moment under the colossal Cristo Redentor statue.

It was easy to share in the excitement as we leant against the thick limestone base. Looking down on the long white beach of Copacabana, we could make out the red umbrellas that shielded sunbathers from the heat of the afternoon sun. Towards the city, we watched cable cars slowly ferrying tourists to the top of the Pão de Açúcar. People who live in Rio, *Cariocas*, have another name for the city; they call it the *Cidade Maravailhosa,* and it was easy to see why.

After two years of planning, we were in the land of carnival, samba and football. Since we arrived a few days earlier we had been preparing to leave Rio, and my feelings had been switching between excitement and nervousness. In part I was impatient to get going, but the wimp in me could think of a thousand excuses to delay our departure.

The first thing on my list was to stock up on food. Travelling by bike meant we were limited as to what we could carry, so we had a carefully planned list to find in the well-stocked supermarket. Avoiding the colourful displays of exotic fruits, we headed to the aisles of non-perishable items, where we filled the basket with items like rice and pasta. We left the supermarket with heavy bags and a painful bill – bread, cheese and tomatoes for lunch had cost £8 alone. Brazil, with its growing economy, was not cheap.

Next, we needed decent maps of Brazil to guide us to the

Paraguayan border. Seemingly, road guides weren't popular with the rollerblading crew of Ipanema, so we headed into the city centre instead, allowing us to investigate life away from the glimmering Atlantic beachfront. We discovered wide boulevards lined with greying buildings that dated back to the days of colonial rule. Rio de Janeiro was a major city under the Portuguese, who arrived in 1502. From 1763 to 1960 it was the national capital and, with this in mind, I'd imagined the centre would be well-maintained like the beachfront; so the crumbling pavements, dirty streets and parks overrun with feral cats were a surprise. Rio had been neglected when the purpose-built city of Brasilia took over the title of capital and the results were obvious to see. There were, though, some signs of improvement, with workers busy resurfacing roads and upgrading the transport system in time for the 2014 FIFA World Cup and the 2016 Olympic Games.

The map hunt continued. The bookshops had none, and we struggled to make ourselves understood as we explained to a magazine stallholder what we were looking for. As most of the countries in South America spoke Spanish, we'd been learning that. Portuguese, we'd been told, was very similar and if we spoke Spanish most people would recognise it. It hadn't worked out that way. If somebody did get the gist of what we were trying to say, then we couldn't understand a word of their response and had to resort to using hand gestures to get our point across.

We decided to continue our search in the city of Niteroi, across the water from Rio. When the Portuguese first arrived in the area they thought they had found the mouth of a huge river, and as the month was January they called it the *Rio de Janeiro*. The name stuck long after they realised it was actually a bay. As we crossed on the ferry, I was transfixed by the long, high bridge that links the two cities and wondered if Paddy would make me cycle over it if we made it back to this point. Finally, we found a road atlas in a small waterside kiosk and headed back to Ipanema to consider the course of our trip.

It was hard to know which beachfront café to opt for; they all looked inviting. In the end, we settled at one of the empty tables belonging to a man with dark brown skin, heavy with wrinkles. He expertly crushed ice, squeezed limes and poured generous shots of *cachaça*, so we felt confident of our first *caipirinha* being a good one. A friend later told me to follow the rule that one of these Brazilian cocktails is a dream, two are dangerous and three a disaster, but that evening the sweet, potent combination slipped down easily and I drank naively as we excitedly plotted our route.

I regretted my indulgence as I nursed a spectacular hangover over breakfast. Fortunately, we weren't cycling yet; we were heading to an after-school project supported by Action for Brazil's Children, a charity we were raising money for. The project was based in Brazil's largest *favela*, Rochina, just one of more than 600 shanty towns in Rio alone.

Our taxi driver checked several times that we had the right address when we asked him to stop at the entrance to the *favela*. Finally, having convinced him to let us out, he took our money and sped off back to the safety of the normal tourist spots. Alone, we nervously waited for somebody from the project to meet us, acutely aware of Rio *favelas'* reputation for crime and violence; the narrow winding streets where we stood had been the battleground for gangs since the 1970s.

We stood on the wide main road which disappeared through a tunnel dug into the mountain, on which the *favela* sat. Below us, blocking the view towards the ocean, was a sprawling secondary school; while above, a steep, narrow, potholed street was lined with shops selling cold juices, mobile phones and an assortment of other goods. Tooting drivers, wearing bright tabards, ferried customers about on the back of motorbikes, swerving around pedestrians and piles of rubbish.

Eventually, a shy teenage boy with smooth brown skin and dark eyes walked over to us, pointing at his T-shirt to indicate he had been sent to find us. He led us up a flight of uneven concrete steps, past elderly ladies carrying heavy parcels, until we reached the doorway of the community centre, where we managed a breathless "hello" to the waiting class. The English teacher led us into one of the functioning classrooms, only half of the building being habitable because a tree had fallen on the roof. Laughing at us good-naturedly, she explained that there was a plan to introduce a mechanical walkway; we obviously weren't the only ones who struggled.

She continued that it was part of a government agenda to

develop all *favelas* by 2020. Programmes were in progress around the city, with the elite police battalion, BOPE, clearing *favelas* of drug gangs, before Police Pacification Units moved in to deliver law enforcement and social service programmes. It would be several months before clearance squads arrived in a dawn raid to drive the drug barons out of Rochina, so for now the project supplemented the learning of students who only had government school classes for half a day.

We sat down with the class and tested their English with questions about football, a topic we had already discovered nearly every Brazilian had an opinion on. They were fiercely proud of their Brazilian stars but had little interest in the English Premier League teams, looking blank-faced when Paddy said that he supported Everton. They were only slightly more impressed by my team, Manchester City, who had recently had the Brazilian star Robinho playing for them.

After class the teacher took us to the rooftop where, looking out across the hodgepodge of red brick buildings stacked together, we pondered the harsh realities of *favela* life. There was nothing temporary about the settlement; the buildings stacked on top of each other had blue plastic water tanks on their roofs, and a complex web of power cables wound around the narrow streets delivering energy to those who could afford it. Looking out across the *favela*, a narrow strip of houses had been painted in vibrant oranges, reds and purples in an attempt to brighten up the appearance of the shanty town, yet it only served to highlight the drabness of the other buildings that clung to the steep mountainside.

Over dinner that evening we agreed we had spent long enough in Rio to get a feel for the city. Trips to Rochina and the centre had opened our eyes to the disparities in the country and we were keen to see beyond the tourist spots. Also, it was hard to relax while we were nervous about leaving – we needed to get on the road. With a rough route towards Paraguay in mind, there was one final piece of preparation needed; to work out how to safely leave Rio.

That's how we had ended up leaning on the Cristo Redentor statue watching the priests huddle for their photo. Edging through the crowds of tourists, we made our way to the western point of the viewing platform where we could see waves crashing on the headland at the far end of Ipanema Beach, after which the road turned sharply out of view around a steep hill. For the other sightseers this was simply the direction to São Paulo, but for us it was the road that would lead to Paraguay, Uruguay, Argentina, and beyond. We had our bearings. It was time to get pedalling.

On day one, soon after the *favela* past which we had hurriedly pushed the bikes, I crawled up the first hill of the trip. It was tiny, but to me it felt like a mountain. Over the past few months I had dropped visits to the gym in favour of goodbye drinks, and I wasn't prepared for riding a loaded 60 kilogram bike uphill in sticky, tropical heat. The sweat dripped off me, my legs ached, and as the road wound through lush green suburbia, I wondered if I could really do this.

There was little time to ponder that now, however. The traffic was heavy as we continued out of the city, crossing confusing junctions, getting lost and disagreeing about which way to go. The surroundings changed quickly, from the shiny Ipanema beachfront to bustling market towns on the outskirts of the greater Rio de Janeiro metropolis, where my senses were overloaded with new sounds, sights and smells. My stomach was twisted with nerves, and I seemed to spend the 75 kilometres we covered that day in a state of bewilderment, as I slowly adapted to our new way of life.

Late in the afternoon, I began to wonder where we might sleep that night and started scanning the busy roadside for somewhere to put up the tent. Lost in thought, I was slow to notice the man jump out in front of me, gesturing frantically and shouting. When I did, my first reaction was, "Oh no, it's happening." Here we were about to have all our belongings taken, we would be back in the UK before the banners had been taken down from our leaving party.

However, it was a surprise that this bandit spoke English. I expected them to have a heavy Latin drawl, none of which I would understand, and they would communicate by pointing guns. Our would-be attacker was empty-handed and, actually, he seemed more excited than aggressive, beaming at us as I pulled on the brakes and stopped face to face with him.

He was Manfred, a German gardener living in Brazil with his

wife and son. Years earlier, he explained, excitedly shaking our hands, he had cycled around Europe on his own adventure. They didn't see many cycle tourists in Brazil and he was thrilled to spot us. When he invited us to spend the evening at his house, we were a little nervous. At home we would never have accepted an offer like this from a stranger, but we reasoned this was part of the adventure. If we wanted to learn about life in South America, what better way than by spending time with local people?

We followed Manfred to his house which was hidden behind high gates off the main road, and locked our belongings inside before driving down to a seafront restaurant. On the way, we passed a strip of food stalls serving steaming bowls of rice and beans to hungry customers perched on plastic stools. He explained they catered for commuters who travelled into Rio de Janeiro and back every day for work, sitting on a bus in heavy traffic for hours to get to a low-paid job that made living in the city a financial impossibility.

Over dinner, conversation switched to the topic of cycle touring and we listened to stories from Manfred's cycle ride, picking up tips that would prove invaluable over the months ahead. As I lay in bed that night, our host's enthusiasm and kindness was a great comfort after an anxious start to the trip, and I fell asleep dreaming of the exciting adventures that lay ahead.

Diary, 13 May 2011 - *Day two! We set off after breakfast and said goodbye to Manfred, who would have hosted us for the weekend, I think. But we can't stop cycling after a day! What a great person to meet. Over dinner last night he was telling us all about the political and economic problems in Brazil, all very interesting as we see signs of that poverty cycling along.*

We hit Santa Cruz in the early morning and stopped at a bike shop as our puncture patches aren't working. The guy in the shop couldn't get his head around any of it, even when we showed him the 'magic letter' [short letters in Spanish and Portuguese that explained our trip, including a map of our route], he just kept saying "Ipanema" and pointing in the opposite direction to where we were heading.

Brazil is the world's fifth largest country. It borders every nation in South America, apart from Chile and Ecuador, and occupies almost half of the continent, with the terrain changing drastically between north and south. The very north is dominated by expansive rainforest, while inland from the narrow coastal plains there are central savannahs, semiarid areas and mountain ranges that rise to 2,000 metres. Whereas, in the southeast and northeast there are the rolling hills, which we found ourselves climbing on our way through the Atlantic Rainforest.

The *Mata Atlantica* was humid and hilly. Brazilians call this luscious section of the coast the *Costa Verde*, and it was easy to understand why. Thick rainforest surged down to the ocean, where luxury yachts bobbed in sheltered coves. It was a tantalising sight as I sweated in the heat, fantasising about diving off the cliffs for a swim. Paddy opted instead for a shower under one of the roadside waterfalls, stepped in too far and returned covered in green slime.

Unfit and struggling with the heat, it seemed to take me 20 minutes to reach the top of each hill, but only two to get down the other side. Towards the top of one climb a car pulled over, the people inside pointing at us. As I approached nervously, the passengers jumped out and started taking photographs on their camera phones before clapping us over the peak. I smiled and tried to look as if I was enjoying myself, but I was gasping for breath. They were our first photographers and it felt unworthy applause, as I pathetically struggled along.

The hills didn't just make cycling challenging, riding through steep rainforest also made it hard to pitch the tent. We hoped to wild camp as much as possible, but with our untrained eyes we were struggling to find suitable sites; if we did find somewhere flat there would be water running through it or it was exposed. On our second day we didn't find anywhere suitable and ended up in an expensive, dirty room in the tourist town of Mangratiba. It was day three and we were determined to camp.

Soon after industrial Angra dos Reis, home to an oil refinery and Brazil's only nuclear plant, all signs of civilisation disappeared and we found ourselves cycling along a low causeway above marshland. There was a smooth, wide hard shoulder and thick forest, complete with soothing birdsong. The sun set at six pm and we wanted to be off the road before then to pitch the tent, but as the afternoon wore on there was no sign of the marsh drying up. Every now and then we would spot a flat patch of land and one of us would clamber down the embankment to check if it was suitable, but the grass was too long or the ground sodden. I remembered Manfred's advice to turn back to places we'd identified earlier in the day, but we hadn't seen anywhere for hours.

I was beginning to panic when we were saved by the Brazilian love of football. There was no sign of life anywhere, but down from the road sat a perfectly flat and fairly dry football pitch. Quickly we rolled the bikes down the embankment, pulled out the tent and had built ourselves a home within ten minutes, by which point the sun had disappeared and we were in complete darkness.

Our bikes were secured to one of the tent poles with a coil lock, the theory being that if anybody tried to steal them, they would wake us in the process. We piled our bags in the vestibule of the tent, leaving enough room to crawl to the sleeping area, which was high enough in the middle to sit up in, just. It was a tight squeeze, but everything had a place and we had a comfortable home.

The one thing we couldn't do inside was cook, so we set up the kitchen on the grass. We were worried about setting the tent on fire as, in the hotel room the night before, the stove had produced so much smoke that Paddy had to climb onto the window ledge to cook. Dinner was a vegetable curry made with some of Manfred's home-grown chillies. It was a little over-ambitious; chopping vegetables, cooking, eating and washing up in the dark was too complicated after a long day on the road, and we were exhausted by the time we crawled inside at nine pm.

Paddy: *It was a thrilling feeling to be wild camping for the first time, especially as we were so nervous. Our minds were full of thoughts of waking up in the night to find someone shining a torch through the door or a wild animal trying to get in the tent. It didn't happen, of course, and after a couple of hours reading by torchlight and holding our breath at the sound of cars turning into a side road a few hundred metres away, we drifted off into a deep sleep, too tired to worry about any security concerns we might have. As the sun lit up the tent* *the next morning, we woke with a newfound confidence for camping. That first night was an important moment.*

The road was flatter now and over the day we covered ground quickly, encouraged by thoughts of arriving in Paraty. We had heard great things about the town whose wide cobbled streets are cleaned by the sea once a month, when water washes in during the full-moon high tide. Judging by the large brown puddles we had just missed the spectacle, but the place was charming nonetheless, with pretty white architecture that hinted at the rich history of the town.

When gold was discovered in the late 17th century, Paraty was the first spot along the coast from Rio de Janeiro where the Serra do Mar mountains could be scaled – a 1,500 kilometre-long range that runs along the Atlantic Ocean. A route was cut in the escarpment behind the town, up which gold, supplies, miners and slaves were transported by mule trains, bringing great wealth to the area. The gold trade had long since disappeared and tourism now brought in the money, the white-washed houses hosting trendy boutiques and health food cafés.

After Paraty, the road turned away from the coast. The scenery was less dramatic, and Paddy amused himself by tickling my ears with long grass he plucked from the verge. There was less touristy charm here, just local people working hard, and we stood out glaringly. As we rode into small villages, we smiled and said *"oi"* to people we passed, but often our greeting would be ignored. One afternoon, on the approach into town, we got our first hostile *"gringo"* shout. The area felt uneasy, and we opted to pitch the tent in a campsite rather than find a spot along the road that night.

The local dogs weren't that keen on us either. The first charge of the trip came out of the blue and my attacker had the advantage as I made my way slowly uphill. He shot out of his owner's café, yapping at my ankles and bouncing off my panniers as he attempted to leap at my calves. He was a short, scraggy white mutt, but he had the advantage of speed and there was no way I could out-pace him. After what seemed like an age, Paddy came to my rescue, ringing his bell and aiming his bike at the dog until, confused about who to attack, it finally gave up the chase.

We stopped to recover in pretty São Sebastião with its pale yellow colonial buildings where, from the waterfront, we looked out towards the Ihlabela, an archipelago of islands across the channel. Enjoying the view over a cold beer, we were surprised to see a gigantic tanker slowly navigate its ways into the tiny waterway and dock alongside a floating platform. The waiter told us this pretty spot was the oil terminal for the multinational energy corporation, Petrobras.

Signs of Brazil's booming economy were everywhere now that we had crossed into the state of São Paulo, the industrial and economic powerhouse of Brazil. Thankfully, the trucks avoided the windy coastal road, as it was hard enough pedalling over the hills, which had returned, without having to contend with heavy traffic. Our bodies were still getting used to riding for up to seven hours a day and our bottoms were suffering particularly. We were using Brooks leather saddles, which are designed to soften to the shape of your derrière, but breaking them in is notoriously uncomfortable, and each morning, we would smother our behinds in cream to numb the pain. My bum hurt, my hands ached, my legs were tired and I was starting to feel sorry for myself.

The feeling was exacerbated as we climbed up the steepest hill we'd encountered so far. The road wound through thick, cool forest, at times sloping upwards at gradients of over ten per cent. There was no hard shoulder, just a narrow strip of road between traffic on one side and a slimy storm drain on the other. We had been climbing all morning, it seemed we would never get to the top and the gradient continued to grow steeper; I was not in a good mood. Frustrated by a set of road works, which broke up the little momentum I had, I dismounted in a huff and started pushing. I was contemplating throwing the bike into the gutter when two cyclists appeared, freewheeling downhill.

When they spotted us, they pulled hard on their brakes and rolled over to where we were stood. It turned out that Chris and Debs lived just a few miles from us in London and were cycling to Rio from Bolivia. They had picked up their bikes on the road, and the aluminium frames were covered in stickers and toys that Debs had collected. We listened as they enthused about travelling by bike, picking up tips about the road ahead. This was the worst hill they had seen in Brazil, they said, which gave me some encouragement. After so long on the road they were more relaxed than us, and meeting them gave me confidence that this trip might be possible after all.

They promised us that after the hill the ground would level out, which it did, and over the next few days we had a gentle ride along the coastal plain to the island of Santos. There, along the wide white beach, we found a cluster of vans with striped awnings offering *pastéis* – stuffed, deep-fried, pastry parcels that oozed cheese. They were highly calorific, delicious washed down with icy Brahma beer, and became our favourite meal over the next few days.

We were stopping in Santos for the football, which had arrived in Brazil via British workers on the Sao Paulo railway project. Brazilians now argue theirs is *o País do Futebol*, and they have a good case, having won the World Cup more times than any other nation. We had tickets for a match between Santos and Internacional, and followed the stream of black and white shirts that flowed through nondescript suburban streets to the stadium. Inside, it was like stepping into an English ground from the 1980s. The ground was only half full, and we stood on the terraces behind the goal for a clear view over the high fences. Unusually, the players entered from opposite ends of the stadium, through inflatable tunnels that stretched a third of the way down the pitch.

Santos' young superstar, Neymar, who was rumoured to be heading to one of the big European clubs, did little to stand out, and the match ended one-all. The atmosphere, though, was mesmerising, with fans chanting through a long repertoire of songs. Hawkers climbed the steep steps selling drinks to fans reluctant to miss a moment of the action, the saleswomen doing better business than the men, who were distracted by the game. I was reminded of evenings spent watching my local town's team; it was difficult to believe Santos was one of the richest clubs in Brazil. By the time the final whistle blew it was late, the match having started at nine pm to make the most of the cooler night air, and as the players returned to the dressing rooms, we headed home. We had an early start the next morning to visit the nearby state capital, São Paulo.

Pedalling into the third largest city in the world would have been a virtual suicide mission, we realised, on seeing the drops on either side of the road up to the high plateau on which the city sits. Instead, we were taking a bus into the city, on a Sunday to avoid the weekday commute when 20 million people journey to work. Traffic jams and crime were so bad in São Paulo that the rich used helicopters to get around, landing on the top of high-rise towers.

We headed to the spot where Jesuits founded the city in 1554. Initially São Paulo grew slowly as a meeting post for sugar growers and fortune hunters heading into the interior, until coffee growing began and immigrants, from as far as Japan and Italy, arrived to work on the plantations. The foreign influence was evident in the architecture of the city's food market, where we sat eating pastries. Below, traders enticed customers to their stalls with slices of exotic fruits from the colourful variety on display. It was a little haven after hours spent pounding the streets, weaving around homeless families asleep on the pavements. São Paulo was interesting, but it was a bustling, gritty city and I was relieved we hadn't attempted to cycle there.

Soon, however, we would have no choice but to head inland. We had just one day left riding along the ocean, and to make the most of it we decided to cycle along the firm beach. Our speed was good, at least when we weren't playing around, forming figures of eight in the sand with our thick tyres. As the sun grew hotter in the afternoon, though, the lack of shade made it draining to ride through the sand, which had grown soft and deep. Having lost sight of the road hours ago we were forced to continue on, stopping regularly to wade through drainage channels and, by the time we rolled our bikes into Peruibe, the sun was beginning to set and we were exhausted.

Since Rio de Janeiro we had covered over 800 kilometres, were feeling fitter and gradually settling into a routine. We were getting to know Brazil but we wondered what life would be like in the interior of the country, a place with little tourism and where pasty-white foreigners on bikes, with terrible Portuguese, would stand out. We hadn't confirmed our route towards Paraguay yet, because everybody we spoke to had a different opinion on the best way; it was clear people from the coast rarely journeyed as far inland as we intended to go.

So, we laid the map on the floor and drew a wiggly line towards Paraguay along the smallest roads we could see. Our guidebook ignored this area completely, meaning we had no idea about where we would be heading, but it was exciting to get off the beaten track. I went to sleep happy; we had a plan.

The Atlantic Ocean was soon behind us as the road wound inland. The air was heavy with the dampness of the forest, which in its determination to expand had forced through the hard shoulder and turned it into thick grass. As we slowly climbed, we were forced to share the narrow road with speeding trucks that shook the ground as they rushed along with precariously-loaded sugar cane cargos. There was just enough space for them to overtake us, but when other trucks headed downhill at the same time, we were forced to the side. Shaking, in the bristly undergrowth we would curse the drivers until we found the courage to get back into the saddle.

It was with relief when, late in the afternoon, we reached the town of Juaquia where we hoped to camp. We were surprised to find on the outskirts a large, temporary army base, guarded by soldiers dressed in light green combats and soft caps, who were friendly, but insistent we couldn't ride into town, which they said was dangerous. They found a female medical officer with perfect English to help, who took me into the local council offices where I stood in the empty lobby, smiling nervously at the officials. It was agreed we would have to sleep in the next-door dingy-looking hotel that we had been hoping to avoid, and reluctantly we lugged our bikes and bags upstairs. The room was dark, the walls were covered in red graffiti, and a dilapidated ceiling fan hung precariously above the bed. The decoration did little to improve my mood after a long day.

Fortunately, off the main highway, quiet roads and big scenery made the region an enjoyable one to cycle through as we headed along the Rio Riberio, a calm river that snaked through banana plantations. The trees, with green fruits growing upwards in bunches and a drooping, phallic, red flower, were packed closely together, cooling the air as we rode along. We laughed with a shopkeeper at her small children, who giggled nervously as they accepted sweets from us, and an old man welcomed us to his village with an explanation of its history. His fast Portuguese was largely lost on us, but that didn't dissuade him from wildly gesturing about the strategic importance of the site where three rivers met to form a wide waterway.

As the road continued, the scenery grew wilder and we found ourselves ascending through thick rainforest on a dirt road cut into the side of a hill. Small black monkeys swung from the trees, teasing us at how easy it was for them to traverse between the caves and waterfalls that peppered the landscape. As we cycled up above the treeline, a view opened across the Alto Ribeira Park – a green blanket, like dark broccoli florets, over which parrots soared. It was cool up here, and by the time we had reached the town of Apiaí later that day we were wearing fleeces for the first time in Brazil.

We stopped for directions on the edge of town and were taken under the wing of Chico, a middle-aged white man with dark hair and a greying beard. He escorted us in his pickup, waiting patiently as we caused a traffic-jam, crawling up the steep hill to the centre. Having negotiated a good rate for us in a guest house, he returned an hour later with cake and an English-speaking colleague who acted as translator as Chico bombarded us with questions about the trip. In return, we quizzed him about our route and whether it was always so cold here. The two men laughed, and Chico told us there was a 95 per cent chance it would snow that evening, the first time since 1975; shivering in our thick down jackets, I believed him.

It didn't snow, fortunately, but it was a chilly start the next morning all the same. Paddy's map case contained a sketch from Chico with a short-cut to Bom Successo de Itararé, our next destination. We were to take a dirt road, negating the need to ride along two sides of a triangle. Our map didn't correspond with the scrappy bit of paper, but after some searching we thought we had found the track on the edge of a small village.

Locals pointed further down the road, but that didn't make sense according to our map or the sketch, so we continued on. The village was built into the side of a steep hill, and we pushed our bikes up a dusty track, bouncing over stones and through potholes to get to the top. We were watched by bemused villagers who looked more indigenous than people on the coast, with light brown skin, dark eyes and thick black hair. Many of the local place names stemmed from the Tupí language, including Itararé, the town we were heading for next: *the stone that the river has dug*.

As we climbed above the village, we discovered a narrow track winding along a ridge connecting tiny hillside settlements together. There was little space to manoeuvre around loose stones on the pathway and, hitting one, I skidded and fell sideways, taking Paddy with me. It took a while to untangle ourselves, but we were unhurt, although a little dusty and with a growing sense this wasn't the track that Chico had meant. When we finally hit the main road and saw a signpost pointing back to Apiaí, our suspicions were confirmed. After a full morning of work, we'd cycled 30 kilometres yet were only ten kilometres from where we'd started, in the process passing through the 1,000 kilometre mark for the trip. I collapsed on the ground with exhaustion and exasperation.

My rest spot was against a farm gate on which sat a life-size, faded cut-out of a panda. Tragically, a year ago to the very day, a friend of mine had died unexpectedly soon after his 30th birthday. Chris Dart was one of the most enthusiastic, positive and fun-loving people I have ever known. We had been part of a group who spent our teenage years in Manchester's indie clubs, dancing to Stone Roses' tracks and moshing at Ash gigs, and we kept in touch when I moved to London. Coincidentally, Chris was obsessed with pandas; including, a few years before he passed away, travelling to China to spend time looking after them. I had no idea why there was a picture of a panda on a locked gate in the middle of Brazil, but it reminded me of Chris and his incredible lust for life. I realised how lucky I was to be doing this trip, stopped feeling sorry for myself and got back on the bike.

Having failed on the dirt tracks we returned to the tarmacked road. We had little idea where we were, but the looks we were getting suggested we weren't in the right place. Concrete houses were painted in vibrant pinks, blues and greens creating a cheerful appearance, yet people watching us from their doorways stared straight through us.

Diary, 28 May 2011 *- Some of the looks we get as we cycle along are unnerving. I don't understand it; it mainly comes from younger people too who I'd expect to be more friendly. Is* *it because we are so unusual here or what?*

We decided to wild camp away from the town as it didn't feel safe there. We found this spot in an unfenced pine forest which isn't too steep, but it wouldn't surprise me if we roll downhill during the night. Despite the setting, there's nothing romantic about it – more a case of hiding away for the evening.

It was quiet when we left the next morning. Judging by loud noises throughout the night, there had been a party in a nearby field and the revellers were sleeping off hangovers away from the freezing fog that had descended over the hills. Our fingers stung from the vibrations of the handlebars each time we hit a bump, but with the road to ourselves there was at least time to weave around the bigger potholes. The only attention we attracted was from dogs tied to stakes outside houses. They choked on their chains as they fought to chase us and, in one sleepy village, we set off a barking relay, the dogs transferring the baton as we passed each house. By the time their owners could arrive to investigate the cause of the commotion, we had vanished into a huge pine forest.

Away from vicious dogs and angry villagers, we rode over small hillocks, some of which had lost their trees to loggers, and began to relax into our cycling. For the first time on the trip we dug out our iPods and powered along to beat-filled, pop anthems. Our favourites were bands like the Foo Fighters or Arcade Fire, but on hilly days I preferred cheesy, cheerful hits by Ricky Martin or Katie Perry that had a good, bouncy rhythm to cycle to.

We had settled into a daily routine that focused on pedalling, eating and sleeping. Our day would start about six when the neighbourhood dogs and cockerels launched a competition to wake the most people and, unable to sleep through the commotion, we would dress, pack our bags and eat breakfast, normally bread rolls or cereal. We'd be on the road by eight and cycle for a couple of hours before stopping for a second breakfast. Lunch would be about midday and we would try to be off the road by dark. If camping, we would quickly cook and probably have fallen asleep by eight after a couple of hours of reading by torchlight. Even in a cheap hotel, we wouldn't last much longer before bed beckoned.

Off the tourist trail, accommodation was much cheaper and

our budget allowed us to stay in basic *pousadas* every now and then. However, after our first experience, we tried to avoid motels. We had spotted the fancy white sign, with bold black letters spelling out the word 'MOTEL' at the end of a tough day in the hills and, excited at the prospect of a bed for the night, we stopped outside the huge gates where a sign directed us to press the intercom button. A gentle female voice responded, switching to perfect English when she realised we spoke little Portuguese. This was unusual, as was the room rate, charged by the hour, and the high-walled courtyard that the mystery woman beckoned us into, directing us via wall-mounted speakers to a garage door that closed automatically behind us.

It wasn't until I turned on the TV to be bombarded with graphic porn, that I finally realised we were in a brothel. Dropping the menu that included sex toys and a list of ladies to order, I hit the remote control to change channel. Seemingly, room service arrived through another door which had a discreet cubbyhole to pass through kinky gifts. We'd heard about love motels, aimed at couples who don't have privacy at home, but there are also the saucier stories, like the Brazilian footballer Ronaldo caught panicking in a room after finding the three prostitutes he'd picked up were men.

Realising where we were sent us into hysterical, childish laughter, and we nervously investigated. Aside from the plastic mattress, a huge picture of a pair of lace-clad breasts, free condoms and a shower-for-two there was little difference from a normal hotel room. It wasn't the best place to sleep though, with Paddy glancing nervously at the door every time he heard one of the ladies-of-the-night moving along the corridor. We left the next morning, having seen nobody other than a flash of red nail varnish belonging to the woman who took payment from us through a cubbyhole.

Back in the saddle, we were deep into agricultural heartland and spent entire days cycling along fenced-off fields belonging to individual farms. Growing in neat rows were soya and corn, planted by descendants of European settlers. Wide-eyed cows watched us curiously, often trotting along with us until stopped by barbed-wire, where they would stand, looking longingly as we cycled off.

We were generally sticking to the bigger roads on our map after another navigating error. This time we'd been following our handlebar compasses south-west, until Paddy hit a bump and his needle swung around to south-east – somehow they had both stuck at exactly the same bearing. By the end of the day we were 65 kilometres away from where we'd been aiming for, a greater distance than when we started in the morning.

Fenced-off farms made it tricky to find good camping sites, but fortunately an abundance of football pitches meant we often found somewhere to set up home for the night. The European influence in the area also meant we started to meet people who spoke English, including a Brazilian couple who had recently returned home after working in Watford. They were perplexed to see people from the UK cycling past and closed their butchers shop for an hour to join us for lunch.

They gave us the details of an English guy a few towns along who owned a *pastel* store, where we called in for dinner, keen for an opportunity to quiz a local in a language we understood. Business was slow that evening, it was raining and Brazilians don't go out when it rains, Shalom explained. So we were able to lazily enjoy our beers while he deep-fried *pastéis* for us and told us his story of how he had moved here after marrying a Brazilian woman.

He was right about people staying indoors in bad weather. The roads were much quieter whenever it rained, which was increasingly often now that winter was approaching. I felt sorry for the farm workers we passed, who must have been cold in their makeshift shelters built from sticks and plastic sheeting. The shacks were squeezed onto narrow strips of grass between the main road and barbed-wire fences of the farms, and I assumed, initially, that they were temporary as they looked so basic. Yet at second glance, the livestock tethered to trees and the well-worn dirt in front of the homes suggested they were permanent. It was the first time we had seen such poverty since the hillside *favela* in Rio de Janeiro, now far away.

Rio was 2,000 kilometres behind us, to be precise. We reached the mark as we navigated our way through heavy traffic on the outskirts of Foz do Iguaçu on the border with Paraguay and Argentina. It had taken 18 days of riding to reach here from the coast, and we now had stripy suntans and red bottoms from hours spent in the saddle. Yet, we were enjoying our new drifter lifestyle, being able to explore different places each day. I felt healthier than I had in years and free from the stresses of everyday life. My priorities were food, sleep and riding, and I loved it.

I did need a break, however, and I collapsed on the mattress Fabio had laid down for us in his pool house. He had offered to host us for a few days after we had contacted him through the Couchsurfing website – a site that connects travellers, some looking for places to surf and others offering couches or spare rooms for people to stay for free, as part of a cultural exchange.

Fabio lived with his mum and niece in a large, secure house in a suburban street. The family owned a fried chicken restaurant, where Fabio helped out. It was Chris and Debs who had recommended Fabio as a fantastic host, and we were grateful that he offered to take us in on hearing this, as it was our first Couchsurf experiment and our online profile had no references yet. It was a new experience settling in to somebody else's home, but Fabio was a seasoned host and welcomed us warmly, and before long our clothes were hanging around the garden and Paddy was hosing the bikes down on the patio. In return for his hospitality, we bought Fabio a bottle of his favourite whisky to share as we recounted tales from the road and tried to answer his question about what we thought of Brazil.

We now understood Brazil was much more than Rio de Janeiro and the Amazon, that there was a complicated mixture of landscapes, cultures, history and economics within the borders of this huge country. Having worried about the bandits and 'bad people', we had instead been overwhelmed by the kindness of individuals we met, who went above and beyond to welcome us. The beaches and rainforests had long ago given way to huge farms where crops grew in abundance, in spite of morning frosts. We hadn't expected to be cold until we reached Argentina, but already our warm kit was in frequent use and memories of sunbathing on Ipanema Beach were just that.

As we sat down with Fabio's family for a meal cooked by his mum, we explained that we felt much more positive about our chances of success. Everybody had said Brazil was so dangerous but, although I'd been nervous at times, we'd never felt seriously threatened.

The family nodded as Fabio translated. "So," asked his mum, "where are you going next?"

"Paraguay" we replied, at which she grabbed Fabio's forearm as a look of fear spread across her face. Turning to her son, she said,

"No Fabio, tell them they cannot go to Paraguay. It is very dangerous there. It is full of bad people."

3. Paraguay

The border crossing into Paraguay was straightforward, if a little slow, as we followed Brazilians walking across the Friendship Bridge to stock up on cheap goods in the border city of Ciudad del Este. Billboards advertised offers on everything from iPhones to bed linen, while market vendors bellowed out daily rates from behind wooden carts. Eager to escape the mayhem, we weaved around cars abandoned in the middle of the road by drivers who'd gone off to shop.

It was only after a couple of miles, once the chaos had subsided, that we began to relax into our riding and could celebrate our first border crossing of the trip with a high five. We were now in the *heart of South America*, as Paraguay is known, thanks to its position in the centre of the continent. Unlike in Brazil, with its extensive road network, here there were only three main roads connecting the principal southern cities in a triangle. We were following the one heading west for a four-day ride into the capital, Asunción, before turning south-east towards the border with Argentina.

It looked to be a straightforward few days in the saddle, with a flat road and a tailwind helping us along. This was confirmed by Edgar, a Colombian cyclist heading the opposite way on route to the tip of the continent. His face was wrapped in a scarf as protection from the easterly gale he was battling into. He looked as if he hated headwinds as much as me. Hills are tough, but they are achievable with a proportionate amount of effort; cycling into wind, however, requires a huge amount of work to cover a disproportionately small distance.

Meeting Edgar provided an opportunity to test our Spanish, which it turned out was now confusingly peppered with Portuguese. We managed to understand that he was sleeping in fire stations and was carrying very little, just a backpack over his shoulders and a small sleeping bag strapped to the front of his mountain bike. It was only a short conversation, Edgar had a long afternoon ahead battling into the wind if he was to make the next fire station before dark.

As in Brazil, the security warnings we'd been given seemed overblown and I slowly relaxed about being in 'dangerous' Paraguay – although a poster with black and white mug shots of people wanted by the police did make me a little nervous. For the most part people we met were friendly and interested in our trip, like the owner of a pizza restaurant who kept our beers topped up as we chatted to him in a mix of Spanish and English. When we asked what he suggested we see in his country the question seemed to stump him, until he finally suggested a village with abandoned buildings and railways that had once been run by the British. We were confused: Spain had been the colonial power here and we hadn't seen any railways; something must have been lost in translation, we assumed.

We were now halfway to Asunción and spent the days riding past fields of soya plants and tired donkeys pulling carts. Much of the crop was bound for China as livestock feed, the soya industry being one of the greatest contributors to Paraguay's economy. With up to 35 per cent of the population living in poverty, the country is one of South America's poorest nations. As we passed through a shallow valley, we saw families living in wooden shacks, perched precariously on stilts above dusty ground. It wasn't the dirt they were escaping, but water; their homes were built in the middle of a shallow, wide river, currently dry but clearly not always.

Finding available space to build homes was difficult in Paraguay. The problem stemmed from the policies of the dictator Alfredo Stoessner who, during his 35 years in power, handed out huge areas of land to military officials, civilian supporters and foreign corporations. By the time the sitting president, Fernando Lugo, came to power in 2008, small farmers, who made up 40 per cent of the population, owned only five per cent of the country's arable farmland. The families we saw had nowhere to go.

We stopped later that morning for a break and, while Paddy went inside the small supermarket to buy drinks, I sat outside with the bikes, enjoying the warm sun on my face. I was only shaken back to reality when the metal frame of the shop shuddered violently. I turned around to see Paddy in the doorway, his feet flying in the air before he crashed to the ground on his back; he had forgotten to duck as he came out of the shop and had smashed his head into the low door frame.

It was like something out of a cartoon and I laughed nervously, only it wasn't funny. The concerned Chinese owner came running out and helped pick a dazed Paddy up off the ground. He also brought us water and painkillers while his little cat curled up in Paddy's lap as if to offer comfort. Paddy normally shrugs off pain, but he had a dark red line across his forehead, and it was over an hour before he felt well enough to move on again. In hindsight, we should have called it a day then.

When we finally set off again, I was in the front as usual, setting the pace so that Paddy didn't zoom off without me. With the road dominated by trucks, we were stuck on a hard shoulder littered with speed humps every 50 metres, making for a bumpy ride and we put our iPods on as a distraction. After a few hours of banging up and down over the bumps, we stopped for another break and, while Paddy once again went inside to purchase snacks, I tried to work out what looked wrong with his bike. Suddenly it clicked and my stomach turned.

When I walked into the shop, Paddy was examining the shelves. Trying to appear calm, I approached him:

"Hey. Have you got your pannier in here with you?"

"What?"

"Your back right pannier, it's not on the bike. I wanted to check you have it."

"You're kidding me, yeah?"

"No. Your pannier isn't there. Are you saying that you don't have it?"

The look on his face said it all; he threw the snacks onto the shelf and rushed outside. I walked slowly over to the window and watched as he walked hopelessly in circles around the bike. I dreaded going outside, because I knew the missing bag contained every item of Paddy's clothing plus our emergency cash and cards. Part of me reasoned if I stayed inside I could ignore what was going on, but instead I smiled at the confused sales assistant and walked out to a distraught boyfriend.

I couldn't ask how he hadn't notice the bag fall off while he looked so crestfallen. Instead I confirmed he'd had it when we stopped last, which meant it had disappeared over the last 30 kilometres. Hopeful of finding it by the side of the road, he stripped the bike of the remaining bags for me to watch and set off to retrace our route. In total, he went back and forth three times: once by bike, again in a car belonging to the petrol station assistant and finally by bus. It was a futile search; we never found the bag and Paddy lost all of his clothes, including the specialised cycling and waterproof gear we had painstakingly resourced and bought over the last few years.

> ***Diary, 16 June 2011*** *- There was £100 in local currency in the bag, but it's the clothes that we took so long to pick out that sting, and the fact that it will be a hassle to replace them. Paddy is understandably upset, totally crushed, frustrated and angry with himself. He has gone to take the bus back to see if he can spot it – I'm not sure how he will manage to buy a ticket as we only have a few US dollars now. There's no way he'll find the bag, but I understand why he has to do it. I hope he is OK and comes back soon. It was horrible seeing him go off looking so sad.*

Part of me wanted to shout at him for his carelessness, but I knew it was just a wretched accident. The worst thing was thinking of somebody searching through our belongings. We stood out so much that whoever had it must have seen us – somebody in a car would have driven past us on the road, or a pedestrian would have seen Paddy searching for it. We knew it was our fault for losing the bag, but we were disappointed that nobody tried to return it.

As if to rub salt into our wounds, the next day the heavens opened for the first time since Brazil. For a while I kept my waterproofs off in solidarity, but ultimately covered up while Paddy got drenched to the skin. My focus was on reaching Asunción to get him some new clothes, instead of concentrating on how wet and greasy the road had become after the last downpour. Consequently, I noticed late the deep, flooded hole at the bottom of the hard shoulder that I was freewheeling down.

There was no way I could ride through it without somersaulting over the handlebars but, reluctant to lose my speed, I ruled out the sensible option of coming to a stop. If I was going to get around the pothole I would need to move onto the road, but the five-centimetre lip between it and the hard shoulder made for a complicated manoeuvre. I continued at full kilter while considering the best angle by which to approach, as the pothole rapidly grew closer.

Ultimately, I hesitated too long and suddenly it was a case of act now or crash into the hole. I swung the handlebars sharply towards the road, forcing the bike to bounce up the kerb. The frame wobbled but, momentarily, it seemed I would stay upright; it wasn't to be. The back of the bike spun out from under me, like a bucking bull determined to dismount its rider. As it whipped me around, my shoulder was thrown into the ground and the back of my head smashed into the tarmac forcing my helmet over my face.

When I came to a halt, I was in the middle of the road looking back up the hill. It had happened so fast that my feet were still attached to the pedals by my cleated shoes and I was pinned under the bike. I could see Paddy rushing past my strewn pannier bags towards me. A sharp pain throbbed in my head as I watched an old woman, who had been carrying firewood, throw her bundle into the wet grass and rush over to help. Soon I was surrounded by a crowd of locals, including the police commander who ushered me into his office down the road. Fortunately, the damage was minimal with the bike suffering nothing more than a twisted handlebar, and although I was shaken, I had only a few grazes, bruises and a dull headache. In fact, Paddy looked worse than I did.

> ***Paddy:*** *I saw that Laura was going to crash, I think before she realised herself. She was perhaps 50 or 100 metres ahead of me, and it was too late to warn her. The lip back to the road and the greasy surface was always going to be tricky but it was the angle she approached from that caused the accident. I watched helplessly as her bike slid out from under her, and I felt sick as her shoulder struck the ground and a split second later her head banged onto the tarmac. The hairline fracture that ran along her helmet showed how very serious it could have been.*

> *After feeling so annoyed at myself over the last 24 hours, the gloom lifted as soon it was clear that she was OK. I was so concerned about her that I realised the really important things in life are the ones we so easily take for granted. That was a turning point for me. I was still angry and upset at myself, but I was now able to accept the bag situation and I set out to try and be positive about resolving it.*

Apart from being a little stiff, riding was fine and I was soon distracted by the heavy traffic as we approached the urban sprawl of Asunción. The road was four-lanes wide and buses zoomed past like Formula One cars, swerving around us only to stop immediately in front to pick up passengers. As we neared the centre things improved, thanks partly to the one-way streets of the city's grid structure that slowed down the traffic. This system had been introduced by Paraguay's first president, Dr Francia, who, convinced of plots to kill him, insisted on being able to see in all directions at every corner. It made it easier for us to navigate to our hotel in the tired Plaza Uruguaya, with its scrubby grass and children in tattered clothes.

Not wanting to worry my parents, I decided to edit recent events when I called home that afternoon. Powering up Skype on our tiny laptop, I thought back to backpacking around Africa when I was 18. Keeping in touch was a nightmare with intermittent internet and unreliable phone lines. Now it was so much easier with WIFI in hotels and restaurants; we could even maintain a website about the trip. Today though, I wanted to call as it was Mum's birthday.

I didn't tell her about the fall, but the lost bag came up when she asked about our plans in Asunción. Replacing Paddy's clothes was the priority, but at 195 centimetres tall it wasn't going to be easy in a country where the average height was below 140 centimetres. Fortunately, in a shiny mall that was completely out of place with the poor Paraguay we had seen so far, we managed to replace the basics, leaving just a few more specialist things to get from home, like trousers and waterproofs. We ordered the items online to be delivered to his parents, ignoring the fact we had no idea how to get them to us in South America.

Both feeling better now Paddy had some clothes to wear, we

set out to make the most of our time in Asunción. Established by the Spanish in 1537, the city was in festive mood as Paraguay celebrated 200 years of independence from colonial rule. As a land-locked country with access to the sea only along the Río Paraná, the newly independent government adopted a policy of isolation. Foreign technicians were invited to develop the state, including British railway engineers who built the Estación de Ferrocarril. The grand brick structure, with pointed towers and a wide, corrugated iron roof, housed an old steam train that presumably once ran to the abandoned village the pizza restaurant owner had talked about.

We walked down to the bay of the Río Paraguay to visit the white, ornate Palacio de Gobierno, but were more struck by the neighbouring shacks, where children balanced on sewer pipes to launch homemade kites in the pungent breeze. While two police officers stopped to help a group of boys whose strings were tangled in the branches of a tree, we paused to read a board outlining development plans for the area. It seemed these children's families would soon be forced to find another precarious piece of land on which to live.

The path around the palace was blocked by armed officers so we retraced our steps past a naval crew preparing their ship. It seemed funny that a landlocked country would need a naval fleet, but the Paraguayan Navy had an important role in the country's history, especially during the 1932-1935 Chaco War with Bolivia, when it carried troops and supplies to the front lines via the Río Paraguay. The campaign for oil in the north of Paraguay was a fruitless one, and caused the deaths of 50,000 Paraguayans.

The victims were remembered by a grand monument on la Plaza de los Héroes. The numbers who perished in the Chaco War were huge, but seemingly insignificant compared to those of the War of the Triple Alliance for which the memorial was built. The 1865 to 1870 conflict against an alliance of Brazil, Argentina and Uruguay, 25 times larger than Paraguay's forces, left the country's population halved and 90 per cent of all males dead. It was this war that brought an end to the country's affluence.

Leaving Asunción, it was a relief to find the bumps of the previous stretch gone, along with the heavy traffic. The route was a cyclist's heaven with each small town specialising in tasty delights, like bright, sweet oranges and sticky, doughnut-shaped honey bread. The constant was Paraguay's traditional bread, *chipa*. Made from cheese and tapioca flour, it was crunchy on the outside, squishy in the middle, and squeaked when we chewed it. It was best eaten warm, bought from men on motorbikes, who roared between villages selling rolls from huge wicker baskets strapped to the seat behind them. We would flag them down and hand over a few *Guaraníes* before selecting our pick of rolls from under a starched white cloth.

Villages were separated by wide grassy plains upon which cattle grazed. We would know we were approaching a settlement upon seeing large statues guarding the entrance. Cows and horses were popular figures, as was San Miguel Arcángel. Paddy's yellow Sylvester the Cat children's waterproof, that he had bought from a petrol station, looked like the warrior's cloak and I insisted he pose for a photo next to the statue. The similarities made us laugh for the first time since losing the bag.

It was still raining and Paddy's tyres had decided to puncture constantly. At least my back wheel waited to burst until we arrived in the gloomy service station room, where we were spending our fourth anniversary. We celebrated the occasion with a bottle of red wine, while patching up the inner tubes that had punctured over the past few days.

> ***Diary, 23 June 2011*** *- A wet, wet day – damp when we started, then a heavy downpour mid-morning. Paddy looked frozen and very uncomfortable in his kid's mac. I was annoyed that he refused to consider waterproofs on sale in a shop this morning. For £20 he'd get something that would make a world of difference, even if they were a bit short. It was so grey that there wasn't much scenery to see. It really was about head down and cycle.*

The incessant wet weather was making us grumpy, and when the stove played up as we tried to cook dinner, it did nothing to improve our mood. As Paddy struggled to get it lit, the noise from the courtyard of the *hospedaje* grew, and I poked my head outside to find a group of locals wrapped in blankets, cooking on an open fire. The friendly landlady, on seeing our stove problem, kindly beckoned me across the yard to use the hob in her apartment.

Her room was simple; the walls were bare concrete against which was pushed a collection of furniture that turned the space into an office, kitchen and bedroom. While I slowly boiled pasta on the two-burner gas stove at the back of the room, her daughter watched me with fascination under layers of blankets in her cot-bed. The other rooms around the square courtyard were less sparsely furnished, and were occupied by workers with dark, weathered skin and white smiles that flashed in the firelight as they sat around the communal cooking pot. The majority of Paraguayans are classified as *mestizo*, a result of Spanish settlers having children with indigenous Guaraní women. Theirs remains an official language in Paraguay and is understood by about 90 per cent of the population, which meant our Spanish was even less successful than usual that night.

The traditional setting of the *hospedaje* was in stark comparison to our discovery the next morning of one of the most modern pieces of engineering imaginable: the Yacyretá Dam. While in Foz do Iguaçu we had visited Itaipu, the world's second largest hydroelectric dam which supplies electricity to Paraguay and Brazil. Yacyretá had only recently opened and the water had not yet reached its final levels.

We couldn't see the actual dam that sits on the Río Paraná near the southern border with Argentina, but the consequences of the flooding were all around, with bus stops poking out of the lake, their graffiti half submerged, and abandoned houses on the water's edge waiting patiently to be consumed. 40,000 people were displaced by the construction of the dam and local species and fish levels were affected, yet, the dam made Paraguay self-sufficient on renewable energy and able to sell leftover electricity to neighbouring countries.

When the road we were cycling along disappeared underwater, we turned onto a new viaduct that bridged the reservoir. We were in awe at the engineering efforts of the project and fascinated by the physical reality of the flooding, the water having encroached as far as the border city of Encarnación. Our two-year-old maps were already out of date, many roads having been submerged, which made for an unusual navigating problem.

We were taking a few days off here to recuperate and explore some local Jesuit ruins built in the early 1600s to educate the natives about Christianity. Religion still played an important role in Paraguay where Roman Catholicism was widely practiced. Our Couchsurfing host, Caesar, took us to visit his favourite church on the banks of the river where there was a clear view across to Argentina. While he said a short prayer inside, we looked out over the water to the city of Posadas where we were due to head next.

Caesar was an English teacher and he told us his class hadn't believed him when he said he had two English cyclists staying at his house. His family also seemed intrigued by our trip and had organised a special lunch in our honour with a huge spread of delicious homemade pastries and rice. I really needed to improve my Spanish to say thank you properly for the hospitality of people like Caesar's mum, and borrowed a dictionary to make a list of essential words to learn as we cycled along.

As I made notes, Caesar brought out a pewter pitcher with a long metal straw resting inside; a *mate* cup he explained, from which to drink tea. *Mate* drinking is a stereotypically Argentinian tradition but is popular throughout the southern region of the continent, and *mate* is one of the main industrial crops in Paraguay. The ritual is as much about sharing among friends as it is refreshment. Leaves are put into the bottom of the cup and hot water is poured on for the first person to drink, once they finish it is topped up and passed on to the next person.

Caesar served a sweet variation with desiccated coconut and milk that I preferred to the bitter green tea. We slurped away with the family who were watching Argentinian football on television. It was our last night in Paraguay, a country that had thrown us curveballs in the saddle but had captured our hearts, and it felt special to finish our time here with new friends as we emptied the *mate* flask. We could have stayed longer but we were heading to Uruguay next via Argentina, countries we were excited to explore.

Saying goodbye to Caesar the next morning, we headed to the immigration post, where we bumped over a set of old railway tracks and past a defunct steam train; the British had been here too, it seemed. Paraguayans didn't seem to hold anything against us for Britain's involvement, but we were aware that people might feel differently in Argentina as the 30th anniversary of the Falklands War approached. As we set off across the 2.5 kilometre wide bridge, we agreed to play down our Britishness and not to mention the war.

4. Uruguay

From Paraguay, we were welcomed to Argentina by a cantankerous official who insisted we push our bikes to the border control. The bureaucracy irritated me and further fuelled my grumpy, first-day-back mood. I rarely enjoyed getting in the saddle after a few days off; my legs would groan at having to work again and I would have to force my head to re-accustom to life on the road. Having to walk across a blustery bridge on the whim of a grouchy customs officer didn't help.

We were heading to Uruguay, via a few days in Argentina and a very quick jaunt through Brazil. Borders in this region wiggled around, a consequence of the power struggle between colonial powers, which, in 1828, culminated in the creation of Uruguay as a buffer state between Brazil and Argentina. These two states shared only a short border, where a thin section of Argentina reached up to the Foz do Iguaçu waterfall. It was this stretch we needed to cycle across to reach Uruguay.

My first-day grumpiness was just that. By the next morning I was back to enjoying the subtle changes in scenery as we followed the Río Uruguay south past rolling fields of *mate* plants and cows standing in flooded marshland, munching on green stalks. The campsite in Santa Tomé was waterlogged where the river had burst its banks and we opted not to stay there despite the recommendation of a Colombian cyclist heading in the opposite direction. His bike was loaded with plastic bags and a basket of freshly-picked 'magic' mushrooms. He was heading north to Rio de Janeiro, he explained, as it was cold in Argentina, and he wished us luck as he moved slowly off.

We were making quick progress, helped by the wind at our backs, and after only three days and 360 kilometres, we approached the border town of Paso de los Libres across the river from Brazil. As we neared the entrance, I spotted a man waving excitedly at us further along the road and pulled on the brakes to meet Juan, a retired judge and keen road cyclist. He insisted we stay with him, the first such invitation since Manfred's, leaving

Rio de Janeiro.

Moments like these were something we hesitated telling our families about when we called home. They were concerned about us staying with strangers, and it was hard to reassure them that most people who offered to host us were kind, friendly individuals, who wanted to hear our stories from the road and share their local knowledge. We always trusted our instincts when we met people. If we felt unsure about a situation we would politely make our excuses, but we mainly met fantastic people through chance encounters like these.

> ***Diary, 29 June 2011*** *- Juan warned us that the entrance to town wasn't very safe, so he met us about ten kilometres before and escorted us in his Alfa Romeo. We ended up racing along a dirt road at 20 kilometres per hour trying to keep up with him; we'd already done 100 kilometres – it totally finished me off! He has a lovely house and he and his wife, Noemi, are so nice. Juan has a garage full of bikes and trophies from road cycling competitions; he loved our Rohloff hubs and he and Paddy spent a lot of time discussing mechanics – quite hard in a language you don't speak. We met some of his cycling friends tonight, none of them spoke English either but they seemed to understand us – I think the wine helped! Noemi had put on an amazing spread of spinach and egg pie and local red wine, which is so cheap and so good that it's impossible to refuse.*

Over dinner we explained our plan to head to Uruguay via Brazil, but it drew shakes of the head from around the table. Cycling was prohibited across the busy bridge into Brazil, they said, suggesting instead Juan would drive us. It was a kind offer, but a difficult one to accept. We had wanted to cycle every metre of our route around South America, and although we recognised the chances of success were slim, we had hoped if we did need help it would be in the face of a more extreme obstacle than bridge-bureaucracy. Of course, accepting assistance had no bearing on the success of the trip. This was a personal adventure; we weren't trying to break any records, so taking a lift a couple of kilometres wouldn't upset anybody other than us.

Resigned to the situation and grateful for Juan's help, even if it wasn't what we wanted to do, the next morning Paddy strapped the bikes into the pickup and we headed to the border. It was strange being back in Brazil; the names of shops and banks in the centre of the confusingly named Uruguaiana were familiar, but being much further south it was cold. Juan opted not to ride with us into the bitter wind that blew off the river and, waving goodbye to him we pedalled away, our legs pushing hard to ensure we covered the 65 kilometres to the border before dark.

We hurried past the deserted control post into Uruguay where a smiling official pointed us towards the sleepy border town of Bella Union. It felt European with its plaza lined with boutiques and bakeries, but riding around the cobbled streets in search of an ATM to withdraw some *Pesos*, we found our foreign cards were spat out with distaste. It would be days before we would find another bank, so we reluctantly dipped into the stash of US dollars hidden inside our seat posts, which we exchanged in time to check into a basic hotel before kick-off of the 2011 Copa America, Latin America's football competition. We were looking forward to watching the tournament while we were in Uruguay and Argentina, two football-mad nations. Uruguay had hosted and won the first ever FIFA World Cup in 1930 and their current squad looked good, having reached the semi-finals of the competition in 2010.

It was to the birth town of one of their star players, Liverpool's striker Luis Suárez, that we were headed next. As we made our way south towards Salto, past vast fields of soya, wheat and grazing cattle, we saw few villages. There was little sign of life along the roadside, and we pitched our tent one evening in a quiet wood, hidden by thick bushes. The next morning, huddled in our sleeping bags, we peered out of the tent to see branches twinkling with silver frost; winter had arrived.

In the cold our bodies craved hot food, but we had misjudged our supplies which were gradually running out. On the day we arrived in Salto, we cooked our final batch of spaghetti for lunch, huddling around the stove for warmth as the water boiled. It had been a long morning in the saddle, and not the time to let the lid slip when draining the pan. The pasta slopped into the grass, and without a word, we lunged forwards and scooped it into our bowls, soil flecks and all.

Several hours later, we knocked on the door of our Couchsurfing host, Andrea. We had been in touch for a week already and, as well as hosting us, she had agreed we could send a parcel of replacement clothes for Paddy to her address. There was no sign of the package yet, but there were thermal baths to enjoy in town, where we tried to hide our cycle suntan marks from giggling school children. There was also local wine, which we shared with Andrea and her boyfriend as we watched Uruguay draw with Peru in the football. We hadn't realised that wine was made here but it was really good, particularly the Tannat, a deep red, similar to a Bordeaux wine. Even France had given it the mark of approval, Andrea told us. She said the French imported large quantities to be bottled as French table wine – emphasising the subtle difference of a wine being produced in a country or being bottled there.

The cold weather continued and the national news led with footage of people wrapped in scarves and hats, shivering as they scraped ice from their car windscreens. It was apparently the coldest winter Uruguay had seen in years. One evening Andrea returned home with a pile of clothes for Paddy to borrow; her mother was worried about him wearing flip flops and shorts. The clothes kept him warm, but did nothing to improve his look when paired with the wiry beard he had been growing since we left Rio.

> ***Diary, 5 July 2011*** - *At the moment Paddy looks like a homeless person. He's wearing borrowed pale denim jeans that are too short for him and a woolly green jumper, the kind that a fisherman would wear. He has holes in his socks, long hair and a scraggy ginger and black beard. It's not a good look – mainly the beard, but he refuses to shave it off. I realised today what it reminds me of – pubes. Where did my lovely, handsome boyfriend go?*

I gave him an ultimatum: either he shaved, or the photos went on Facebook for all his friends to see. Even he realised he looked bad, and by the end of the day he was clean faced. I think he expected me to feel guilty, but I couldn't hide my delight.

Eventually, through Andrea, we discovered the parcel was sat in customs in the capital Montevideo awaiting payment of an import duty. We were frustrated the delivery company had not told us earlier, but at least now we could set the ball rolling. It would take several days for the parcel to arrive in Salto, and impatient to get cycling we decided to leave; Paddy would return by bus when the package turned up.

For once, it felt great to be back pedalling. The high sun gently warmed our backs and a tailwind helped us cover 250 kilometres in two days to Mercedes. We were in excellent spirits after an email from Andrea saying she had the parcel, and I was cycling along day-dreaming about what adventures lay in store, when Paddy called me to stop; there was something wrong with his brakes. On inspection, the problem was even more serious, a small crack in the rim was causing the rear wheel to wobble and catch on the brake pads. This was a massive blow, and we stood in silence staring at the fine line in the dark grey metal. The carbon rim was specific to the Rohloff hub and the likelihood of finding a replacement outside of a major city was slim. For the moment, there was little we could do and after releasing the back brake, Paddy headed down the road at top speed, venting his frustration on the pedals, which was probably not going to help.

Later, while he headed off to retrieve the parcel, I researched a solution to the problem. The online advice was not to ride on the rim, as if it cracked completely it would leave the wheel unable to support any weight and burst the inner-tube. If we absolutely had to cycle, I read, we should remove the luggage from the back wheel and take it slowly. Of course, with the replacement bag finally having arrived, we had more weight rather than less, and I argued that we should be sensible and not ride on. In his new clothes, however, Paddy was in an upbeat mood and insisted it would be OK. I could only warn that if we broke down in the middle of nowhere, on his head be it.

Paddy: *I was in denial about the severity of the problem. I wanted to convince Laura it would all be OK, and, subconsciously, if I believed it myself then perhaps it would turn out to be. I felt guilty for slowing our progress, first with the lost bag and now this. Neither of us is particularly patient, and this was really stretching our limits.*

Fortunately, the bang of the inner tube exploding happened as we were approaching the riverside town of Nueva Palmira, 80 kilometres along the road. He looked at me sheepishly; the rim was destroyed. We pushed the bikes into town, and over a bottle of wine agreed our only option was to catch a bus to the city of Colonia del Sacremento, 100 kilometres away. From there we could take a ferry to Buenos Aires where, we hoped, we might find a replacement. Our mood was low as we contemplated our recent streak of bad luck. Life on the road was turning out to be as much of a mental challenge as it was physical.

The bus journey the next morning did nothing to cheer me up as I listened to the bikes bouncing around the hold each time we hit a bump. The landscape zoomed past and I couldn't help thinking how much more enjoyable it would be viewed from the saddle of a bike rather than a stuffy bus. At the coach station we detangled the bashed bikes and headed to a hostel; we wouldn't be riding anywhere for a while, and that was becoming an all too familiar story.

As keen as we were to get cycling, there was no rush to move. The company who made our bikes, St John's Cycles in Somerset, had agreed to send a replacement rim to a hotel in Buenos Aires, meaning another wait. The rim had most likely cracked, we discovered, due to the tyre pressure being too high for it to handle. We had followed the tyre manufacturer's guidelines, but hadn't realised the rims could not take the same kind of pressures, nor had we factored into the equation the weight that the wheel was carrying. It was frustrating that the whole thing might have been avoided, but at least we had a plan to resolve the situation.

Fortunately, there was plenty to see around Colonia del Sacremento, a city built by the Portuguese from 1680 to resist the Spanish across the Río de la Plata in Buenos Aires. We spent the days wandering around the pretty, old centre with its colonial buildings and cobbled streets, watched football in bars packed with cheering Uruguayans as their team progressed through the tournament; and we visited the local shopping mall for a pair of jeans to replace my trousers, now held up with safety pins because I had lost weight since leaving Rio.

The initial plan for our South American adventure was to cycle to every single capital in the continent, but thanks to the broken rim we were forced to abandon any hope of arriving in Montevideo by bike. Instead, we made do with a bus trip on a cold grey day which did little to bring out any charm the place may have had. We wandered around the tightly packed streets admiring a huge statue of the national hero General José Gervasio Artigas who, in 1811, had launched a revolt against Spain; while across the Plaza Independencia smartly-dressed soldiers awaited the arrival of the current president, José Mujica, a former prisoner under the military government who ruled Uruguay from 1973 to 1985. There wasn't too much else to discover in the small city, so we took our time over lunch in a food market styled to look like old railway carriages.

We could have been in a European city; the colonial influences of the Spanish and Portuguese were there in the food, culture, buildings and the look of the people themselves. This wasn't how we had expected South America to be. Where was the exotic continent of myth and legend, we wondered?

The next morning, we made our way on foot to the ferry terminal in Colonia del Sacremento, reluctantly abandoning the bikes in the terminal hall as we queued for immigration; I crossed my fingers that they would arrive in Buenos Aires with us. Uruguay hadn't been our luckiest country so far. The last few weeks had tested our patience, changing our plans and forcing us to adapt. These were important lessons which would help us further along, but not ones we necessarily appreciated at that moment. As the Argentinian immigration officer stamped my passport, I hoped his country would be more fortunate for us. Little was I to know, but Argentina was going to be good in ways I could never have imagined.

5. Argentina

People expect my standout memory of Argentina, perhaps of the entire trip, to be the moment I turned around to see Paddy on bended knee asking me to marry him. But at the time I was so surprised that I remember little of it. I think I mumbled something along the lines of, "Yes, of course. Don't be stupid; get up before anybody sees you." Which isn't the most romantic of replies.

In my defence, if you take your girlfriend on a tour of Mendoza's vineyards and propose to her after a morning of wine tasting, you should anticipate a somewhat confused reaction. I was expecting the tour guide to come back to collect us and was embarrassed she might walk in on us. Paddy knew she wouldn't, however, because he had planned this moment very carefully. It was perfect too; he was proposing on the vineyard's balcony, looking out over straight rows of neat vines to the snow-capped Andes Mountains beyond.

It is, actually, our first sight of these white peaks a few days earlier that is my strongest memory of Argentina. Riding along the road to Mendoza in the winter chill, I had suddenly noticed faint jagged shapes in the sky, peeking out through the thin white cloud. It was only when the sky cleared to reveal the mountain tops sparkling in the sun that I realised we had made it to the Andes.

Of course, it was a long way to Mendoza and getting there hadn't been straightforward. In fact, if 'Super Dad' hadn't turned up, we would probably still have been in Buenos Aires the day Paddy proposed.

Our arrival in Argentina was not emphatic. Because of Paddy's broken rim, we left the ferry terminal in Buenos Aires pushing the bikes. As we navigated packed pavements on our way past universities and grand colonial palaces painted in pastel shades, I felt conspicuously in the way.

We anticipated another wait for the replacement rim, but at

least we were in Buenos Aires, one of the most vibrant places in South America. In ornate churches built by Spanish colonialists, we were amazed by the quantity of shining gold adorning decorations from floor to ceiling; we browsed markets selling antique ornaments, vibrant paintings and general bric-a-brac. On the cobbled streets of San Telmo, we watched couples tango with long, elegant strides as they danced out the story of a prostitute and her pimp, a tradition which originated during the 1800s in the lower-class districts of Buenos Aires. We wrapped up warm for sun-downers in the trendy bars of the converted docks, and at night we fought our way off heaving metro trains to eat in Palmero restaurants that served curries and vegetarian dishes that tasted like heaven after two months of pasta.

We were escorted around the maze of narrow passages of the Recoleta Cemetery by a chubby black and white cat who had worked out this was a good spot for a feed and a stroke from the hundreds of tourists who passed through daily. The cemetery was packed with grand white stone monuments dedicated to the great and good of Argentine society, including an elaborate Art Nouveau statue of a beautiful young girl accidentally buried alive in the early 1900s. The most famous occupant was Eva Perón, or 'Evita', the wife of former President Juan Domingo Perón. From a poor background, she grew to be adored by the *descamisados*, 'the shirtless' urban workers, because of her charitable work establishing hospitals and schools, and since her death in 1952 at the age of 33, she had been revered in Argentina. We might have missed the small bronze plaque marking her burial place, were it not for the long queue outside the closed doorway to her family's tomb; decorated with pink and yellow carnations, it added colour to the sombre, monotone surroundings of the cemetery.

Buenos Aires was a city bursting with stories to tell. As we wandered through the Plaza de Mayo, we stopped to watch a group of elderly women holding placards. They were the *Madres de la Plaza de Mayo*, the mothers of adults who disappeared between 1976 and 1983 when Argentina's military dictatorship killed and abducted tens of thousands of political opponents. To this day, 500 children born to activists in prison remain missing. It is thought they were adopted by families associated with the regime and, since 1977, their mothers and grandmothers have demonstrated in front of the presidential palace demanding information about the whereabouts of their loved ones. It was sobering to think that atrocities such as these could have occurred during our lifetime and, moreover, that we had no idea about them.

This sentiment was only increased when we spotted a sign marking the place where locals, *porteños*, threw boiling oil on British invaders during the Napoleonic Wars. This made no sense to us – neither of us was able to recall discussion in history class about Britain fighting in Argentina. Some online research confirmed, however, that it was in fact true; apparently, in the early 1800s British forces twice tried to take Spanish-controlled Buenos Aires, but were sent packing both times. So much of what we learnt in school about our country's past was based on the victories and achievements, with little time devoted to the defeats and culpabilities. I loved how travelling allowed me to discover new stories and versions of history.

There was plenty of time to read up on Argentina's history while we waited for the rim, but I would have preferred to be cycling. After a week of hanging about, I was growing bored.

> ***Diary, 20 July 2011*** - *Rubbish day – suffering massively from cabin fever. Spoke to somebody on the phone who said the parcel was at the big post office near the railway station. Waited there for ages, only to hear it wasn't there. Apparently the hotel refused it yesterday and it's now being sent back to the UK. The hotel deny refusing it so we have no idea what is going on. We had to call a number who said they would look into it, so there was lots of waiting around in the hotel room. I am in a foul mood. I just want to get going, this is massively frustrating.*

Our other problem was how the extended stay in the capital was eating into our budget. Argentina had once been a cheap place to visit from Europe, but since the financial crash that hit the country in 2001, the *peso* had bounced back. Now we were finding our British pounds didn't go very far in this expensive city.

Our limited budget wasn't intended for treats, like tickets to watch the Copa America quarter-final between Brazil and Paraguay. But it was a once in a lifetime opportunity, we reasoned, as we made our way through security to the stadium in La Plata, 60 kilometres south of Buenos Aires. Inside, supporters mingled in anticipation of an explosive game, their replica shirts turning the stands a bright mix of red and gold. In spite of Brazil's superior strike force, they were unable to take their opportunities, forcing the match to a tense penalty shootout which culminated in a deafening roar from Paraguay's supporters when Brazil missed the final spot kick. It was a shock result and as Brazilians quickly made their way out of the stadium, Paraguayans cried and hugged each other in ecstasy. Their team would go on to the tournament's final, but the trophy would be lifted by Uruguay; on the day of the final, we could imagine the euphoria in Salto where the red wine would be flowing.

Arriving back from the match, the hotel owner met us excitedly in reception with the much awaited news that the parcel had finally made it to the central post office, and first thing next morning Paddy headed down to collect it. We tore open the cardboard with the excitement of children on Christmas morning, and then we swore, a lot. The bike shop had sent a rim with too many holes, and whatever we tried there was no way we could get it to work with the Rohloff hub. We were exasperated, and although the shop apologised and offered to send a new one immediately, we really couldn't afford to take another week off in terms of time and money. As I sat on the bed clutching a bottle of red wine and wondering what on earth to do, the phone rang. It was 'Super Dad' and he told us not to worry, he was hurtling along the M4 to Somerset to save the day.

Paddy's dad, Kevin, had worked as a pilot for British Airways, but he was now retired and on the lookout for new adventures. He is an older version of Paddy; people are often amazed how similar they look, and it's fascinating to watch them walk together with their identical rolling gait. They both have a love of maps and charts, and Kevin was tracking our progress online daily, sending us emails about things we might find on the road ahead. Now, he had the perfect excuse to join us. We spoke to him shortly after he left the bike shop with a new wheel that we could fit straight to the bike. Not long after, he was on a flight out of Heathrow and was in Buenos Aires in time to eat breakfast with us the next morning.

Rather than just a rim, SJS had sent a new wheel complete with hub that we could put straight onto the bike, avoiding rebuilding the entire wheel. Kevin had promised to return our defunct wheel when he arrived home. It was the best news we could have hoped for, and we were too excited at the thought of getting on the road to dwell on the fact that we had been rescued by one of our parents.

Moreover, it was wonderful to see a familiar face after so long and, over dinner in a steakhouse, we persuaded Kevin to accompany us on the road. We couldn't let him head straight back to the UK after flying all this way, so we proposed an arrangement where he would escort us by car and we would let him carry our bags; he didn't need much convincing. The next morning, as we left him to collect his rental car, we adjusted to riding without panniers as we made our way out of Buenos Aires on blissfully empty Sunday streets. We were heading west for the first time, pedalling across the Pampas, South America's fertile lowlands. A steady headwind negated the advantages of a pancake flat road, but we were still hammering out 100 kilometres per day in delight at cycling again, and thanks to Kevin's support.

Each morning we would agree recce points for the day, and he would meet us with hot coffee, banana sandwiches and cheese rolls smothered in Marmite from the tub he had brought from home. We did lose each other a few times, once in the city of Lujan, 68 kilometres from Buenos Aires. It looked inconsequential on the map, but riding through the narrow streets we discovered a main square dominated by a gothic red-brick basilica with two pointy, delicately-carved towers, that was dedicated to Argentina's patron saint, the Virgin of Lujan. Normally we might have stopped to investigate but we needed to find Kevin who, driving along the main road, hadn't realised the site existed. It was a reminder of the advantages of travelling by bike and the freedom it allowed to adapt our plans as we rode along.

We were both enjoying Kevin's company, especially the opportunity to have a conversation with somebody other than each other. As we ate lunch behind the disused railway station at Tres Sargentos, a striking yellow and white building that no longer operated, we noted how well Kevin had adapted to our nomadic way of life. He seemed to enjoy the opportunity to lay his head down in a different location each night and to discover new, unexpected places. That afternoon, we informed him, his task was to find somewhere for us to sleep about 40 kilometres away, and afternoon tea would be appreciated we added cheekily, as he waved us off in the sun.

Although Kevin seemed to be enjoying himself, I felt disappointed for him that he had joined us at a time when the scenery wasn't the most spectacular. The Pampas must have made for boring driving, they certainly weren't interesting for cycling across; the road was as straight as an arrow and surrounded by field after field of green crops of unchanging variety, or cows occasionally being rounded up by gaucho cowboys. With no other distraction, I pedalled along lost in thought with my music playing and my legs working hard to bash out the kilometres before dark. So, when Paddy gestured me to stop and suggested I put on my waterproof jacket, I wasn't impressed.

"Why? It's sunny and hot," I replied grumpily. "Do you want me to turn off my iPod as well?"

He looked at me and pointed to the sky ahead. "It might be wise, it's going to get wet."

Glancing up, I had never seen anything like it. We were stood under a bright blue sky but one kilometre along Ruta 7, dark grey clouds were tumbling towards us. I pulled on my waterproofs just in time, as five minutes later the sky above us had transformed from bright blue to black. Sheet lightning shot ferocious forks of silver through the dark sky and the wind picked up. We were struggling to keep the bikes upright and battling to stay on the narrow gap between speeding traffic on one side and the long wet grass on the other.

> ***Paddy:*** *The already-black cloud kept getting darker, but the traffic continued at the same speed. I was scared as hell that a car would clip us off the road – they probably wouldn't even have realised. All I could think about was James Cracknell's accident in America when he got clipped by a wing mirror and ended up with a horrific head injury. In the end, the only sensible thing to do was push through the long grass verge. It was hideous.*

I had never felt so exposed. In the surrounding fields there were only short, stubby crops and no trees – we were prime targets for the flashes of lightning that brightened up the sky. Normally, we would have erected a shelter with our tarpaulin, but we had left all our equipment with Kevin. Moving at less than five kilometres per hour it would take five hours to get to the next town; I was terrified and the fact that Paddy, who is normally unflappable, looked worried, highlighted the severity of the situation. Our only hope was that Kevin would rescue us before something terrible happened.

Of course, being Super Dad, he did, but those 30 minutes we spent desperately watching out for his car seemed like hours. He looked as fraught as we did when he pulled over onto the verge. After searching for over an hour, with the lashing rain and speeding traffic impeding his view, he had only just seen us. We crammed into his car, the bikes hanging out of the boot, and escaped to the safety of a roadside hotel, where we sat in the sparsely-decorated room drinking beers to recover from the afternoon's experience.

Unbelievably, an hour after Kevin rescued us, we were looking out over sunlit fields. The storm had moved on to wreak havoc in Buenos Aires, raging through the city at 86 kilometres per hour. The wind tore apart buildings, picked up trucks and knocked down trees; two people were killed and several injured. When we saw the scenes on the news, we realised how lucky we were not to have got into serious trouble.

The next day, Kevin presented us with high visibility sashes to wear; they were his parting gift. Without the replacement wheel, we would probably still have been in Buenos Aires waiting for another parcel to arrive. Instead we had enjoyed a fun week on the road together, and we were sorry to see him go.

Back carrying our own bags, with no catering assistant and stuck with each other for conversation, our mood was low and our progress slow as we battled into a lip-cracking wind. As we avoided football-sized tumbleweeds that blew across the road, I felt relieved that we were not heading south to the tip of Argentina. As much as we wanted to explore the region which is renowned for its beauty, the gales there were notorious and, more importantly, snow had begun to fall, cutting off many roads for the winter. Instead, we continued west into the state of San Luis where the scenery changed little aside from decorated shrines with fluttering red flags along the roadside. Traditionally, they were built in memory of a cowboy known as Gauchito Gil who was executed after deserting the army in the mid-1800s. Nowadays, they were found at the site of fatal road traffic accidents.

Some of the shrines may have been erected in memory of people whose mangled vehicles now lay stacked behind Fraga's police station. We had stopped there to ask if we could camp in the garden, but we went off the idea as Sébastien, the police chief, showed us around, explaining in gruesome detail about the number of fatalities from each accident. I was shocked at the sight of cars with their roofs caved in and trucks with fronts ripped off. What was astonishing was not necessarily the damage done, but the sheer number of motors in such a small space, and this police team only covered a short stretch of the route along which we were cycling.

After our tour, we were ushered into the staff room and served fresh fruit and *mate* while an officer was dispatched for the keys of an empty house belonging to the village mayor. Sébastien had organised for us to stay there and to eat at the mayor's restaurant as his guest, which we didn't realise until he refused to give us the bill. I think he found it amusing we had joined his other patrons around a bulky television set in the middle of the restaurant, to call out answers to the Argentine version of the *Who Wants to be a Millionaire?* show that was playing.

The quiz was still ongoing when a tall, dark-haired policeman arrived to drive us the few hundred metres back to our accommodation. He took a long detour, smiling as he turned on the flashing blue emergency lights and whacked up the stereo to belt out Katie Perry's *Hot n cold*; in the back seat we sat laughing along, giving each other 'this is totally random, ridiculous and awesome' looks. Our presence was probably a welcome relief from his work responding to the daily traffic accidents.

Early the next morning, we returned the keys of the mayor's house to find the team searching the scattered load of a truck that had overturned during the night. The driver had fallen asleep, sending the vehicle crashing through the central reservation, the impact of which had caused a baby to fall, fatally, from the driver's cab. We quietly returned the keys and nodded goodbye to the exhausted team who were busy taking statements in the hazy dawn light. It was a sombre sight and we put on our high-vis sashes as we got back into the saddle, more aware than ever of the need to be careful on this road.

At lunch, still touched by the generosity of the police team, we looked at the photographs from the night before, relieved they hadn't seen our earlier shots of me standing next to a 'Las Malvinas son Argentinas' sign. The Malvinas, or the Falklands Islands as they are known in Britain, are an archipelago of islands about 500 kilometres off the Argentinian coast in the South Atlantic Ocean. Argentina is the closest country geographically, but they came under British control in 1833. On 2 April 1982 the Argentine military government launched an invasion, in part to distract Argentinians from domestic problems, and in the hope that politicians in Westminster, nearly 13,000 kilometres away, would not have the inclination or political power to respond. In doing so, they underestimated the iron will of the Prime Minister, Margaret Thatcher, who sent a task force to relieve the islands. Three months after the initial invasion, British forces defeated the ill-prepared Argentinian military and control was returned to Britain at the cost of 900 lives.

Aside from wondering why either side was intent on owning the islands and assuming it probably had something to do with the offshore oil reserves, we had little opinion on who the Falklands should belong to, which we had explained in our basic Spanish to the police team when they asked what we thought. However, we found the 'Las Malvinas' road signs amusing and Paddy had photographed me posing in front of one pulling an exaggerated frown and pointing my thumbs down. Sat in the staff room, enjoying their hospitality, I was incredibly nervous when they suggested we have a photograph together, that they might see the shot of me in front of the sign; it might quickly have changed their feelings towards us.

Continuing to battle into the wind with our heads down, we were slow to realise we were now riding amongst fields of tightly-packed vines owned by family-run wineries, *bodegas*; we were getting closer to Mendoza. The city sits in the shadow of the Andes Mountains, the longest continental mountain range in the world, running for 7,000 kilometres along the continent, from Venezuela to Argentina. People often asked how we planned to cycle over the Andes, but I never gave it much thought, because, starting in Rio de Janeiro, I couldn't imagine reaching them. Over the past few weeks, as we realised we were getting closer, we had discussed the practicalities more, but that hadn't prepared me for the moment a gap cleared in the cloud to expose a cluster of Toblerone-shaped pyramids, dusted with a sprinkling of snow.

Diary, 9 August 2011 - *We decided to try out the old road that runs parallel with Ruta 7 and it was great. Hardly any traffic at all which meant plenty of time to admire the fabulous views of the Andes which came into view early on. They are beautiful – shimmering with snow. The closer we got to Mendoza the bigger they look and we still have some distance to cover to get to them. We were both incredibly excited and I was cycling along with a ridiculously huge grin and tears in my eyes (I may be a little hormonal!). It's incredible to believe we have got here by bike. We talked so much about this moment. I can't wait to cycle over them and get over the nerves and excitement of it.*

We had actually already started climbing; the seemingly-flat road from Buenos Aires to Mendoza had brought us to a height of 746 metres. There was a further 2,454 metres to climb to the Paso Internacional Los Libertadores and the border with Chile. Tour de France cyclists probably don't prepare for a mountain stage with a visit to the local vineyards, but that is exactly where we were headed. During evenings spent planning the trip, we pored over maps and guide books in the company of a good bottle of velvety Argentinian Malbec, and we were keen to see for ourselves how the wine was produced. Mendoza, producing two-thirds of Argentina's wine, was the perfect place to do this.

The Argentinian approach to wine tasting was to quaff the entire glass; none of this spitting it out nonsense, which suited us. There were whites, sparkling and reds, plus, at our third vineyard a four course lunch with matching wines. So, outside on the restaurant's balcony, when I turned around to see Paddy on bended knee, my first reaction was that the morning had caught up with him and he had fallen over. When I realised that he was proposing, I was completely taken aback.

Paddy: *In advance of the trip, Laura's father, Rick, was the only person who knew that I planned to ask her to marry me. I'd plucked up the courage to ask his permission driving back from the golf course. I was more nervous than I expected,* *because during our game I lost most of his golf balls and hadn't brought enough cash to pay for lunch. He still said "yes" though, chuckled a bit and then turned the radio back up – he's northern, you see. I didn't say when I planned to do it, as I didn't want to feel pressure on Skype calls home from excited voices asking for "any news".*

Before we left, Mendoza was one of a few places I considered to ask Laura. It was three months into the trip; we loved the wine there, and the backdrop of the Andes would be a great vista to look out on, as well as signifying a large challenge for us on the trip. A week before we arrived, I contacted a wine tour company with my plan, as everything felt right. Both of us had adjusted to our way of life and I loved being able to share together the experiences that each day brought. I couldn't think of not doing this trip with Laura and I felt so lucky that we were doing something we both enjoyed.

On the day itself the wine tasting helped settle my nerves, or at least until the plans had to change. There was another couple on the tour and the guy got sick, leaving the girl to tag onto us. I was going to propose over lunch but it was now gate-crashed. I was so nervous during the meal that I could barely eat, although I don't think Laura noticed. Fortunately, there was a balcony upstairs that I could use and Laura came up there, to find me on bended knee.

The next day, Paddy suggested, we should go shopping for an engagement ring. It hadn't immediately occurred to me that he hadn't given me one, but when it did I was worried there may have been one in the bag he lost in Paraguay; he insisted there wasn't. We picked out a simple, white gold ring with a blue stone which we thought was lovely but hopefully not shiny enough to attract too much attention. I was so excited and couldn't stop staring at the ring. It all felt very right. Our friends and family wanted to know if we would be getting married on the trip, but we had decided to wait until we got home; for the moment we had other things to deal with, like cycling over the Andes.

I had never cycled up a mountain before. I imagined there would be one steep road up to the top and another descending sharply on the other side. It doesn't work like that, I realised, as we trundled slowly into the foothills of the Andes – Mount Aconcagua, the highest mountain outside of the Himalayas, still hidden from view by the cluster of smaller peaks in the foreground. Looking over the handlebars the road appeared flat, and it was only when I stopped a third time to check if my brakes were stuck on, that I realised the sensation of riding through sand was because we were climbing. Although it was a cool day the effort required warmed us, and we stripped to our T-shirts for the first time in weeks as we rode past low rocky mounds, dotted with short dry shrubs.

After several hours of slow riding, we were surprised to find ourselves racing downhill; it was a break for the legs but meant the last hour of climbing had been wasted. The descent stopped at a sparkling blue dam, Embalse de Potrerillos, on the shores of which we camped that evening in the company of a shaggy brown dog who fell asleep on the tent. The next day, our route took us upstream along the narrow banks of the Río Mendoza, which over thousands of years had cut a gently-sloping pathway into the towering walls of rock. The gradient may have been easy to cycle, but the narrow passageway tunnelled a howling wind, forcing us to walk in sections where the gusts were so strong they seemed intent on sending road signs flying down the valley.

I wasn't enjoying fighting against the wind, and I didn't appreciate being photographed by a tourist who stood snapping away as I struggled towards him. So, when I reached him and he turned his back on me and jumped into his car, I was furious. It was strange when complete strangers took our picture, but if people said "hello" or waved, then I didn't mind. This guy, however, was just plain rude and I was flabbergasted as the car took off up the road.

Temporarily distracted, I hadn't noticed our cycle computer tick over the 5,000 kilometre point for the trip as we rode into the incredible landscape of the wide Uspallata Valley. It was framed with crags in shades of gold, red and white that were lit by the sun and, high above, looming grey peaks sported a sprinkling of snow. The dusty gorge floor was split in two by the river, which had made the most of the wide valley to expand and bulge. The movie *Seven Years in Tibet* starring Brad Pitt, was filmed in Uspallata, the surrounding mountains acting as the Tibetan Himalayas.

The following morning we reached the far side of the valley, where the cliffs of cool rock were so high they blocked the sunlight from permeating downwards. Large boulders sat precariously nestled on ledges in the rock face, and scattered across the roadside was the debris of ones that had fallen. By the time we had ridden out of the narrow corridor it was lunch and we stopped in a small workers' settlement, where, too tired to eat, I threw my sandwiches to a small, long-fringed dog who approached us nervously.

We had sat near a sign explaining this was the same route General José de San Martin's second division of the 'Army of the Andes' took in 1817 on their way to liberate Chile from Spanish rule. Wanting to maintain an element of surprise, he led his 4,000 troops by an unusual route through the mountains, losing a third of his men during the 21 days it took to reach the Chilean capital of Santiago. The army had marched during the Argentine summer, and we were soon to learn why.

An hour later, turning out of the cold valley we had spent the morning pedalling up, we found a blanket of white; we had cycled up to the snow line. It was exciting to have ridden so high and we stopped to celebrate with a snowball fight, but the snow was icy and clung to the rocks, resistant to being used for ammunition. We carried on past button lifts and snow ploughs to a tourist hotel in the ski resort of Los Penitentes. There was just 20 kilometres of road left to the border with Chile which we could easily cover the next day, and we drifted off to sleep under layers of blankets, delighted with our progress.

It was a surprise then, to wake up the next morning and see absolutely no sign of the road. Thick snow covered the entire resort. We walked outside to investigate, traipsing through snow that buried our shoes, laughing at the craziness of the situation; we were going nowhere, so settled down with books in front of a roaring fire. Over breakfast the next day, we were delighted to see a snow plough shuffling downhill after clearing the road higher up, and we quickly collected our stuff and jumped on the bikes before they could close the route again.

We had the road to ourselves as we rode up to Puente del Inca. The air was still and bitterly cold, but there was no snow and I pedalled along savouring the sharp white scenery. After our worries of the previous day, we were moving again and it felt incredible to be so close to Chile. So, on leaving the village, when snowflakes began to fall and the road became slippery with ice, I could understand why Paddy wanted to ignore the situation and carry on riding. My bike was skidding out from under me, however, and in a couple of minutes the cycling had gone from glorious to dangerous.

Each time I stopped to steady myself, my metal cleats slipped on the icy road when I tried to push off. Three men wearing heavy overcoats and rubber boots who had followed us out of Puente del Inca had soon overtaken us, nodding at us indifferently as they headed towards an outhouse further along the road; stomping through the snow, they could move far faster than us on the tarmac. When my back wheel skidded out from me, leaving me fighting to hold the bike upright, I decided it wasn't wise to continue and headed back to the village, leaving Paddy to battle uphill alone.

Soon, he joined me in the tiny wooden café where I had already ordered two mugs of creamy hot chocolate. The owner shook his head with a laugh when we asked if the road was open, saying more snow was expected and it would be at least two days before they opened the route to the border; it was disappointing news, we were just 16 kilometres from Chile. Despondent, we sat next to his wood-burning stove, cradling hot chocolates and pondering our options: camping was not possible in the snow, accommodation in the tiny, tourist hostel cost far too much, and we were short on supplies and cash. Yet, the thought of having to cycle down the mountain after all our effort climbing made me want to cry. While we were discussing the best thing to do, a bus arrived to return stranded locals to Uspallata. The driver said his was the final transport until the road reopened and, not wanting to get stuck, we resigned ourselves to returning to town until we could move on again.

The next two days were a waiting game; every few hours, we headed to the bus station for news, but nobody knew anything. Lorries lined the high street and the road into town, while the truck park was stacked with row upon row of transporters waiting to make their way into Chile. By the end of our second day in Uspallata there were about 2,000 trucks waiting to make the crossing. We realised when the road finally reopened there was no way we could cycle back up the mountain next to these monster transporters, but neither could we afford to hang around and wait for them to pass in case another snowfall closed the road. So, at the bus station we pleaded with a driver to squeeze us into his bus; encouraged by a sizeable tip, he agreed.

On day three there was at last some good news and we crammed into the stuffy, two decker coach where passengers had been sleeping since the bus arrived in Uspallata days earlier. We joined the long throng of traffic heading for the border, looking away in sadness at the point where we had been forced to abandon our climb. I knew there was no way we could cycle, there were icy patches and thick snow was piled against the side of the road, but I was still disappointed. We didn't even see Mount Aconcagua; grey clouds obscured the peaks and we only knew we had passed it because a sign pointed in its direction.

We had two entrance and two exit stamps for Argentina, but on none of those crossings had we managed to cycle across the border. In between, however, we had some fantastic cycling and once in a lifetime moments, including getting engaged. The bus slowed as we approached the immigration post, and I felt disappointed not to be leaving the country under our own steam; our departure in Argentina was as unemphatic as our arrival in Buenos Aires all those weeks ago. I hoped in Chile we might finally make some progress on our bikes.

6. Chile

The impatient bus driver dragged us by the arms, gesturing that we should collect our belongings that, oddly, were now strewn in front of the concrete immigration building. We had been inside collecting our passport stamps, so I had no idea what was going on, but I did as I was told and carried my panniers into a cold metal hut, where a line of officials scanned and inspected our bags with the upmost suspicion. Unlike most borders around the world, the officials were concentrating their search on food rather than drugs, I realised, looking at the posters covering the grey walls. Our fellow passengers rolled their eyes as one of my bags was held up and a surly female official directed me to empty the contents on the desk. She suspected I was carrying a watermelon and looked disappointed not to be able to issue a hefty fine when, instead, she pulled out my compressed sleeping bag.

The cloud cover was thick and the bus' headlights cast the only light on the road as we wound round the first of 29 tight switchbacks, cut into the mountain face. We edged slowly downhill along a narrow stretch of cleared tarmac, between piles of glistening snow that had been pushed to the sides. I couldn't help but notice a lack of guardrails to stop us careering over the edge if we skidded, and I spent the journey to Santiago staring at the red digital clock above the driver's cabin, trying to ignore the rolling sensation each time the bus turned into a bend.

It was midnight by the time we had offloaded the bikes, bent the mudguards back into position, refitted the wheels and cycled to the hotel that was to be base while we explored Santiago. We had read positive things about Chile's capital city and soon slipped into the relaxed way of life there, enjoying the city's international food and culture. Our hotel was in the *Paris* region, a quiet area with cobbled streets and old terraces with ornate stonework, lit by art-nouveau lamp posts, from where it was only a short walk to the central meeting point of the *Plaza de Armas*. Bordered by grand buildings, the heart of the square was an area where locals and tourists gathered to meet friends under the shade of tall leafy trees, surrounded by fearless pigeons scrounging for food.

Although the mountains were several dozen kilometres away, they seemed part of the city; the backdrop of the snowy peaks was visible from almost every street corner through the ever-present haze that hung low over the city. Students carrying leather satchels owned the streets, drinking coffee at tables squeezed onto pavements, or waving placards outside the university campuses, calling for free secondary education for all. The city had a relaxed vibe and, as in Buenos Aires and Montevideo, I had the feeling of being in Europe rather than South America.

Santiago had not always possessed such a calm atmosphere. In the impressive Museum of Memory and Human Rights, we learnt about offences committed by General Augusto Pinochet's government which, in 1973, when it came to power in a military coup, ordered the imprisonment and exile of Socialist supporters. Within a year, several thousand had been killed and over 30,000 people removed from Chile. It was a gruesome time in the country's history, but it was encouraging to see that during the last 40 years things had changed and protesting students no longer seemed to fear violent repercussions from the authorities.

Our last afternoon in Santiago was spent exploring a mall where every sport imaginable was catered for. It was grander than anything we'd seen in the UK and indicated the wealth floating around Chile, the only country in South America not to have been hit by the recent worldwide recession. After buying new T-shirts to replace the smelly, sweat-ingrained ones we had been wearing since Rio, we headed off to sample the local *pisco sours* – frothy white cocktails made with grape brandy that slipped down very easily.

The next morning, we hit the road with fuzzy heads, but it was a straightforward ride out of the city along the smooth Route 68. There was even a passenger service for cyclists, operated by road maintenance vehicles through two tunnels, the longest being almost three kilometres under the foothills of the Andes. Heading west, it took two days to cycle from Santiago to the seaside resort of Valparaiso, and although descending from 520 metres to sea level should have been easy, a heavy rainstorm rolled in from the ocean slowing us down. Visibility was so poor that a concerned driver jumped out of his car to tell us we were almost impossible to see. From his backseat he pulled out two fluorescent tabards for us to wear – the vests came around South America with us, time after time highlighting our presence to rushing drivers on busy roads.

We avoided the gushing drainage channels at the side of the road as we freewheeled towards the Pacific Ocean. For many days, Paddy had been reciting the closing lines to his favourite film, *The Shawshank Redemption*, by saying that he hoped "the Pacific is as blue as it has been in my dreams"; he was disappointed, under a dreary sky the choppy waters appeared sludgy grey instead. However, we were still thrilled we had made it from the Atlantic to the Pacific and a few rainclouds couldn't dull our mood.

Valparaiso grew in the 19th century as a stop-off point for boats sailing between the two oceans. The wealth of the city led to an influx of European immigrants, who developed clever techniques to settle in a landscape dominated by steep hills rising sharply from the narrow coastal plain. They built box-like houses that clung to the face of the slopes, and painted them in bright shades of pink, blue and yellow to brighten up the city on dreary days. As the population grew, a network of funiculars was developed – cable-driven elevators that carried people from home to work. The lifts still operated, some of which were beautifully elaborate, but the one heading towards our hostel resembled a cardboard box on wheels, giving us little option but to push the bikes up the slippery cobbled streets instead.

In town, we went in search of Paddy's favourite reading material: maps. A bookshop owner, upon hearing about our trip, pulled out a chart from behind the counter and, before we knew it, was excitedly drawing a wiggly line up to the Bolivian border for us to follow. From his motorbike adventures he knew the area well, and suggested we ignore the main roads and leave town by the coastal route that climbed over low hills, northwards for the first time on the trip.

It was easy riding with calming views of the ocean crashing onto the rocks, and my mind drifted off. Today was my grandad's funeral. Over the past few years he had been battling cancer and Parkinson's disease, and before we left he was already very sick. I knew then I wouldn't see him again, but I didn't want to upset him with a full-blown goodbye, so we had simply shared an extra-long hug, as we usually did if I was going travelling. As we cycled along, I was sad not to be there to say goodbye properly.

It was a downside to the trip that we were too far away to get home for important moments like this, or the weddings of friends and cuddles with their new-born babies. However, although we weren't there in person, countless hours in the saddle gave me time to think about them more than I probably would have at home; my grandad's passing, especially, weighed on my mind. Henry Pollitt was a traditional, northern working-class man of his generation; known to his friends as Harry, he enjoyed a pint while playing snooker at the clubhouse with his friends, had a wit as dry as a bone, and could fix any electrical gadget using the collection of wires in his garden shed. He had retired while I was still a baby, and although there were regular catch ups with old friends and sometimes a trip with my gran to Blackpool, generally, his days passed happily and uneventfully. Between them, my grandparents had been abroad to Europe only a handful of times; neither had much desire to travel, preferring instead the familiarities of home.

I, on the other hand, have always loved to explore. Aged 18, I announced that I wouldn't be going straight to university; instead I was heading to Africa with my backpack, where I spent several months travelling by bus from Kenya down to South Africa. Through the people I met and things I saw, I learnt more about the way the world works than I ever did in a lecture room, and ever since have been hooked on exploring the world. I generally last about two years in a job before my feet started twitching and I find myself poring over guidebooks as I plan my next escape. I often wondered as we rode along, if I would be able to return from an amazing trip like this and settle down to a 'normal' life.

It was late August, the Chilean avocado harvest had just begun, and as we turned inland from the coast, trucks rattled along, heavy with crates of fruit destined for market. On the bookshop owner's advice, we were avoiding the busy Pan American Highway, a road that stretches from Alaska in North America to the tip of Argentina, and instead found ourselves riding along old mining trails that regularly disappeared through narrow gloomy tunnels. One afternoon, after summiting several false peaks, we finally reached the head of the valley, where we were rewarded with views across a lush green basin surrounded by barren hills, their slopes dotted with shadows of wispy clouds. We stopped for photographs and, not wanting to hold him up, we declined a pickup driver's offer of a lift through the next tunnel. He looked confused by our decision and about a third of the way along, we realised why.

Paddy: *After donning our reflective vests, we entered the heavily rutted tunnel. As we bounced along the rough tarmac the dim light from our head torches picked out gravelly potholes. The walls were damp with water running down through the hill and about a third of the way into the tunnel we realised why the driver had looked at us strangely when we refused the lift. A large pool of water had collected, it came up over our ankles and spread the entire width of the tunnel. Under the light of our head torches it sat dark and oily, but we had no choice other than to wade through it.*

Laura went first and I could hear her swearing from the shock of the cold water seeping into her shoes. I followed close behind, stumbling into hidden potholes but at least it was easy to push the bikes, the panniers seemed to float on the water and kept the frame upright. About halfway through, a truck appeared heading towards us, he waited for a bit but then got impatient and edged forwards past us. What an idiot. We had to squeeze up against the wall so he could get past, splashing us with cold, dirty water as he did.

When we finally stumbled into the light, we were in a quiet valley of sandy hills and stubby bushes, the dry leaves of which rustled in the wind. Our route meandered through Las Chinchillas National Reserve, parallel to an abandoned railway line along which donkeys wandered freely. Wild colonies of long-tailed chinchillas lived in the park and my eyes scanned the grey rocky landscape for any sign of the furry critters without success. It was a distraction, at least, from the two hour climb out of the reserve, a crunching ascent up a set of switchbacks that had us grinding slowly along in first gear. It was exhausting work and, having collapsed on our backs at the top, we joked that although it might have been easy for the bookshop owner on a mountain bike, we were ready to head back towards the coast in search of friendlier gradients.

We were greeted at the gate of our campsite for the evening by a burly St Bernard, a vivid blue peacock and a gnarly goose, the welcoming noise of which brought a girl running to check the cause of the commotion. She explained the campsite was closed for the winter, but let us pitch our tent on the overgrown lawn under the supervision of the animals. A few hours later, I was questioning whether wild camping would have been preferable as I hid on a child's climbing frame to escape the pantomime below.

We had set up the stove on one of the picnic tables, which attracted the attention of the St Bernard who had decided that, in Paddy, he had found his soul mate. He hovered around us as we cooked our pasta, accompanied by his admirer, the goose. The peacock was more obsessed with scratching the earth for food, but if it ever did so near the dog, the over-protective goose would attack. It had all been quite amusing until the peacock flew over my head to escape, followed by the goose hanging onto the blue tail feathers. We hurried to the climbing frame to escape, eating dinner ten feet up as the St Bernard looked up at us with the pleading eyes of a hen-pecked husband.

By mid-morning the next day we had arrived at the wide, quiet Pan American Highway and thanks to easier terrain, within just a few days had passed into the Atacama Region. The Atacama Desert, a 1,000 kilometre strip of land along the Pacific coast is the driest desert in the world. It was our second 'Triple A' challenge of the trip, so-called because we had identified the Andes, Atacama Desert and Amazon Rainforest as the three biggest obstacles on our route around South America.

That first evening in the Atacama, we camped on an old river bed: it was the only cover from view of the road that we could find. Although the desert is about three million years old, I didn't know if occasionally there was rain and whether we needed to be concerned about flash floods. Paddy was finding my dithering irritating, I could tell, and he impatiently told me not to worry, before letting out a loud yelp. Bending over to pick up a bag, he had accidently brushed against a cactus and now had thick, prickly spikes, each about five centimetres long, embedded in his backside. He swore loudly as I carefully pulled them out and sprayed his backside with antiseptic; then we moved the tent, again.

Initially, the scenery was rather dull, consisting of little more than brown rock after brown rock, plus the temperature had soared and the undulating terrain made for brutal days in the saddle. So, we were delighted to discover one morning, that parallel to the highway a new road was being built. Aside from workers we had to weave around every few hours, it was completely empty and smooth. It was a real treat to be away from the traffic and we ate lunch in the middle of what would soon be a major highway, before setting up camp for the night in a cutaway under the road.

We awoke to discover a grey blanket of marine mist covering the desert. Known as 'la Camanchaca', this fog enables delicate purple flowers to bloom in one of the driest places on earth, creating a welcome break in the brown landscape. Underneath the desert surface, the earth was packed with gold, silver, coal, copper and iron. In August 2010, just north of the sprawling city of Copiapo, 33 miners were trapped when the San Jose copper mine collapsed. They spent 69 days deep underground, until they were dramatically brought to the surface in narrow rescue capsules.

We had a tailwind as we left Copiapo and, heading west towards the coast were flying along, easily covering 75 kilometres by lunch. If I had been in any doubt about the support we were receiving from the wind, the pained expressions of the four Russian cyclists heading the other way confirmed it; wrapped in headscarves to protect their faces from sand, they looked to be having a miserable time. They were scientists from the Russian Geographic Society and were cycling, rowing and walking around the Pacific Ring of Fire, a 40,000 kilometre horseshoe where earthquakes and volcanic eruptions occur in the basin of the Pacific Ocean. They seemed significantly under-equipped in terms of their cycle equipment; their panniers were waterproofed using plastic bags, while they each had a wire basket mounted to their handlebars that held, amongst other things, bottles of vodka.

Under this weight, it was no surprise they were moving slowly, but they were travelling light compared to the Mexican we met further on. From his weathered face it was hard to tell his age, but he looked over 60. He had left his home in Mexico months earlier, he told us, and was headed south, seemingly with all his worldly belongings in the cart he pulled behind his bike; plastic bags, thermos flasks, blankets and a long wooden stick poked out of the top. He was dressed in an eclectic mix of Lycra shorts, long leggings, a cotton jumper, high-vis vest and a thick woollen hat from which his ears protruded.

As we rode through the Pan de Azucar National Park the next morning, it took a while for our legs to warm up after covering 169 kilometres the previous day – our longest yet. Our bikes felt heavy under the weight of the extra supplies we had packed to get us through 400 kilometres of desert before the next town. The quiet coastal track hugged the Pacific, and riding over black mounds of ancient lava, and past untouched white beaches, I felt privileged to be in a place few people ever visit. We ate lunch in a small bay where hundreds of pelicans pestered local fishermen for their catch, before spending the afternoon climbing the gentle gradient of a dry riverbed back to the Pan American Highway and into a hot rusty-red landscape. That night we set up the tent behind a small hill, and it was the most perfect camping spot.

> ***Diary, 9 September 2011*** - *I'm sat here admiring the most amazing views. Rolling desert, peaked hills, endless valleys and what looks like the cone of an old volcano with three flows of white, far away in the distance. Just had our pasta and tomato sauce and now waiting for the stars to come out. This is what this trip is all about!*

The next few days provided some spectacular cycling. The earth was barren, but the hues of red made it look like the surface of Mars and it was a beautiful, unique landscape to ride through. The traffic was infrequent and the few passing drivers seemed happy to see us, as we got friendly toots from truckers and some even stopped to donate juicy oranges and biscuits to our supplies; "*Por energia*", one said, slapping Paddy cheerfully on the back. He was driving non-stop from Lima, Peru to Santiago, which would take him two days, and he bellowed a deep belly laugh when we told him it would take us three months to cycle between the two.

The undulating terrain was hard on the legs and the heat parched us, but it felt liberating to be out in the wild. Each evening we pitched our tent off the main road, away from the headlight beams of trucks which drove throughout the night, and then set about trying to rub the red dust off our skin with baby wipes, which were no substitute for a hot shower. After dinner we would lie looking up at the clear sky counting the stars, the dry desert air providing great visibility for amateur stargazers and also teams of professionals with gigantic telescopes that were dotted around the region. Early one morning, I was woken by the sensation of the ground moving beneath my sleeping mat – it felt as if I was lying on a water mattress that somebody was gently shaking. The earthquake's tremors were so gentle that Paddy didn't even wake up and I soon drifted back to sleep, rocked by the movement of the earth underneath me.

Normally, we found cover for the tent behind small mounds that had been dug by local mining companies. Mining had long been an important industry in the area, and we cycled past the yellow crumpled ruins of Ruinas de Britania and Alemania, where British and German companies had once processed nitrate. Nitrate, or 'white gold' as it was known, was once a huge industry for Chile who exploited the colossal supplies beneath the dusty sands of the Atacama. However, in 1909, German scientists discovered how to create nitrogen in a laboratory and the industry collapsed, abandoning settlements across the Atacama, like Britania, for the desert to slowly reclaim.

Once a day, we would pass a *posada*, a trucker's rest stop. Here we were able to fill up our water bottles and sometimes found an ice lolly to stuck; absolute nectar in the middle of the desert. A few hours after leaving the Posada San Francisco, a turquoise wooden shack where we had hugged bottles of Pepsi in an attempt to cool down, we saw a strange sight; a cyclist with a birthday banner flying from his bike trailer was heading towards us. It turned out that it was Piers' 30th birthday, and the Dutchman was delighted to meet his first cyclists since he started riding in the north of Chile. He was on a seven week adventure to Santiago and, alone, he was finding the empty roads tough work mentally. We would have loved to chat longer, but Piers needed more water before nightfall and we didn't have enough to share, so we waved goodbye with cries of "Happy Birthday" as we headed in our different directions.

It was lunchtime the following day before we arrived at the next *posada*. The morning ride had been relatively easy and we were in high spirits, but low on water, so were relieved to reach the wooden hut. Only, when we rode up to the gate there was no sign of life, the doors were padlocked, and we couldn't access a tap. There was no need to panic, it was 35 kilometres to the next *posada* and we should arrive within a couple of hours. We rationed our water and ate our last biscuits and oranges; they didn't provide much energy, but we didn't expect the next few hours to be too challenging.

Back into the saddles, however, we found the wind had changed direction and intensified. We entered a narrow passage between hills that forced the ferocious wind straight at us and I could only manage to power the bike to four kilometres per hour, a ridiculous speed considering we were heading downhill. Our progress was excruciatingly slow and, in frustration, I found myself crying, but without tears as I was so dehydrated. My mood was made worse when a kind, but speeding, driver threw us oranges out of his cab window, and the juicy fruit exploded on hitting the road. I dismounted and let the bike fall to the ground in despair.

> ***Paddy:*** *There wasn't too much I could say to Laura other than to give her a big hug and reassure her that we could do it and, more to the point, that we had no other choice but to carry on. After a sit down and some disgustingly warm water, we set off with me in front, trying to provide as much of a windbreak as possible. I focused on my cycling computer and aimed for a steady ten kilometres per hour but in the gusting wind it was difficult to achieve, and instead I spent most of the time looking over my shoulder to see Laura, head down, pushing hard on the pedals with the miserable expression of a tired toddler post-tantrum.*

We finally arrived at the *posada* at 4.30pm; it had taken us four hours to cycle 35 kilometres downhill. By the time our food arrived, we had drunk two litre bottles of cold, sweet Pepsi. I had never been so thirsty. The sun was beginning to set by the time we had refuelled, and, exhausted, we decided to pitch the tent at the *posada*. While Paddy unloaded the bikes, I went in search of a suitable place, walking around the corner of the building straight into a sleeping pack of wild dogs.

One by one they lifted their heads off the dusty ground, eyeballing me with menacing stares that caused my heart to pound. It was an ugly, inbred collection, many looked alike. They must have lived off scraps from the big rubbish bins lined up behind the *posada*, but they obviously fancied making a meal out of me as well. Slowly, not wanting to show how terrified I was, I backed away until I was around the side of the building and out of their sight, and then I ran.

Two kilometres further along the road, we found a mining mound off the road which would provide enough cover for the evening. After collecting a number of melon-sized rocks to anchor the tent down in the wind, we crawled into our sleeping bags for one last night in the desert.

The next morning, the wind had turned again and we covered 30 kilometres in the first hour as we made our way to Antofagasta. It was a fabulous way to spend the last day of my twenties and I freewheeled towards the Pacific Ocean with a girlish grin at the relief of feeling the sea breeze again, and the joy of seeing the ocean and bright flowers after days of endless red desert. After four nights of camping we looked like vagabonds, and it took some persuading to convince the reception staff to allow us to stay at the beachfront hotel that Paddy had booked as my birthday treat.

The hotel, with its hot showers and fluffy white towels, was just one of the surprises Paddy had arranged; there were balloons, cards and messages from friends and family, and even a relaxing massage that my aching limbs adored. If I had been in London I would have been rather melodramatic about turning 30. I have never taken ageing well and major milestones were the worst; yet, on the road, the number didn't matter. I was having a fantastic time with a wonderful guy – I was living my life.

Cycling uphill to leave Antofagasta was tough after several days of eating and drinking. It didn't bode well for the next stretch of the journey up to the Bolivian border, which required us to climb higher than at any point yet. Our first port of call was Calama, 200 kilometres away at an altitude of 2,260 metres, where we planned to acclimatise for a day before climbing up to the border at 3,920 metres. Only, it didn't look as if I was going anywhere. I was leaning over my handlebars at the base of the road that disappeared into the hills, feeling incredibly sick with a swollen stomach. I was so exhausted, I felt ready to collapse; we had no choice but to head back into town.

This wasn't the first time my body had given up and delayed our progress. On a few other occasions I had crumpled along the roadside in a heap and we'd been forced to abandon riding for the day. We didn't know what was causing the acute nausea and bloating, or the extreme exhaustion, when my limbs felt too heavy to lift. When we returned home I discovered I have food intolerances, particularly to gluten, the sticky stuff in wheat, barley and rye. In South America we were living off a high gluten diet with lots of bread and pasta. Unbeknown to me, the food I was eating in huge quantities to power me along the road was making me sick. Since I've cut out these 'bad' foods my symptoms have all but disappeared. I wish I had known there was such an easy solution. It would have been difficult to follow such a strict diet, but it could have made a big difference to my energy levels.

The delayed departure wasn't totally bad; Paddy was able to carry out maintenance on the bikes and, when I woke up, it gave me the opportunity to order my wedding dress. After our engagement we realised that neither of us was keen on a big wedding in England, and we had started to hatch a plan for something different. My parents had wanted to visit us, but during their available dates we would be in Venezuela, which they didn't fancy. Instead, they had offered to pay for us to take a two hour flight to Barbados and meet them there for a week's holiday. The arrangements had been made before we got engaged, and it seemed a great opportunity to organise a small wedding. Our parents and siblings seemed understanding and quite keen to spend a week in the Caribbean in February, so the wheels were in motion for a wedding in five months' time.

It would be a very simple affair, with only ten guests, so there was not a huge amount to organise; however, I did need a dress. The decision was made easier by having limited options, as the sun had got through the mesh of my cycling shirt to imprint a sports bra outline across my back. Looking online I found just one design I thought might cover the marks, and as I could order it made-to-measure, I decided to take the plunge. Paddy borrowed a tape measure and sized me up, I entered the details into the website and pressed send; perhaps the quickest purchase of a wedding dress ever.

When we finally made it to Calama, there was plenty of time to rest and acclimatise as the town was closed for a public holiday. From here it would be eight days before the next opportunity to restock, and when the shops finally reopened we bought so much food that the bikes were their heaviest yet, mine weighing in at about 65 kilograms and Paddy's 75 kilograms. Consequently, it was slow going as we started the climb out of Calama.

The sky was clear, baby blue and, on either side of the exposed road the land was sandy and rocky. There were few points of interest aside from the spectacular volcanoes on our horizon, with their jagged edges and snow-capped peaks. By nightfall the tarmac had ended and we camped off the road in the dusty outline of an old riverbed, the wind snatching at the canvas. The volcano cones continued to elude us the next day, as we struggled with the altitude and gradients.

> ***Diary, 21 September 2011*** - *God, this is much harder than I expected. We managed to cover just 35 kilometres today. Started off into a headwind, which really didn't help. By the time the wind changed this afternoon we were both exhausted and struggling with the altitude. I am completely lethargic and wobbling about the place. Paddy's suffering with his head and stomach. Stunning scenery with the volcanoes, but I'm not really taking any of it in.*

By the time we called it quits for the day at lunchtime, we had climbed to 3,500 metres. The combination of altitude and physical exertion was clearly affecting us – we could hardly drag the bikes into cover, let alone cycle. It took almost an hour to pitch the tent as we needed to sit down to catch our breath after pushing each peg into the ground. Altitude sickness affects everybody in different ways and there are a range of symptoms, some of which can be fatal. At 2,500 metres people start feeling the effects, but over 3,500 metres symptoms are often worse because the lower air density means less oxygen to inhale.

By resting up, most people can normally acclimatise to the altitude and, lucky for us, the next morning our acute symptoms had disappeared. We covered 51 kilometres, summiting a 3,965 metre pass where we were rewarded with views of an incredible extinct volcano that had erupted sideways leaving an exposed pattern of coppers, yellows and reds that were tinged with patches of white snow. It was an awe-inspiring sight, yet I kept my eyes on the road as we wound through a series of minefields, marked by large yellow signs.

This area had been contested by Chile and Bolivia since Simón Bolívar established Bolivia in 1825. He granted the new nation access to the Pacific coast, something which Chile strongly disputed. In the late 1800s, the Santiago government defeated Bolivia and Peru in the War of the Pacific to annex the nitrate-producing regions and leave Bolivia landlocked. In 1913, as compensation, Chile opened the Arica-La Paz railway which stretched 440 kilometres from Chile's most northerly port to the capital of Bolivia, La Paz. The line gave Bolivia access to the sea for its exports but only a few goods trains made the journey still, one of which was huffing slowly uphill towards us.

From the minefield, we arrived in a workers' camp, where dust-covered men stood chatting. They seemed nonplussed to see *'gringos'* as they called us and instinctively pointed in the direction of a water pipe, which they correctly assumed we were looking for. Their camp was on the edge of the Salar de Ascotán, a soggy salt plain that in areas had turned to black slush under the weight of trucks traversing it. The salt pan was too long for us to cover in a day and, on seeing a pit where we could camp, I lowered the bikes down to Paddy and we chose the driest patch on which to pitch the tent. We cocooned ourselves in our sleeping bags and donned every piece of warm kit we had, as during the night the temperature fell to minus eight degrees; our water bottles iced up, and when we woke we found a thin layer of our frozen breath lining the tent.

By the time the day finally warmed up we had entered a beautiful valley where mountains reflected off the salt lake. We even spotted a vicuna, a smaller tawny-brown relative of the llama, as we climbed a rocky path up to 4,000 metres from where we could see across the white Salar de Carcote, divided in two by the railway line. The road we were following was rough with stones and from our vantage point we could see it continued around the salt pan. Paddy reasoned that we could cycle across the *salar*, which would be a shorter route and would avoid the rough road. I wasn't convinced; a bad road it might be, but it was surely there for a reason. However, he was so keen that I capitulated and he set off exclaiming, "Let's go have an adventure!"

I thought we already were but, nevertheless, I followed him onto the salt pan where it seemed as if Paddy had been right, the going was smooth and, for a while, we made good progress. However, about an hour in, gaps started to appear in the surface, revealing murky blue water beneath and the slushy salt stuck under our brakes. We were halfway across the *salar* and laziness, rather than optimism, meant that neither of us wanted to turn around and recover our steps. So we continued on in stony silence until the salt pan deteriorated to such an extent that our wheels began to sink into the wet crust.

If we were to continue forwards, our only option was to ride along the railway line that stood at shoulder height, unfazed by the water sloshing at its embankment. As I bounced on the wooden sleepers I gritted my teeth with determination, gripping the handlebars to keep the wheels steady between the slippery metal tracks. Every now and then I would inadvertently hit a large stone that the train had thrown onto the sleepers, and the bike would judder and veer dangerously towards the edge of the embankment. The most I could do in response was to pull sharply on the brakes and thrust my feet down to come to a skidding halt, where I would stand composing myself for a few seconds before pushing off again.

The situation became even more challenging when a loud toot announced the imminent arrival of an oncoming train that was chugging across the *salar* with a cargo of gigantic red buckets loaded with minerals. As it grew closer, the ground began to tremble with the weight of the freight and we scrambled off the tracks, pulling the bikes down the embankment and resting them on the soft crust while we let the train pass.

Night was falling by the time we finally reached the edge of the lake and, to my frustration we were far from the road. For now, we set up camp among the ruins of a railway outbuilding on the edge of the *salar*, clearing the ground of fallen bricks to create a patch to pitch the tent. It was dark by the time we finally coaxed the stove into action, the altitude and evening mountain winds playing havoc with the flames, and we crawled into our sleeping bags straight after dinner, exhausted from our day's 'adventure'.

It took several hours of pushing through thick sand the next morning to reach an eerie, deserted town where we rejoined the main road. Not for the first time in the last 24 hours I shot Paddy a look that said, "You idiot". The surface was smooth and well-maintained, and we would have had a far easier ride the previous day if we had stuck to the designated route. I was tired and grumpy, and it was only when I had refuelled on fried egg sandwiches at the border post of Ollagűe, that I could begin to see the funny side of Paddy's desire to go adventuring.

I felt a real sense of achievement on reaching the border with Bolivia. Having cycled up to the Andean altiplano through some awesome scenery and over inhospitable terrain, I felt a growing confidence that I might actually be able to do this bike touring thing. We had taken on two of our 'Triple A' challenges, riding through the stunning and harsh Atacama Desert and had climbed into the Andes twice.

I was excited about cycling into Bolivia, and hoped there we might find a different version of South America to the European-like countries we had discovered so far. My wish was granted sooner than expected. Leaving Chile's smart brick immigration building we entered a dusty stretch of no-man's land, at the end of which lay the silent Avaroa railway station. Looking around at the sleepy border post, I felt as if I had ridden into a different world.

"At last," I thought, "this is where the 'real' South America begins."

7. Bolivia

There was nobody in sight as we rode across the border into Bolivia unchallenged. Resting our bikes against a rickety metal fence in the train yard, we headed across the worn railway lines in search of an immigration office where we could get our passports stamped. There were only a few buildings along the platform of the dilapidated station and we guessed that the hut displaying a hand-painted sign of the Bolivian flag and a llama was the one we wanted.

We tapped gently on the blue door, hoping the tattered sheet of paper listing the office's opening hours was wrong, as it should have already closed for the day. To our relief, the entrance was swung open by a smartly dressed man with dark hair and light brown skin, who, in a silent movement, handed us forms before shutting us out again. Slightly confused by the welcome, we crouched down to complete our applications, to the disinterest of three old men sitting on a bench further along the platform, watching the world go by. Their creased faces suggested they had spent a long time over the years sitting in the mountain sun.

Forms completed, we tapped nervously at the hut, upon which we were permitted into the cool, sparse office. There was no fee to pay for our visa; in fact, in the whole of South America we were only charged to enter Suriname. Yet the official had plenty of stamping to do until, with a final bang, he suddenly smiled up at us and handed back our passports. Our new friend accompanied us to the door, pointing past abandoned railway carriages rusting on the tracks towards a T-junction where, he said, we would find the road to the Salar de Uyuni.

We could only see, however, a criss-cross of tracks heading in all directions across the plain. After much deliberation, we opted for one of the firmer trails that followed the railway line into the distance. Our route was across a wide off-white salt flat, bordered on all sides by stubby, rocky peaks in rusty shades of red, crowned by a fine sprinkling of snow. Above us the sky was clear with only a few wispy white clouds for decoration, allowing the sun to beam down and vividly light up the landscape. We were completely out in the wilds; only one car passed us the whole day, driven by a German couple who helpfully confirmed we were heading the right way. There was little shelter out on the open plain and, with thoughts of camping we headed towards the hills in search of cover from the wind that was gaining in intensity as the light grew dimmer. We followed the track around the hills until, rounding an outcrop, we suddenly found ourselves at the entrance to an odd-looking army camp, and face to face with three very bored soldiers.

They were sat on a low wall belonging to the camp's crumbling railway station and motioned us to wait while they collected supplies from the heavy train that was puffing towards them. Once they had unloaded their boxes we asked if we could pitch the tent in their camp, and the two younger soldiers turned to the third who shrugged his shoulders nonchalantly in agreement, before leading us into the deserted barracks of the Chiguana Camp. A two metre stone wall enclosed the base which was comprised of an assortment of run-down outbuildings and ten crude, dome-shaped huts painted grey with big square windows that were mostly devoid of glass.

The camp was a base for the army whenever tensions with Chile rose over the border, but for now it was deserted apart from the three soldiers tasked with guarding it, and their snappy dog. Our home for the night was the central dome, officially Chiguana's operation room. The floor was covered with threadbare wooden boards and the walls were decorated with peeling white paint and hand-painted images of Bolivian generals. Under the fading portrait of the South American liberator, Simón Bolívar, stood a concrete lectern painted in green and brown camouflage and across the room there was a scale model of the entire area around the Bolivia-Chile border. Piles of sand had been moulded to look like nearby volcanoes and a cardboard train, complete with loaded buckets of grit, made its way along matchstick tracks. For me, with a BA degree in War Studies, this was insanely cool, and while Paddy unloaded the bikes I stood behind the lectern issuing orders at him.

Our first day in Bolivia had gone smoothly, and it really did feel like we had arrived in the 'real' South America. The laid-back attitude, indigenous faces and slight disorder is what I had expected to find around the continent but, up until today, aside from otherworldly landscapes like the Atacama, things had felt comparably European. I was excited to be here and was looking forward to the weeks ahead cycling across the Bolivian Altiplano, a high plateau that sits between the two parallel chains of the Andes that run through the country. My knowledge of Bolivia was limited; I anticipated some spectacular scenery, women wearing bowler hats and, because the country is one of the poorest in South America, I expected to see signs of poverty. We had heard of cyclists who had been attacked on the road and of another who had his bike stolen, so for the first time since Brazil and Paraguay, I was back to being extra concerned about security.

We crept out of camp the next morning, successfully managing not to wake the guard dog. As we rode further away from the border, 4x4s packed with backpackers began to appear, racing each other on the wide plain. A couple of times I had to pull sharply on the brakes as a driver swerved towards me so that the tourists could take a photograph of us, their long-lens cameras sticking out of the windows. "If you find us interesting, then stop and speak to us," I thought. Their rude point, shoot and then bugger off policy really annoyed me. How must local people have felt getting snapped outside their home or walking down the street, because some westerner thought their brightly coloured shawl or bowler hat would make a cool picture? I didn't take photographs of people without their permission, principally because that's just polite, but actually a picture meant so much more when we had spoken to the person and knew their story.

We diverted off the main track to escape the 4x4s and made our way slowly across the salt pan watching our cycle computer tick over to the 7,000 kilometre mark. Our ritual for reaching a significant distance on the trip was to cover the last few hundred metres riding side by side so that we could high five as the digits clicked over. Then we would take a picture at the precise spot to mark the moment. This time we took out our foldable bike stands and etched a large '7,000 kilometres' into the salt surface. "That will confuse the backpackers for a while," I thought, "or at least until the jeeps drive over it."

Rio de Janeiro was a long way away. After five months on the road we were slimmer, toned and fitter, our skin glowed a deep bronze and Paddy's hair had grown outrageously. Our bags and bikes sported grey patches of duct tape to cover tears and chips, while our panniers had faded in the sun and were covered in the layer of dirt that clung to everything we carried. We may have looked like adventurers, but we continued to like our luxuries, and we succumbed to those on offer in the tourist lodge in the remote village of San Rosario de Juan, with its comfortable rooms and hot water giving us the chance to shower for the first time in five days. I spent the evening pumping tap water through our portable filter to avoid having to buy expensive bottles of mineral water. It was the first and, as it turned out, the last time on the trip that we used the filter, as we were hardly ever so far away from civilisation that is was impossible to find drinking water.

By the time we reached the edge of town the next morning, the road had deteriorated into heavy washboard, an effect made by fast-moving vehicles pushing a sandy surface into tight ripples. It made for a bouncy ride, my boobs ached with each bump in the road and I stopped to tighten my bra straps under the watchful gaze of llamas who stared at me with glossy brown eyes. Herds of the Bolivian national animal – a mishmash of brown, black, white and tan long furry coats – meandered across the plains grazing on low shrubs. They seemed unfazed by humans, even the group of road sweepers dressed in bright yellow from head to toe.

This group, under the glare of the sun, were literally sweeping the road, using shovels and brushes to even out bumps. It was a thankless task; they couldn't have cleared more than a few hundred metres a day which surely would quickly get mashed up again. There were three men, and one younger woman dressed in a bright yellow cotton dress, cut in the indigenous Bolivian style with long sleeves, a square neck-line and a wide skirt that flared at the waist and ended at her knees. Her face was protected from the sun with a wide-brimmed yellow hat, keeping the sun off her face better than the simple caps of her male compatriots.

We stopped briefly to exchange pleasantries, but we all had long days ahead, theirs significantly harder than ours. A lack of drinking water in the village and now manual road sweepers – we were starting to realise how poor Bolivia actually was. In 2009, the World Bank estimated 50 per cent of the population lived below the poverty line, this in spite of the fact that Bolivia has huge amounts of natural resources. The Spanish exploited these materials under colonial rule and after independence production continued, yet by the 1980s the country's economy was in a dire state, hit by the collapse of the price of tin, which left thousands of miners jobless. Many were forced to look for work in the lowlands, where they grew coca, some of which was destined for the Colombian drug trade. At the age of 12 the current president of Bolivia, Evo Morales, was one of those who made such a journey, and when he came to power in December 2005 as Bolivia's first indigenous leader, it was on the promise of land reforms to help peasant farmers.

Apparently, Morale's administration had stimulated growth, but it was difficult to see the effects as we continued along the bumpy track looking for a village on our route called Colca K. We had no maps of this area other than a hand-drawn sketch from another cyclist, so when we spotted a rusty sign pointing off the road, we were temporarily delighted. Two hours later, at the top of a steep sandy track, the road ended abruptly in the centre of a village where shy locals insistently pointed us back along the trail; there was nothing to do but turn around.

Back on the flat, and as the afternoon wore on we started to grow concerned that we were lost; we hadn't seen any signs of life in hours, so when a 4x4 appeared in the distance, we waved frantically and thankfully the driver diverted towards us. He was a tour guide from La Paz and pointed out the direction we needed to be heading. By car, he said, it was a ten minute drive to Colca K, but the road was bad and, looking at our bikes, he suggested it would take us over an hour. He restored my faith that not all drivers around here were crazy, and we thanked him before setting off along the road that deteriorated as he had promised, worse than anything we had come across so far. In parts the sand was so thick that it buried my tyres, and I would have to drag the bike to the surface before launching off again.

Consequently, the sky was growing dark by the time we finally made it to Colca K and the lure of a backyard lodge was too much to resist after a long day in the saddle. At £3.50 per night the room was understandably basic, and the beds, covered in thick woven blankets, were not made for tall people, but wonderfully it had a solar powered shower that pumped out hot water.

> ***Diary, 26 September 2011*** *- The ladies in this village are all wearing the traditional Bolivian clothes – the pleated skirts, bowler hats and brightly-coloured woven shawls. I read somewhere that Europeans introduced the skirts and hats. I don't know if it's true, but I quite like the story that British workers on the Bolivian railroad received a shipment of bowler hats from home that were too small, so they gave them away to the locals who liked them because they were less likely to blow away in the wind. Everybody seems very friendly and gentle, although Paddy said that in the village where we got lost one woman put her head down and ran past him when he was looking for directions – perhaps she was intimidated by the fact he was almost double her height.*

The next morning, we met a French couple heading south. It was the first time we had seen a female touring cyclist since Debs on the Brazilian coast. In fact, we only met one lone female rider the whole trip and just two sets of women who were riding as pairs. Cycle touring seems more popular with men, yet if anybody inspired me to take to the road it was the Irish writer, Dervla Murphy. I first discovered her while I was at university, trying to get my head around the conflict in the former Yugoslavia. I read her book *Through the Embers of Chaos*, an account of her travels by bike through the region at a time when everybody else was heading in the opposite direction. Then I moved on to her tales of riding to India, told with her usual sense of calm and understatement. Reading her stories, it's hard to know how anybody could fail to fall in love with cycle touring.

To be fair, although riding a heavy bike is physically demanding, anybody with mental determination can do it. As a woman, I could complete the same route as Paddy, but just a bit slower. The biggest hassles, for me, were more basic things like not being able to go for a wee at the side of the road quite so easily. At times when there were dead snakes and caimans lying along the roadside, I was envious of being able to point and shoot like a man. Then there was the time of the month issue – the logistics of trying to be hygienic when we were on a stretch with limited water supplies and no toilets. My biggest worry, however, was safety. Some of the looks I got from men when Paddy wasn't with me made me realise that his presence gave me much more freedom and security than if I had been attempting this ride alone. I don't know whether if I had been by myself, I would have been brave enough to camp in the middle of nowhere, stay in some of the very basic accommodation we did, or accept invitations from strangers to stay in their homes.

By mid-morning, we arrived at the shores of the Salar de Uyuni, the world's largest salt flat, covering approximately 10,000 square kilometres. Salt pans form when water cannot drain off a lake. Instead it remains on the surface where it will evaporate, leaving behind a layer of the minerals that have dissolved in the water. The starched white plain, that looked like rock salt compacted by a steam roller, was in fact a crust of salt over a lake of brine.

It was an unnerving idea to cycle across a lake topped with a thin layer of salt, but it unflinchingly held the weight of the 4x4s that raced across the surface. The crust changed throughout the year and at certain times was unnavigable; it was late September when we rode onto the *salar* and the surface was beginning to show small holes that offered a vantage point into the murky ice-blue water below. Estimates suggested there was over 100 million tonnes of lithium under the *salar*, at least half of the world's total supplies. The Bolivian government had not yet started to exploit it, but there was so much wealth buried underneath that it could only be a matter of time.

The French couple had ridden from the eastern side of the *salar*, along the road which leads to Uyuni and the mining city of Potosí, where the production of silver from the mid-1500s made Bolivia, temporarily, very rich. We, however, were heading north in the direction of La Paz. It was a distance of 80 kilometres to the other side of the *salar* and we hoped to cover it in less than two days. There were no roads across the salt plain, just a network of criss-crossing vehicle tracks, so we navigated by sight, aiming for the just-visible peak of Cerro Tunupa, a 5,321 metre-high volcano on the other side.

Our intention was to reach the Isla Incahuasi, a rocky outcrop in the middle of the *salar* by evening so that we didn't have to pitch the tent on the salt surface. The crust began smoothly and we whizzed along at 20 kilometres per hour, in spite of the headwind; it was a cyclists' playground. There was no traffic, no fighting for road space, plus a flat surface to pedal along as we practised riding looping circles, no-handed. Our excitement was immense, this was a moment we had talked about since we sat at our kitchen table, staring at the huge white blob on the map of South America.

We had joked that the remote *salar* was the perfect place to cycle naked without being seen, but I went off that idea after seeing the peeling nostrils of the French woman, where the bright white salt had reflected the sun inside her nose; there are some places you just don't want to get sunburnt. After lunch, Incahuasi finally came into view: a hazy, dark blob in the distance that offered something more palpable to point our front wheels towards. Our pace had slowed thanks to the salt surface having morphed into hexagonal cobblestones that looked as if somebody had laid a set of bumpy tiles, 40 centimetres in diameter and almost perfectly symmetrical. The edges were bordered by a thin fence of hardened salt that stood about a centimetre high, making the surface excruciatingly bone-jarring to cycle across.

By the time we finally arrived at the island it was getting late and the 4x4 tour groups who had been climbing the rocks were gradually disappearing back to their comfy lodges on the mainland. We set up camp on the edge of Incahuasi, wedged in between a wall of rock and giant cacti, and as the last jeep set off we sat down to watch the sun slowly set across the westerly peaks. We had one of the most incredible natural features in the entire world completely to ourselves.

In spite of the perfect campsite, I slept badly. The altitude was affecting my sleep and I reckoned on the Altiplano I had only been getting four good hours a night; I was beginning to feel exhausted. An easy day would have been nice but the surface had deteriorated further and at one point we were moving at just seven kilometres per hour. The holes in the surface had grown in size, and by the time we approached the edge of the salt plain there was enough open water for pink flamingos to wade in. Back on land the route didn't get any easier, and we found ourselves pushing the bikes up a rocky path around the flank of Cerro Tunupa. Every 100 metres I would have to stop – I simply couldn't inhale enough air and felt constantly winded; it was a scary sensation and the more I struggled to breathe the more anxious I became.

Paddy: *It was frustrating to see Laura struggling. I had adjusted to the altitude and found it hard to appreciate why she hadn't. I knew that it affects people in different ways but her symptoms were not consistent and because of this I didn't realise Laura was getting into a state before it was too late. The shortness of breath caused her to panic which then made her even more breathless – it was a nasty cycle. I couldn't get her to take a rest, to try and slow her heart rate, because we were near the top and she just wanted to get down the other side.*

When we at last reached the small town of Salinas de Garci Mendoza, we realised we needed to take my reaction to the altitude seriously. The next 120 kilometres were along a reputedly bad washboard road, and I was terrified my breathing might get worse in the middle of nowhere, away from help. It was a risk to carry on along such bad terrain in the state I was in, and we even wondered if we would have to head towards the coast rather than to La Paz. In the end we decided to skip the dirt road section and see if I improved on the tarmac.

Fortunately, we managed to get the last two places on a local bus, Paddy sitting up front between the driver and his wife, while I slumped into a seat at the back. The state of the road was so bad that even the locals who regularly travelled this route let out a scream and shouted "*Bolsas*!", as luggage came flying out of the overhead compartments when the bus hit a bump less than 200 metres into the journey. It was a typically terrifying South American bus journey.

Paddy: *The driver navigated the narrow streets out of town, at times using his knees to steer so that he could shovel coca leaves into his mouth from the plastic ziplock bag in his lap. He didn't share his supply, using it all to stay awake during the long journey. It was the first time I had seen somebody chewing the leaves, which, although they are used to make cocaine, don't produce such an extreme high when chewed – they need to go through a chemical process for that.*

Chewing coca is a big part of the local culture and apparently increases energy, reduces hunger and helps against the effects of altitude. As the driver added leaves, he developed a large green ball in his mouth that caused his cheeks to bulge and forced the corners of his lips into a smile. His eyes focused constantly on the road as we sped along the ripio, creating the feeling of aquaplaning, a horrible sensation for anybody not in control of the vehicle.

By now his jaw was in mastication overtime, keeping him alert to the dangers of the road: the animals that casually strolled out in front of us, and people that rushed out of their tiny, mud huts to flag us down. An hour into the four-hour journey, the bus was already struggling to accommodate standing passengers. When we finally reached the glorious tarmac and stopped, we thanked the driver and wife with a small tip that they seemed quite taken aback and delighted by. We were just so grateful not to have attempted that stretch of road by bike.

It was such a joy to be back on tarmac that it took several hours before I started complaining about Paddy having chosen a route around South America that meant we were always cycling into a headwind. It had become a daily 'joke', which he would counter with a detailed explanation about prevailing winds, while I over-dramatically rolled my eyes at him. In spite of the wind, it took just two days to reach Oruro, Bolivia's second largest city where we set about restoring the weight we had lost over the past few weeks by devouring curry in a Hare Krishna-run restaurant.

Oruro grew from the silver and, later, tin trades as a hotchpotch of narrow streets in a tight grid. The wealth that once existed here was apparent in the grand, neatly-kept squares where we slurped slush puppies before heading to an internet café to search for a wedding venue. We found a villa where the ceremony could take place and a woman who organised weddings in Barbados, to whom we sent a couple of quick emails. This meant most of the main planning was done, allowing us to focus on the job of riding to La Paz.

A few miles out of Oruro we met Matthew and Matt, an American and Canadian duo, who were cycling to Ushuaia. Their priority in town was to fill up on food, as like us, they were finding it difficult to buy supplies in Bolivia, there being only small shops with limited produce. We were struggling to find our usual staples, like pasta, so were being more adventurous with our meals. Eggs were easy to cook, but they were tricky to carry and regularly I opened my panniers to find a crushed, gooey mess inside. Sometimes we would find local Aymara women, wrapped in colourful shawls, sitting along the roadside, selling white heavy cheese in a round the size of a saucer. It tasted of little but it was cheap, good fuel and palatable with a spreading of Marmite.

Late one afternoon we summited a hill to a puzzling sight below. A static snake of trucks and cars stretched out across the valley, edged by a slow stream of people carrying suitcases and bags, like refugees fleeing a conflict. This was the main road connecting Bolivia's two largest cities, and consequently the queue of vehicles was growing by the minute. We joined the throngs of people milling about, and a group of miners relaxing on the grass waved us on when they saw us hesitating about whether to continue. Reassured by their friendly demeanour we pushed our bikes past the waiting traffic for a couple of kilometres to a small village, where we found the cause of the delay was a barricade across the road. We were allowed to pass but we weren't sure what to do; we had planned to camp along the side of the road, but that whole stretch was jammed with traffic and we didn't fancy setting up the tent in front of lots of people.

Instead we asked in a *hospedaje* for a room, where we stumbled upon the strategic centre of the operation. The first floor was covered with thin mattresses, on some of which lay sleeping miners who were working in shifts to man the barricade until they would all depart noisily at four o'clock the next morning, taking the waiting traffic with them. Thankfully for us, the lodge owner had one room left that we could lock ourselves in for the night, because although the atmosphere in town felt resigned to the event, the miners in the *hospedaje* seemed tense, and I was happy to hide away until the protest had run its course.

We did venture outside briefly in search of the town's public toilet. There was no running water in the lodge and the owner gave us directions to communal ones, a common sight in poorer parts of Bolivia, but we couldn't find it anywhere. We obviously weren't the only ones; somebody had left a clear plastic bag of urine hanging from one of the hooks on the wall. Desperate for a wee ourselves by now, we emptied two large water bottles and took one each to use. For Paddy it was pretty straightforward, while I got a chance to use the 'she-wee' I'd been carrying, a plastic funnel for purposes like this. After contorting myself into a strange position in the cramped room, I managed to get everything into the bottle successfully, but it wasn't a process I was keen to repeat regularly. Peeing through a funnel with my back to my boyfriend was pretty weird, and I wondered if getting married could ever make us closer than experiences like this.

Initially, we assumed the demonstration was about working conditions in the mines, but a few days later, sitting in our hotel in La Paz, a huge boom rattled across the sky and we looked out of the window to see a stream of miners marching down the street. They carried banners and dynamite launchers which they aimed skywards at the end of each rousing song, protesting against plans for a new road that would cut through the Amazon Basin. The highway was a Brazilian project to provide access to the Pacific coast; it would bring trade to Bolivia, but the route was through indigenous territory which would be destroyed at great environmental and cultural costs. A few weeks later, the protestors discovered their efforts had been worthwhile when President Morales announced the plans for the highway were being shelved.

The next morning, concealing our bottles of pee in plastic bags, we rejoined the now quiet road, where a few miles along we poured away the contents. Two days later we reached the outskirts of El Alto, so called because, sitting at 4,050 metres above sea level, it is one of the highest cities in the world. It was once a small suburb of La Paz, but now bulges with simple red brick buildings that house people who moved from rural areas in search of work. Directly below, in a bowl-shaped valley, sat La Paz, Bolivia's administrative capital – Sucre has the honour of being Bolivia's legal capital, a city just north-east of the mining town of Potosí. At just 3,500 metres in altitude, I enjoyed the treat of freewheeling 13 kilometres down the steep road into the centre.

Diary, 6 October 2011 *- We went for a wander around town today, it's such an interesting place. The roads are incredibly steep and the buildings seem to cling to the sides at all kinds of angles. The streets are packed with people eating at roadside stalls run by women with round bellies and big smiles, and vendors sell everything you can imagine. Paddy brought back two plastic bags filled with mango juice and a straw tied in the* *top – an ingenious way of serving it!*

I loved La Paz's mixture of old colonial buildings, rickety homes in need of repair and the bright modern structures that suggested not all areas of the country's economy were in dire straits. The atmosphere felt different to the Bolivia we had seen so far; the city had its unique way of doing things and an amazing variety of food on offer, more than anywhere we had visited so far. Many restaurants catered for backpackers who used the city as a base to explore the North Yungas Road, 'the world's most dangerous road'. Tour companies offered day cycling trips along the stretch with steep drops and no crash barriers, but we saw enough treacherous roads on our own bikes, so opted instead for a tour of the ruins of Tiwanaku, about 70 kilometres west of La Paz.

From around 300 AD to 1000 AD, before the time of the Incas who built Machu Picchu in Peru, a flourishing community existed at the site, which was a spiritual centre for worship and human sacrifices. Only a small area had been uncovered, but the giant stone monoliths with their block faces and huge square eyes that stared directly at us, gave an insight into how grand the site must once have been. Many of the stones used to build Tiwanaku were dragged from Lago Titicaca, and a few days later as we cycled to the lake, I wondered how they had managed such a task at this altitude.

***Diary, 11 October 2011** - I want to go back down to sea level. The altitude is miserable. This morning in La Paz was bad enough, not being able to finish sentences or walk upstairs because of losing breath. But now we're back on the Altiplano and being on the bike is completely rubbish – I am literally gasping for breath every couple of kilometres and on the slightest incline. It didn't help that we cycled into a wind all day. As well as making it harder to pedal, the air blows into my mouth and winds me. It also dried my mouth out, and swallowing makes me skip a breath, so I'm short again. I lost count of the number of times I threw my bike on the verge needing to sit down immediately and gasp for breath.*

We met several cyclists heading the other way, all looking much happier than us as they were blown towards La Paz. I was happy to stop and chat to take a break from pedalling, and if it wasn't for Paddy reminding me we needed to keep moving, I would have stayed all day with them. We were heading to Copacabana, Bolivia's largest town on the shores of Lago Titicaca. Our route took us across the narrow Tiquina Straits on a rickety wooden ferry at a point where the lake was 500 metres deep. We watched, captivated, as a bus driver manoeuvred his wobbling bus onto the platform. Understandably, his passengers declined to accompany him, opting to follow on the next boat instead.

From the lakeshore the road took us on a crunching climb, packed with false horizons, up to the highest point of the trip yet, 4,300 metres, where we were rewarded for our efforts with a 13 kilometre descent into town. As we rolled downhill I looked over the handlebars to admire the spectacular view of the turquoise water stretching across the landscape. The novelty of having cycled from Rio de Janeiro, with its Copacabana Beach, to its namesake high in the Andes was not lost on us.

We would soon be leaving Bolivia, the sixth country of our trip, and one I had fallen in love with. The country's mountain landscape was my resounding memory of Bolivia – the vast barren valleys, enormous salt lakes and towering snowy peaks. The country had some of the most varied and outstanding scenery I had ever seen, and that was without visiting the thick forests in the east.

The lowlands would have to wait for our next trip. We were on a tight deadline and needed to get a move on if we were to reach Cusco in time to meet Paddy's parents who were joining us for a few weeks. If I needed a reminder to pick up speed, it came in the shape of a black and white dog who chased me to the border. As I rode past his farm, he started barking from a few hundred metres away. I laughed as if to say, "whatever dog, you're never getting me", but I had underestimated his desire to attack. When he got halfway across the field I realised he would actually catch me, at which point my legs sprang into action, turning the wheels fast in my highest gear.

I rounded the corner and was out of his territory just before his snapping jaws reached my back tyre. "Bye-bye crazy dog", I thought. "Goodbye Bolivia."

8. Peru

After Brazil, Peru was the country in South America I felt I knew most about. Travel books unanimously raved about the traveller's mecca, where Peruvians welcomed tourists to sites built by ancient civilisations, geoglyphs drawn in the desert and cities once covered in gold. I was expecting to have a great time exploring the country.

Two days in and, so far, little had changed as we continued cycling around Lago Titicaca, the largest lake in South America. At 3,812 metres, it was the highest navigable expanse of water in the world, and was so wide that only on clear days could we make out the hazy peaks of distant mountains on the other side. A few kilometres offshore from the city of Puno, bobbing on the lake's surface, were the floating islands of the Uros people, a tribe predating the Inca civilisation. Made from strong tora reeds that grew in the lake, they were anchored by ropes and sticks and could be moved, an important thing for the first inhabitants who lived under threat of attack from the mainland.

A community still existed on the islands, with residents travelling back and forth to Puno for school and business, while tourists visited in droves, enjoying trips on reed boats. Considering the lake's importance to local communities, we were surprised they seemed to use it as their rubbish dump. Plastic bottles and food waste bobbed in the water and we watched one man drag a wheelie bin full of bin bags up to the water's edge and tip the contents in.

The most significant difference from Bolivia was the addiction Peruvian drivers had with beeping. They pa-peeped the horn when they approached and passed us, only stopping when they were well ahead. We couldn't work out if they were saying hello, warning us to get out of the way, or what. Every driver seemed to do it, and it grated on our nerves like somebody dragging their nails down a blackboard.

Our progress was good, aside from impromptu stops thanks to

Paddy's stomach. We could trace the problem to a piece of chicken he had eaten in Bolivia – weeks later he was still experiencing severe cramps and sudden bursts of diarrhoea. One afternoon, out on a wide, exposed plain, he suddenly went pale, clutched his stomach, dropped his bike and ran off to find cover.

> ***Paddy:*** *I knew that Laura could probably still see me behind the slightly-raised railway line, but I couldn't care less as I squatted down. Each time I thought it was over, my stomach would lurch again and I would quickly bob back down. After the third bout, as I stood up, I was really dizzy and only narrowly missed stepping into my latest contribution to the arid landscape. I felt so rubbish that when two shepherdesses who had been herding their flock slowly towards me finally reached me, I didn't have the energy to get out of their way, and the sheep just wandered on past. Laura was really good and gave me salt tablets to help with the cramping as I lay flat on the tarpaulin clutching my cramping stomach. It had been going on for weeks now, and I was fed up to the point of considering joining her in becoming vegetarian.*

The heat of the high sun didn't help Paddy feel any better, and we headed for shade wherever we could find it. In Juliaca, we sheltered under the billowing brass skirt of a dancing statue to eat our lunch of bread and cheese, where we were joined by two panting dogs hopeful of scraps, as we rehydrated with bottles of sticky, sweet *Inca Kola*. It tasted like *Vimto* and the fluorescent yellow colour suggested it probably wasn't the healthiest thing to drink, but it quenched our thirst perfectly. The soda, made from lemon verbena, was created in the 1930s by a British immigrant called José Robinson Lindley. Peruvians loved it, and it soon became one of our daily staples.

Away from the lake, I started to enjoy the cycling more, as we made our way along quieter roads through rolling green valleys, where sheep, llamas, alpaca and cows roamed. In the bustling town of Ayaviri we spotted two heavily-laden touring bikes propped up outside a café; their owners were inside, two Belgians en route to Ushuaia. We sat down to eat *almuerzo* with them – a cheap, set-lunch that became a daily favourite as we rode through the Andes. They were not the first cyclists we had met in Peru; a few days earlier we had chatted to two Australian girls taking the same route, their knickers unashamedly drying on top of their panniers as they rode along.

We also met a French woman. She looked to be in her forties, but it was hard to tell: her face was deeply tanned and she wore several bulky jackets, a big woolly hat and sunglasses. She had started in Caracas, Venezuela and was heading to Ushuaia. Her adventures to date were dramatic; she had been robbed, attacked with stones in her tent and had fallen off the bike, fracturing her shoulder, but she was determined to continue.

We lost the Belgians as we rode towards Ayaviri's main square, when Paddy's back wheel punctured for the umpteenth time in the last few weeks. The rim tape had pulled away and was slicing the inner tube, so we replaced it with a layer of electrical tape – our go-to solution for most mechanical problems. Thankfully it worked, and the next day we continued on to reach our 8,000 kilometre mark in the middle of a flat, grassy valley, where the local houses were built from adobe bricks, made using a mixture of clay, water and straw. It was a poor area and a stark juxtaposition to the smart blue carriages of the train that rattled past us on the way to Cusco, with tourists taking pictures out of the windows.

Half-heartedly, I stuck my hand out to hitch a ride, but the driver only waved, leaving me to remount for the climb up to the Abra la Raya pass – at 4,338 metres, the highest point of our entire trip. Paddy exhausted himself early on by racing two young boys who had music blaring out of a mini beat-box on their handlebars. The boys soon realised the craziness of climbing all the way to the top and turned for home, leaving us to continue the slow climb alone. It was late afternoon when we at last reached the top. The lofty peaks of nearby mountains cast dark shadows onto the pass, and we stopped only briefly to admire the views; there was still 800 metres to descend before we could finish for the day.

People often talk about Colombia being the most dangerous country in South America, but I have heard more stories of travellers being robbed, attacked in their tents, kidnapped and even killed in Peru. A few months before we arrived in the country, two cyclists riding along the northern coast had been shot at in an attempted robbery, their bike frames and panniers were hit but they escaped unhurt. When we reached the area we needed a police escort to cover that stretch of road, it was deemed so dangerous. Fortunately, having things thrown at us was the worst thing that happened, but even that left us feeling shaken and unwelcome.

The first occasion was on our way down from the Abra la Raya pass. We should have had a relaxed 40 kilometres of freewheeling, but that changed as we entered a large farming community spread out across a narrow, steep valley. As we approached the village we slowed down, alert to the possibility of children or animals running out into the road. A woman and her two young daughters were walking along the side of the road, and I smiled at them. *"Hola, qué tal?"* I asked the mother.

She stared at me blankly but her elder daughter, who looked about eight years old, suddenly sprinted towards me and started kicking wildly at my turning back wheel. Her bare short legs flew dangerously close to my spinning spokes as she chased me down the road. Startled by the unprovoked attack I was slow to react, until my instincts took over and I swung the bike sharply away from her, pushing hard on the pedals to escape. Safely past, I turned around to see the child gesturing angrily at me, while her sister stood in the middle of the road with a football held above her head ready to launch it at Paddy's wheels, but he had anticipated her moves and dodged the throw.

The mother didn't bat an eyelid, but I was shocked and shaken. If the girl had managed to kick my wheel, her foot could have caught in the spokes and she could have lost her leg or worse. These thoughts were rattling through my mind when, out of the corner of my eye, I saw a man on the side of the road pick up a handful of dirt and launch it at my face as I passed. The earth crumpled in the air and I rode on untouched, but I was furious. "What's the fucking problem with people here?" I thought.

Most Peruvians we met were friendly, but there were a significant number who seemed to feel animosity towards travellers. The main roads which transported excited visitors to Peru's popular tourist spots invariably ran through poor villages in rural areas. I imagine villagers must have resented rich foreigners racing through their villages in big cars, the speed of which threatened the safety of a child or loose animal that wandered into the road at the wrong moment. We would also see tourists sneaking photos of locals without asking permission, so it didn't surprise me some people might feel exploited by travellers, especially as they were unlikely to receive little direct benefit from tourism.

There was also historical resentment left over from the colonial period. In 1527, the Spanish arrived at Tumbes along the north coast, where they discovered a wealth of gold and silver, and Peru quickly became a principal target for them. Three years later an expedition of 100 foot soldier and 60 horsemen under the control of Francisco Pizarro returned with thoughts of conquest. At the time Peru was under the control of the Incas, yet when Pizarro arrived the leadership was in turmoil following the death of the emperor, Huayna Capac, from smallpox – the disease had been brought to Mexico by Europeans and was now spreading through the Andes. Capac's half-brother, Atahuallpa, was currently in control and Pizarro set off to meet him in the city of Cajamarca. For some reason, although the Indians kept a close eye on the invaders, they did not attack and the Spanish were able to settle in the city, where they invited Atahuallpa to a meeting.

The Inca leader arrived in the Cajamarca square, escorted by 6,000 men, but was surprised to find no Spaniards waiting. At last a priest appeared who handed Atahuallpa a Bible, but having never seen a book before, the confused Inca tossed it to the ground, at which point the Spanish, who had been hiding, attacked on the grounds that he had repudiated the word of God. Between 6,000 and 7,000 Indians were killed and Atahuallpa was taken hostage. He tried to buy off the Spanish with a huge offer of gold which took several months to arrive from Cusco, but when it did, instead of sending the emperor into exile, Pizarro had him garrotted— a brutal form off execution using a tightened iron neck collar. In November 1533 Pizarro's forces arrived in Cusco, the heart of the Inca Empire, and took over the city. The Spanish conquest of Peru was long, bloody and treacherous, and it was easy to understand why Peruvians might still feel animosity towards *gringos*.

The next morning we had another 20 kilometres of descent, but it would have been more pleasant cycling uphill, the wind blew so fiercely against us. We stopped off for lunch in a fly-infested café where *queso frito* was on the menu. This had fast become my favourite Peruvian dish, a bowl of boiled potatoes served with a huge chunk of fried cheese, and this time there was rice as well; at just £1, it was a bargain.

A few hours later we stopped for ice creams. Sat on the pavement licking away, two policemen came over to chat, and soon we were surrounded by a crowd of children eager to see the map that Paddy had opened. He had developed a routine when explaining our trip to people; slowly, he would trail his finger around the map, tracing the route we had travelled. When he reached the point where we currently were, the crowd would nod with recognition of local place names, and then he would continue to Rio, at which point people would shake their heads, slap Paddy on the back and break into laughter.

By now we had heard from Paddy's parents, Linda and Kevin (TAPs – The Aged Parents – as they called themselves for short) that they had landed in Lima and were already driving to Cusco. I was excited to see them, not only for the obvious reasons, but they were bringing me a new saddle. After a long battle with the Brooks, I had conceded defeat; my bottom was covered in a red rash that was excruciating, particularly when riding up demanding gradients. Fortunately, the ascent into Cusco was fairly gentle.

> ***Diary, 21 October 2011** - Once we hit the outskirts of the city it got very busy and dirty with all the fumes and dust. They were doing works so the road was terrible, but we were able to cycle along a walkway briefly. I was following Paddy for a change, and it was scary watching the cars scrape by him with millimetres to spare – usually he gets that view of me. He really let the crazy drivers get to him, and was so frustrated that he actually slammed his fist on a bus that cut him up.*

When the Spanish arrived in Cusco in 1533, they plundered the city for the silver and gold that adorned the Inca's buildings, then they razed the temples and palaces to the ground to build their own Christian churches and grand mansions. It was a brutal process, but the results were undeniably spectacular. The city was laid out on the traditional design of Spanish conquistadors across the Americas – in the centre was a grand, imposing square around which were the most important buildings, like the governor's residence and church – and buildings were painted white with red roofs, giving an ordered Mediterranean feel to the city. The cathedral in the Cusco's Plaza de Armas was particularly impressive: a wide red structure with elaborate carvings and huge green metal doors that, from our balcony table overlooking the square, we could see tourists streaming in and out of.

We had taken TAPs to sample a Peruvian *pisco sour,* which differed from the Chilean version by the addition of Angostura bitters and egg white that gave a fluffy finish to the cocktail. They had acclimatised well to the altitude, which was great news as we had been worried that heading straight from sea level to 3,500 metres might be a bad idea. It meant we could head off to visit the 'lost' Inca ruins of Machu Picchu.

Of course, the Inca site was never really lost. When the US professor, Hiram Bingham, 'discovered' the ruins in 1911, a small group of locals was farming on the stacked terraces where the Incas had once grown maize and potatoes. The site, on a ridge between two prominent peaks, overlooks the Río Urubamba and is believed to have been a royal estate, a temporary residence for important Incas visiting from Cusco. It was probably built in the mid-1400s and then abandoned when the Spanish arrived.

I was surprised that the ruins were situated at 2,492 metres; I had imagined the mountain citadel to be at a great height but this seemed low compared to some of the areas we had ridden through. The dates were fascinating too. I thought the Incas were an ancient civilisation, but the empire spanned only 100 years until 1533, about the time the English King Henry VIII was marrying his second wife, Anne Boleyn. While Europeans were building ships for expeditions around the world, the Incas were worshipping sun gods and constructing mountain temples; they did an incredible job.

> ***Diary, 25 October 2011*** - *Machu Picchu! One of the best things I have ever seen, it was so impressive. We were all absolutely blown away by the site, which was much bigger than we'd imagined. The sheer drops on all sides have to be seen to be believed. I swore pretty badly in front of TAPs when Paddy tripped and nearly went flying off the edge of a precipice; they looked a bit surprised by my reaction!*

I had really enjoyed our time in Cusco, particularly watching the Manchester derby on television which City won emphatically, 6-1. It was shown live early in the morning, and I woke up the travellers next door with my excited screams each time another goal went in. TAPs' visit was also perfectly timed, as they brought the wedding dress for me to try. It had been delivered to them in a parcel the size of a sandwich bag, so was easy to stick in a suitcase. Amazingly, the dress fitted, hid my crazy tan marks and had the added bonus of being nice.

TAPS weren't leaving Cusco with us. We had convinced them to take the train to the must-see Lago Titicaca, which would enable us to get some kilometres under our belts before they caught us up. Ours was a steep climb out of Cusco up to a ridge. The road was in poor condition, and an elderly, frail man was attempting to fill in the large potholes with shovels of dirt. As vehicles approached he would hold his hand out to the drivers, hopeful they would appreciate his work and pass him a few *soles*. We had no change to offer, so instead split our cake with him as the three of us sat in silence enjoying the break.

The day finished with a smooth 30 kilometre switchback descent into a humid riverside village, where I stood frozen in fear when a tarantula wandered in front of me, until a six year old boy removed it. We were now in extreme up and down territory, and while the descents were fantastic, at the bottom of each there was, inevitability, a long climb ahead. One day alone we climbed more than the height of Ben Nevis, the highest mountain in Britain. As we approached the top of a pass we would be layered up against the cold, while at the bottom of the valley we would strip down to our T-shirts and load up on mosquito repellent, because, however fast we pedalled, we couldn't escape the small black flies that bit at our ankles as we crawled up the lower sections of road.

Climbing up switchbacks became a daily occurrence, and while I loved standing at the top, salivating over the freewheeling I was soon to enjoy, I would inwardly groan looking across to a route in the distance I knew we had to summit. Paddy's favourite method of climbing was truck surfing. When a sluggish lorry passed, he would pump hard on the pedals to catch it and grab onto a metal handle at the back, so that the truck would drag him slowly uphill. I tried it once, but I didn't have the strength in my arms to hold on for long. Paddy didn't let that stop him, however, and one day he disappeared around a corner and was soon out of sight. I was pretty annoyed and 20 minutes later, when I still hadn't caught him up, I stopped for cake and got my own back by feeding his share to a tan and black dog. It was clearly hungry as it kept me company for the next half an hour, only turning for home when I finally found Paddy again.

Near to the top of that 4,000 metre pass, in the middle of nowhere, we were raced uphill by three wild-looking kids, with cheeky smiles. They moved faster than us, taking short cuts across the steep fields instead of following the curves of the road. One of the little boys was wearing a replica Chelsea football shirt, but he didn't seem to know who they were when we asked if he supported the team; it must have been handed out by a charity. We gave them biscuits, which they seemed delighted with, running off with their treats along a well-worn path that disappeared into the fields.

Later that day, TAPs caught us up. As I cooked a pasta supper for us all that evening, it was unusual to see that, for once, I was the healthiest person in the team. Paddy's ongoing stomach problems had left him weak and tired, while TAPs had succumbed to bad altitude sickness. It was abundantly clear that everybody needed to descend to sea level as soon as possible. Fortunately, we were near to the final pass, from where we could freewheel 100 kilometres down to the coast.

> ***Diary, 30 October 2011** - Paddy and I weren't speaking, or at least I wasn't speaking to him, as every time I opened my mouth he snapped at me, so it was safer to keep quiet. It's only because he's not well, I know, but still, I wish he wouldn't take it out on me. We made up halfway down which was good as it was a really fun road to cycle – or to coast down. The wind was fierce, though, and at times we had to brake to get around corners rather than being thrown into the wall. When we got to Nazca, everybody was so relieved and excited to be back down from altitude.*

It felt so good to be back down at sea level. I had loved our time in the mountains, but it was an amazing sensation to breathe oxygenated air, and within a few hours all of our various symptoms had miraculously disappeared. The last time we had seen the Pacific Ocean was in Antofagasta, Chile. We were now 1,600 kilometres further north along the Pan American Highway in a town called Nazca, famous for huge geoglyphs in the surrounding desert.

The figures covered 450 square kilometres and depicted living creatures, plants and imaginary figures, some of which were several kilometres long. The Nazca people scraped the lines into the dry surface between 400 and 650 AD, and covered them with sand and gravel, which is how they had survived so long. Many of the lines were only visible from the sky, so we boarded a small plane to get a good look. They were incredible creations. My favourite was one that looked like an astronaut, although Paddy said it was an owl, which seemed more sensible considering when the lines were made. Nobody knew what the lines were made for, but the common assumption was they were to please the gods.

Modern day Nazca was a bustling city, built on the traditional Spanish grid system, but the buildings were charmless concrete blocks. In 1996 an earthquake levelled the city and much of what we saw as we wandered the dusty streets had been recently built. We had passed a huge camp of shacks as we rode into town, assumedly people who had not been rehomed since the quake. The whole place had a poor, edgy feel to it and I didn't feel particular comfortable there, a feeling exacerbated by the shrill wolf-whistles I received when we rode into town, even though Paddy was right there with me.

We spent most of our time in Nazca relaxing in the tightly-guarded tourist hostel that TAPs had treated us to. It was pure luxury compared to the usual places we stayed – it even had a pool where we could soothe our tired legs, during our final few days with TAPs. We really appreciated their efforts to come all the way to Peru and had really enjoyed their company.

They left with my new saddle, as it was even more uncomfortable than the Brooks. Oddly, after experimenting without padded shorts, the Brooks turned out to be nicer to ride on, and I managed with that for the rest of the trip. It wasn't like sitting in an armchair, but I was much more comfortable. We were in the desert now and, in the heat, five am starts became the norm, so we could finish before the sun and wind became too much to bear. Squished onto a narrow hard shoulder next to busy traffic, the cycling wasn't much fun.

> ***Diary, 3 November 2011*** *- There were lots of shouts of 'gringo' and people trying to get us to stop, all very dodgy. I got hit on the back by a stone a kid threw from a truck. I protested at him, but he just stared at me with a look of utter hatred. Paddy was fuming. Later, he almost got pulled over by the police after he gave them the finger. We were cycling along and this tremendous beep right at our backs scared the hell out of us. He didn't realise they were police at first, and apparently they didn't look impressed. But what is the fucking need to beep incessantly? I have to say, I'm not enjoying cycling in Peru.*

We inched northwards along the coast, taking an afternoon off here and there when we needed to escape the stress of the road. Fortunately, there were many things to distract us: sand boarding in the red Huacachina dunes; bird watching on the Ballestas Islands, where thousands of birds and seals gathered above the choppy Pacific waters; and a visit to Pisco, the namesake of the cocktail.

Following the coastal road, a bumpy strip of tarmac lined by work plants and piles of stinking rubbish, we arrived in Pisco. In 2007 it was rocked by a massive earthquake that destroyed 80 per cent of the city. Four years on and it still resembled a building site, with land fenced off by tall wooden boards to hide the slow progress of the rebuilding. I imagine most of the city's sleeping residents didn't feel the earthquake that gently rocked our building, causing our furniture to quiver at six am the next morning while I was pulling on my socks. It was nothing in comparison to the quake that decimated the city, but it was a reminder of the high seismicity along the Pacific coast.

Unusually, the sun didn't appear that morning; instead a thick coastal mist covered the area, dulling the landscape. We passed the time by trialling our new strategy for scaring off aggressive dogs. We had discovered that if we shouted loudly and confidently at them, they had no idea how to handle it and froze in their tracks. Paddy enjoyed shouting "fuck off", while I found "go home" worked just fine and was less crude. It was a great way to release the tension we had built up riding around Peru.

We hit the 9,000 kilometre mark just before we arrived in Lima, and stopped for a quick photograph before returning to battle the traffic and huge potholes that lined the city's streets. Many of the streets were named after important dates in Peru's history, and after realising we wanted the 28th January rather than the 26th, we finally arrived at the hostel in the upmarket area of Miraflores where we planned to stay for a few days. At a beachfront restaurant I almost melted eating a Roquefort salad dressed in balsamic vinegar; it was a far cry from boiled potatoes and rubbery cheese.

Lima was founded in 1535 by Francisco Pizarro, the conqueror of the Incas, who wanted a city that was easier to access than Cusco. It was once one of the most beautiful in the whole of Spanish America, known as the 'City of the Kings'. Simón Bolívar knew the strategic importance of Lima in his campaign to free Peru from colonial rule, and after securing the capital in 1824, his troops defeated Viceroy De la Serna's army at the battle of Ayacucho; Spanish power in South America was at last broken.

Modern day Lima was less exciting than its dramatic history; a typical city, with a mix of modern grey buildings and old mansions. After months of exploring old colonial cities, we had discovered there was a pattern to their layout and architecture, and could now tick off the usual tourist destinations of the central square and grand cathedral in one day. We were never particularly interested in the museums or church tours. Instead we preferred to explore the modern culture of a city, which in Lima meant bustling Miraflores, with its fancy restaurants and rowdy bars where patrons passionately followed football on huge televisions.

One evening, we cooked in the hostel. The centrepiece of the meal was a kilogram of broccoli, an item I craved on the road, but Paddy looked far from delighted with his meatless supper. I had been vegetarian since the age of eight, and we were following a veggie diet on the bikes, mainly because it was easier to cook one meal per night, plus fresh meat was difficult to carry in the heat. Paddy didn't mind, especially after having some bad chicken which made him suspicious about what he was eating. Finding something to eat in cafés and restaurants was more of an issue, but even that wasn't too problematic as long as I didn't expect gourmet cuisine. In the Andean countries I survived on rice, potatoes, cheese and eggs, and while big meat-eating countries like Argentina and Brazil were more difficult, there was always salad and often pizza.

We timed our departure for Sunday, our favourite day for leaving cities because the roads tended to be quieter. Departing our hostel at six am, it started well as we rode past revellers stumbling out of nightclubs onto a section of road closed for a running event. The centre was busier though, and as we turned onto the Pan American we found ourselves on the scariest road of the entire trip. There was no hard shoulder, just four lanes. None of the vehicles obeyed the white lines or the speed limit, and drivers cut each other up, veering diagonally across to exit a junction at the very last minute. My legs were spinning so fast that the muscles screamed in pain, and the lyrics of the Foo Fighters' song *Walk* were rattling around my head: "You keep alive a moment at a time.... I never wanna die, I never wanna die."

After what seemed like an hour, the road widened, and for the first time on the highway I turned my head to check Paddy was still behind me. Thankfully he was, but so was another cyclist, and at the first opportunity I pulled into a lay-by so we could introduce ourselves. His name was Joel, he was a swimming teacher in France during the summer, but spent the European winter cycle touring in warmer climes. This was his second season in South America; the year previously he had ridden through the southern half of the continent, including the blisteringly hot northern section of Paraguay. On this trip he was taking a similar route to us up through the Andes, on his way to stay with friends in Panama. He was older than us, and after years of doing the grown-up thing, he had returned to the road in search of adventure.

With the mind-set that three cyclists were more visible, we continued on together. When, 45 kilometres later, the road split, we ignored the 'no cycling' signs and snuck past the barriers onto the *Serpentin*, a winding road cut into the cliff face. It was a shorter, more scenic route, but the opposite side of the road was bordered by a steep drop into the Pacific, which explained why bikes weren't allowed. Looking down we could see a truck that had fallen and caught on a ledge halfway down – I couldn't decide if the driver had been lucky, or not.

The road rejoined the highway a few kilometres on, and we continued as a threesome. Neither of us minded having extra company, Joel was really chilled out and easy to talk to, plus he had lots of experience of bike touring and it was fascinating to hear his stories. It was great to have somebody else to talk to as we made our way along, with the ocean sparkling on our left-hand side, while on the right, expanses of sand covered the rocky ground. Every now and then we would enter a valley where, instead of a white sandy wilderness, we found a green oasis. I loved the sight of crops growing in the middle of the desert, the colour was a welcome relief to the senses and it looked freakishly unnatural. The fields were in fact fed by irrigation channels that diverted water from rivers, a process used in the area for up to 5,000 years.

Days in the saddle were long and hot; we wore long sleeve shirts and hats to protect our skin from the blazing sun and blasts of sand. With two men in our party the speed had picked up and we stopped less often, which tested my stamina. One evening we arrived in a poor fishing town, where the houses were built from adobe bricks and the only place to sleep was a dirty lodge with a filthy shared bathroom. Paddy and I weren't speaking – I had wanted to stop 20 kilometres back, but I had been out voted and we had pushed on to cover 127 kilometres that day.

If we weren't getting on, it was normally because one of us was ill or coming down with something. True to form, the next day I was a cycling zombie, I could hardly keep my eyes open and when we reached Casma after 60 kilometres, I insisted we stop. That evening we had dinner in a *chifa*, a Chinese restaurant; they were common along the coast and because the food was cheap we ate there regularly. I ordered my favourite, egg-fried rice with vegetables, flavoured with a big splash of soy sauce. The next day I felt even worse and spent the day in bed with a swollen belly and high fever as my body attempted to sweat out whatever was attacking my insides. Now, I know soy sauce is full of wheat and gluten, but back then I couldn't work out why rice and vegetables were making me so ill.

It took me a few days to recover in Casma. Understandably Joel continued on, I didn't expect him to hang about for a sick woman he hardly knew, but Paddy had no choice. One afternoon, we went out for a walk around town, and when I started to fade he flagged a tuk-tuk to take us back. These tiny three-wheeled vehicles, normally associated with Asian countries, were everywhere in this part of Peru. It cost next to nothing for a short journey, but we had to pay upfront so the driver could buy the petrol to take us. Compared to the wealth in Lima's decadent suburbs, life here felt significantly harder.

Paddy: *This was a poor part of Peru. After one particularly long, hot morning on the road, we were desperate for a cold drink, but we were in the middle of nowhere and had been for hours. So, riding through a narrow rocky valley, in an old quarry that seemed to be in perpetual shadow, we were surprised to spot a rickety corrugated iron structure set up as a rest stop. The man ushered away chickens and cleared a plastic table for us to rest at while his wife fetched bottle of Inca Kola. This was how they made their living, it seemed, selling cold drinks to passers-by and fixing tyres, we guessed, looking at the small collection of tools in front of the house. The couple had three young children and shyly they came forward as Laura pulled a bag of sweets out of her pannier. As they sat chewing with big smiles, their parents looked just as excited, it was clear candy was an unaffordable treat.*

We met up with Joel again in Trujillo, at a *casa de ciclistas* run by Lucho. *Casa de ciclistas* simply translates as 'cyclists' house', there are several of them around South America, which informally open their doors to travelling cyclists. There is normally a place to sleep, fix your bike and meet like-minded people, doing or dreaming up their own adventures. Most people who cycled through Peru stopped off at Lucho's house, and we quickly understood why as he invited us into the wide garage that doubled as his maintenance room.

Lucho was a small, slight man with thick dark hair and a huge white smile. He was a road cyclist, but welcomed all kinds of riders, allowing them to bunk down in the double storey extension at the back that was patrolled by an over-excitable ginger cat. We were in the same room as Joel, who said he had been attempting to leave for several days, but that something interesting always delayed his departure. He didn't seem too concerned, he had a flexible timescale, and it didn't take much persuading to convince him to hang on one extra day and leave with us.

We enjoyed Joel's company, and I think he liked having people to socialise with too. He seemed happy to ride with us for sections, even though alone he could cover the kilometres quicker. There was a more important reason, however, that we were all keen to travel in a group for the next part, as 50 kilometres beyond Trujillo we would pass the village of Pujan where cyclists had been shot at a few months earlier. Lucho asked a friend to accompany us and arrange the police escort, but the officers didn't try to refuse – either Lucho's name held significant sway, or the threat was so real that they escorted all cyclists.

The police car drove at a brisk pace, but a strong tailwind helped us keep up as we entered a barren stretch of desert. The two officers looked bored, and I couldn't help thinking they could solve the problem if they caught the attackers rather than acting as chaperones. However, they stuck with us even as we slowed when the wind changed direction and started whipping us with coarse sand. To make things worse, one of Paddy's spokes snapped but we kept going, aware that the police were impatient to be rid of us, until they suddenly sped off as the next village, safe territory, came into sight.

As we wheeled the bikes into a hostel two more spokes broke; that unmistakable high-pitched ping would become a familiar sound over the next few days. We'd had the wheel trued in Trujillo as Paddy had been experiencing problems for a while, but it seemed the spokes had been tightened too much. That evening we trawled the streets of Pucasmayo in search of a mechanic to loosen them, and finally found a man who was able to help. Sat on the floor of a workshop crammed with bikes, tyres and an assortment of screws, he secured the wheel in a well-worn vice and twisted each of the spokes until he formed a perfect circle. We paid him three *soles*, about 70 pence, and hoped he knew what he was doing.

We managed 135 kilometres before the next ping. Joel leant us a spare spoke; we were lucky that he had a Rohloff hub too, as we had used all ours. We hoped that the wheel would hold out, as we had a long day ahead if we were to cover 218 kilometres through the empty, vast Sechura Desert to Piura. At five am that morning, we had left the city of Chiclayo in the dark, and were now at the last village before we rode deep into the barren wilderness.

The Sechura was a dry white desert, peppered with brittle, bare trees bent in the direction of the prevailing wind. When we reached our 10,000 kilometre mark, Joel took the celebratory photograph for us and it was nice to share the moment with somebody who appreciated the work we had put in to get so far. Not long after, we stopped to speak to a group of British motorcyclists who were exploring South America. They were amazed to see people attempting this stretch by bike and had their own fascinating tales of getting lost on treacherous roads in the Andes, but we couldn't stay chatting to them for long if we were to make town by nightfall.

We arrived just after sunset, after a very long day in the saddle. Paddy's wheel had made it through the desert, but it was only a matter of time until the next ping. So, in the morning, while Joel continued north, Paddy returned to Trujillo to get it fixed. I left him at the bus terminal an hour before his departure time, as all passengers were put through vigorous security checks prior to boarding, akin to getting on a plane. Online I followed his progress towards Trujillo, thanks to the bus' GPS tracker. These measures were a safeguard against armed robbers hijacking buses along quiet stretches of road and a consequence of Peru's political troubles in the latter half of the 20th century.

In the 1980s and early nineties, a group called *Sendero Luminoso* launched a violent campaign to create a Maoist state in the name of the Indian communities of the Andes. They were once described as the world's most dangerous terrorist movement. The guerrillas held up buses, robbing travellers of their belongings, and in the mid-1980s, a German couple was taken off a bus and executed; their only crime, to be foreign. The terror was widespread but Lima was specifically targeted, suffering a string of bombings, blackouts and assassinations.

In 1990, Alberto Fujimori was elected president and he crippled the group by capturing its leader, Abimael Guzmán. During the civil war some 4,000 people had been disappeared by the armed forces, while 69,000 people had been killed, mostly by the guerrillas, between 1982 and 2000. However, *Sendero Luminoso* still operated, mainly in the remote jungle areas of the south-central highlands, where they were funded by drug-smuggling operations, which is why bus companies took no risks with security.

Paddy made it safely back from Trujillo, and with the wheel fixed we could return to the road. Throughout Peru we had stuck to main routes, so when we saw a rare B-road heading to the surfing mecca of Mancora, we decided to get off the Pan American for a while. The first 15 kilometres were fine; the road meandered through abandoned villages where blonde-haired surfer dudes had set up camp in wooden houses. We asked if this was the correct way and they nodded enthusiastically, so we rode on past security guards who waved us through a gate into the private land of an oil company. The sandy tracks we cycled on ran parallel to large white pipes carrying oil from platforms standing like an invading armada off the coast.

As the road slowly deteriorated, splitting into several narrow tracks, we stuck close to the ocean to maintain our bearings. Gradually the surface became washboard, and in some areas thick sand, where the dunes had encroached over the track. In the end we were forced to push and, at times, even carry the bikes. We weren't the only ones having trouble; we came across a 4x4 stuck in the sand and three men trying to dig it out. Paddy helped, and after considerable shovelling and pushing, the vehicle eventually lifted out. We were still in the middle of nowhere and had run out of water, so when the driver offered us a lift back to the main road we jumped at the invitation. Paddy and I squished into the back seats, our bikes balanced precariously in the back of the pickup and the panniers flapping in the wind as the driver raced across the landscape, using speed and power to avoid getting stuck again.

When we arrived in Mancora, we slumped into the sofas of a hippie restaurant along the main street. Munching on burgers, a guy stopped, aghast; "Are these Thorn Nomads?" he said, pointing at our bikes, beaming with delight when we confirmed they were. Mark had been born in Britain, grew up in Canada, but now lived in Mancora with his Peruvian wife Lindsay and their two gorgeous children. He was a keen cyclist and told us he had been eyeing up the Thorns online for a while now, but he hadn't seen one in person. We offered for him to take one for a spin and he, in return, invited us to stay at his house, where we were treated like old friends. The family leant us their quad bike to visit some local thermal springs and on our final evening treated us to *cerviche*, a local delicacy of raw fish marinated in lime juice and chili. It was a typical meal for fishermen who took a lime and some spice out to sea to accompany one of the fish they caught during the day.

Mancora had a tropical, dry climate and the Humboldt and El Niño currents that met here produced good waves for surfing. The Humboldt Current, named after the explorer Alexander von Humboldt who identified the natural phenomenon, was a cold flow of ocean water from the south of Chile to northern Peru, while El Niño was a band of warm ocean-water temperatures that periodically developed off the western coast of South America, causing climatic changes across the Pacific Ocean. El Niño can have devastating effects, and Lindsay told us when she was younger Mancora was left stranded when heavy floods and landslides washed away the main road on both sides of town.

Joel had headed here to surf, and we met up with him one evening to share a few beers. He was half thinking about leaving with us, but in the morning there was no sign of him, so we left a message and set off. We heard nothing in reply and were beginning to think we may have offended him, when we received an email saying he had been knocked out surfing and had been unable to get out of bed for a few days. We felt bad, if we'd known we would have stayed to help him.

A few days later, just south of Tumbes, we said goodbye to the Pacific Ocean. From here we would be cycling north-east towards Venezuela, and the Caribbean Sea. The last few days in Peru had been relaxing and fun with our new friends and I had almost forgotten how frustrating I had found the country at times, when a nervous policeman pulled up.

We had stopped a few miles before the border, my stomach was playing up again and I was retching by the roadside. The police officer stopped his motorbike, and in hurried Spanish frantically pointed at people at work in the fields. As far as I could tell they had paid us no attention, but the policeman insisted they were all "bad people" and we must keep moving. He wouldn't leave until we set off. For the first time on the trip, I was relieved to be leaving a country – the never-ending security concerns in Peru were draining. I sincerely hoped Ecuador would be a friendlier place.

9. Ecuador

"Dame tu mano y venga conmigo. Vámonos al viaje para buscar los sonidos mágicos de Ecuador."

We paused halfway across the short bridge connecting Peru to Ecuador and turned our iPods up loud, as the 1990s Sash! dance hit blared out: "Give me your hand and come with me. Travel with me to search for the magic sounds of Ecuador." Our faces shone red in the midday heat, and sweat trickled down our backs as we danced in the empty road. I thought back to nights spent planning the trip at our kitchen table, when, distracted from more important logistical issues, I had declared we must ride into Ecuador listening to this track. Now it was actually happening; we were ready to explore the magic of Ecuador.

Although it was the smallest country in the Andes, only slightly larger than the United Kingdom, Ecuador packed in a range of diverse terrain, including the world-famous Galapagos Islands. The archipelago of volcanic islands, where a huge range of species flourished and which influenced Charles Darwin's theory of evolution and natural selection, were perhaps the main draw for travellers to Ecuador, but we wouldn't be visiting on this trip. Even the most budget trip would set us back a couple of thousand US dollars, and in the knowledge that our bank account was rapidly diminishing, we had little choice but to stick to the Ecuadorian mainland on this occasion.

Still, there would still be plenty for us to see as we made our way towards the capital, Quito. The city sits high in the central Andean highland, where the mountains act as a barrier between the thick Amazon jungle in the east of the country and the flat coastal plain in the west. *Equator* in Spanish, the country takes its name from its position straddling the latitudinal intersection of the globe. This pub quiz fact was about the extent of our knowledge of Ecuador. It was a place travellers rarely spoke about with gusto, so we had no highlights to anticipate, nor had we received the usual, overblown security warnings from locals about how people were all thieves and villains. For once, we could set out to explore a country without having many preconceptions.

Our map showed that to reach Quito we could either follow the coastal road north for a while, or head straight into the mountains. While a week of riding along the flat sounded attractive, we opted to turn inland sooner to escape the sweltering heat and the persistent mosquitos, both of which were increasing in intensity the further north we rode. Thanks to the mossies, my tanned legs were now covered in itchy red spots and there didn't seem much chance of respite while we continued through banana plantations where the little critters thrived.

There were fields after fields of banana trees, their bright pink flowers drooping towards the earth. After the collapse of its cacao industry, Ecuador started mass producing bananas in the 1920s and was now the world's largest exporter of the fruit. The closely-packed trees cast little shade across the road, but we kept cool by riding back and forth beneath icy jets of water from misdirected sprinklers. The refreshing feeling of the cold liquid trickling down our backs gave a similar sense of relief as downing a cold beer and we would only move when completely drenched, in the knowledge that within ten minutes we would have dried. Every now and then we would pass wobbly wooden stalls loaded with huge branches of ripe bananas. Although most of the fruit was destined for foreign markers, mainly the USA or Europe, enough could easily be spared for passing motorists and the odd cyclist. The stall owners were usually reluctant to sell us less than ten, but we would point at our already overloaded panniers and they would laugh as they peeled off just enough to fuel us along the next stretch of road.

Pasaje, a town of grey buildings and a confusing maze of wide streets, housed workers from the surrounding banana plantations. As we rode through the centre in search of a morning snack, the roads were quiet and only the odd pedestrian wandered along the pavement, leaving an eerie feeling of a town having been abandoned. So, we were surprised when, from out of nowhere, a stream of bikes crossed at the junction in front of us. Curious as to what was going on, we abandoned our hunt for food and tagged onto the back of the group, following them sharply around a corner into the middle of a huge cycle demonstration.

Riding together in a two-lane wide peloton were cheerful school children, teachers and parents. There were riders of all ages, shapes and sizes; a few rode light, bright racing bikes, but the majority had old-fashioned workhorses with thick, worn tyres and heavy frames. They were united by a piece of white A4 paper tied to the front of everybody's handlebars that ecstatically proclaimed *'Promoviendo la salud urbana'*.

It was a demonstration to encourage people to keep fit by using their bikes more, a teacher explained, as we were swept along by the wave of riders. Dressed in light blue jeans, with a tomato-red top and cap, he seemed popular with his students, who kept close as we weaved around the streets. The police followed closely as the bikes took over the centre of town, before heading to the suburban outskirts and finally back to the central plaza where the parade came to an end.

Tired, sweaty cyclists filled the square, refuelling on ripe yellow bananas that were being handed out to participants from a well-stocked truck. The atmosphere was electric as young people chatted away in rushed, excited Spanish about the ride. Our new teacher-friend gathered us in a huddle with his class and the students snapped away on their smart phones, taking photographs of the strange *gringos* who had crashed their demonstration. Attracted by the crowd that had gathered, a camera crew appeared and asked for an interview for the local news channel. Paddy bravely mumbled a few words of explanation about our trip and why we supported the local commitment to cycling and healthy living.

We waved goodbye to our new friends who pointed us back towards the banana plantations in the direction of the dusty town of Naranjal. Along the main street, mustard-yellow taxis, more synonymous with the bustling streets of New York City, raced back and forth, weaving around vendors peddling their wares. The vehicles weren't the only US imports; most of the bottled water we bought had US labels, and food, like cheese, was also shipped in. The most interesting import, however, was the use of the US dollar as the official currency of Ecuador.

In the 1970s, oil was discovered in the Ecuadorian jungle east of the Andes. High levels of production encouraged public spending and with it the rise of corruption, meaning, that by the

1980s, the country was suffering runaway inflation and growing public deficits. Successive governments failed to deal with the problems and, by the mid-1990s, Ecuador was in a mess: around ten per cent of the population left in search of work in the US and Spain. One of the government responses was to make the US dollar the official currency in order to stabilise the economy.

It felt odd to be paying for our shopping in dollars in the supermarket in Naranjal, the checkout assistant handing us a pile of familiar green notes and small coins in change. We hadn't bought much, as we wanted our bags to be as light as possible for the climbing that lay ahead. Throughout the day, above the tightly-packed banana trees, I had caught occasional glimpses of the foothills to the Andes, grey and gloomy under a heavy cloud that obscured the high mountains behind.

It was our last day on the flat for a while; in the morning we would start climbing, and didn't expect to wave goodbye to the mountains until Venezuela. As keen as I was to escape the heat of the Ecuadorian coast, the idea of riding at altitude again did not excite me. I would have preferred a week's rest by the beach, but we had a tight schedule if we were going to make it to Barbados in February for the wedding.

Diary, 12 December 2011 - *Seven months on the road today and back into the hills. The road is steep. The gradients are much harsher than anywhere before – they seem to build their roads straight uphill. There were a lot of breaks; we stopped every few kilometres to catch our breath. It was a bit better this afternoon as it was cooler higher up, so slightly less exhausting.*

We had a funny moment leaving a village called Bucay. An old woman pulled us off the road and into her house to feed us coffee and biscuits. We didn't really understand her Spanish but she chatted away regardless. When we asked for a photo with her, she took us through a nondescript door that I hadn't noticed at the side of her house. It opened into a little chapel that was painted blue and lit up with Christmas lights and a nativity scene. There were pews and, at the front, an altar decorated with statues of the Virgin Mary. She hugged me when Paddy took a photo.

She was so lovely and kind: I think she would have kept us forever if she could. We had that awkward moment of not knowing if we should give money as a way of thanks, or if that would really offend her. We decided it was better not to and she waved us off beaming, so I think we did the right thing. I wonder why she has a chapel in her house, damn my useless Spanish skills for not being able to understand her properly.

The next day the road was even steeper and, five kilometres in, I stopped. It was the now familiar problem with my stomach and as I sat on the floor shaking from head to toe, it was clear that I couldn't continue. Disappointed, we rolled downhill to a police station and asked the officers if they knew where we could get a lift over the steeper section of road. The buses that raced through the town appeared packed with locals and backpackers, meaning we had little chance of getting us and our bikes on. So, it was a great stroke of luck when the police said they were heading that way right now and invited us to load the bikes into the back of the pickup. I left Paddy and an officer to secure the bikes while I squeezed into the rear seats. The relief of having found a quick solution, however, was short lived.

Paddy: *I was still wrapping bungee cords around the bikes to secure them in the flat bed of the pickup, when the driver gestured for me to hurry up and sit next to them; there was no more room inside for me to join Laura in the cab. We set off quickly, the traffic clearing as the police car pulled out sharply into the road. Within minutes we covered the few kilometres we had climbed on the bikes already that morning; the steep, winding roads providing no resistance to the police car that raced along, oblivious to the dangers of sharp bends and blind corners.*

With one sudden swerve, I felt the bikes jolt and slip, and suddenly I was pinned up against the side of the pickup, the heavy bikes leaning down on me. It hurt to breathe under the weight, but I managed to lift my arm high enough to bang on the window to call for help. The policemen were unimpressed, and I tried to look jovial as I saw Laura's worried face peering through the back window.

The bikes repositioned, the driver sped off again. The tyres screeched as he slid the vehicle sideways around bends in the road and I closed my eyes each time he overtook vehicles blindly at corners. It felt like being in a rally car race, only nobody in their right mind would do that on a narrow road like this, with plunging drops on one side.

By the time the vehicle suddenly came to a halt, my jaw hurt, I had been clenching my teeth so hard, and I was shivering with cold now that we were high in the mountains. Laura jumped out as soon as the car stopped and started helping me offload the bikes. "We're not at the top yet," she whispered, "but I can't do it anymore. We have to get out before we die in there."

The police officers were laughing and kept pointing further along the road to the top of the pass, but we smiled and insisted that we were happy to cycle from now on. We thanked them for their kindness and watched them speed off into the distance, at which point we both collapsed onto the damp grass and gripped each other in a tight hug.

It was a terrifying experience. I don't know how the driver didn't take us off a cliff. We spent the rest of the ride to Riobamba in silence, both lost in thought. There was still climbing to be done, but the shock of what had happened distracted me from the physical objections of my body.

The next morning, however, I couldn't lift my head off the pillow. The recurring exhaustion and sickness had started to have an impact on the trip and was beginning to ruin it for me; I knew that Paddy was finding it frustrating too, although he never complained. After researching my symptoms online, I decided to experiment by cutting bread out of my diet, to see if that was the problem. As much as a pain as this was, it made a big difference and the extreme symptoms mostly went away for the rest of the trip.

That morning, while I recuperated, Paddy went in search of a haircut to tame the curly locks now piled in a cone atop his head. When he returned, I almost fell out of bed laughing. He had found a barber's shop around the corner, where he asked for a trim. He had held up his fingers to indicate about seven centimetres should come off, and the barber had responded meticulously, taking out a ruler and carefully working his way around Paddy's head, taking off an equal amount from each strand. Predictably, the end result was disastrous: the sides were too short, while the top was now shaped in a long soft quiff that floated about on top of his head. When it became wet, it would stiffen into the shape of a volcano cone; it was one of the worst haircuts I have ever seen.

Fortunately, his cycle helmet hid the worst of it as we got back on the road, climbing into what Humboldt named the 'Avenue of the Volcanoes'. Along this stretch of road leading to Quito sit eight of Ecuador's ten tallest peaks, including the 6,310 metre-high Chimborazo, the top of which is the furthest land point from the earth's centre. The position of Chimborazo on the equatorial bulge means that it surpasses all other peaks, including Mount Everest, for the record. As we rode along the avenue, the snow-covered top of the Ecuadorian giant loomed above us, while the lower slopes of the volcanoes, with their lush green patchwork of fields, reminded me of the English countryside – only here the climbs seemed to go on forever as we rose to 3,400 metres on our way towards Atambo.

In the sprawling conurbation of Atambo, we were reunited with Joel for the first time since Peru. He had recovered from his surfing accident to attempt climbing Volcán Cotapaxi and, over dinner, he encouraged us to join him. There was no way, however, that either of us could be persuaded to climb up to 5,897 metres. We were struggling with the altitude as it was a few thousand metres lower, and we said our goodbyes the next morning as we set off towards historical Latacunga.

We had planned a day off here to visit nearby Lago Quilotoa, a cauldron-like volcanic crater filled with gassy turquoise-blue water. The lake was situated along the unpaved road we would have ridden had we not headed straight into the mountains. As our vehicle bounced through deep potholes, I knew we had made the right decision to cycle the tarmacked road.

This was one of the poorest areas we had seen in Ecuador, with children running beside the car, their hands outstretched, begging for change. The villages were built from adobe bricks and the fields cultivated little more than potatoes and onions, our guide explained. In one small village, he pointed out a brick hut with tiny square windows and peeling paint which was where, he said, the current Ecuadorian president had once lived.

Rafael Correa was elected president in 2006 on the promise to sweep away the corrupt party system and give rights to indigenous communities. Correa was a US-trained economist who learned the local Quechua language while working on an agricultural project in Zumbahua, the village we passed through. During his first two terms in power he cut poverty by one third and, in 2013, was re-elected for a third consecutive term with over 50 per cent of the vote; for Ecuador, a country that had eight presidents between 1996 and 2006, this was a significant show of support from the nation.

Back in the saddle, we appreciated the smooth tarmac as we made our way along the highway towards Quito. The road was lined with small yellow road signs, depicting a black exploding volcano above a heavy arrow indicating the direction people should run in case of an explosion. These signs lined volcano alley and never failed to make me smile; how anybody could expect to outrun a raging lava flow on Ecuador's steep roads was beyond me.

Pichincha, Quito's active volcano, last erupted in 1999, covering the capital city in several centimetres of ash. The volcano played an important role in the country's history; in May 1824, during the Battle of Pichincha fought on its slopes, General Sucre defeated the Spanish forces to win independence for Ecuador. The mastermind of the hard fought campaign, the South American liberator Simón Bolívar, merged the territory of Ecuador with Colombia, Panama and Venezuela in what he called the 'Republic of Colombia'. His plan was destined to fail, however, and by 1830 Ecuador was an independent republic.

The city sat in a wide, hilly valley under the gaze of Pichincha. From the ridge overlooking the capital, we were rewarded for our days of climbing with spectacular views and a zippy descent to meet an Ecuadorian who would be our host during our stay in Quito. A middle-aged man, he lived with his wife, their two young boys and a light, red bike that he powered around town on. The invitation to stay with him had been longstanding, having arrived through our website before we left for South America.

The traffic was gridlocked, so he guided us between cars as we made our way through Quito's Old Town, a beautifully preserved area. The city was founded by the Spanish in 1534 after the defeat of the Incas, and it rapidly became a major centre with dramatic churches, wide plazas and a towering basilica. Beyond the cobbled streets, we joined a network of cycle lanes that any European city would be proud of. The route took us through parks, around twisted bike-shaped sculptures, into the suburbs and north towards the family's apartment, about eight kilometres out of the centre.

His family welcomed us warmly and we were dedicated a corner of the living room to lay out our bags and an inflatable mattress on which to sleep, where we collapsed exhausted at midnight when the family went to bed. The clinking of cutlery being laid woke me at six am, and as I peered out of my sleeping bag I could see the family preparing for their day at work and school. We were clearly expected to join them, so I crawled reluctantly out of my warm cocoon. Sitting, bleary eyed, nibbling at my cereal, my body screamed for the prolonged sleep it was used to on a day off. Over breakfast it became apparent we weren't going to be allowed to stay alone in the apartment, which is how at eight am, we found ourselves hugging mugs of strong coffee in a bustling café in the centre of town, trying to work out how to spend the next ten hours.

Meeting local people was one of the best things about life on the road; I loved the opportunity to see a city from their perspective, and appreciated their efforts to show us around and make us feel at home. We were extremely lucky that most people were relaxed about having us around; they understood sleeping and eating were important during our time off and were happy to indulge us these basic luxuries. Everybody who invited us into their homes did so with acts of kindness and generosity, and we never lost sight of the good intentions they had towards us. Sometimes, however, things just didn't work out.

In anticipation of our long day in the city, our host had suggested some sights to see, and we wandered around and drank espressos until it was time to head back. We had offered to take the family out for pizza, our preferred way of thanking people for their hospitality, as it was cheap, sociable and better received by our South American hosts than a home-cooked, vegetarian meal. There was an American-chain pizzeria, Papa John's, not far from the family's apartment and we suggested the six of us head there.

Whist the men ordered, I sat with our host's wife and children who were testing my Spanish because the next day Paddy and I were due to do a series of interviews about our trip. Before we left for South America, we had arranged for a technician to do a survey of our boiler, one of the many administrative tasks needed to rent out our house. Paddy told him about the trip and it turned out he had a friend working for the British Embassy in Quito. We had emailed the embassy a few weeks earlier and they had asked if we would be happy to help promote the Olympic Games which would open in London in seven months' time. We had said yes, but as the children laughed at my tongue-twisted Spanish, I began to think it maybe wasn't such a good idea.

I was distracted from my concerns by the arrival of a stack of pizza boxes, and I shot Paddy a look of 'what on earth have you ordered'; he replied with an expression that made me realise it wasn't of his doing. There were two family size pizzas for the men alone, while we women and children each had a large pizza, plus there were boxes of chicken wings and dips. It was a ridiculous amount of food for six people, the four large pizzas would have been enough alone, and not surprisingly, we didn't finish half of what arrived. The bill, Paddy told me on the way home, was $70, and that was after he had done some negotiating to take off other items.

$70! I was furious and upset. $70 could have paid for at least three night's accommodation in a nice, central hotel room where I could sleep as long as I wanted. Out in the countryside, that was almost a week's budget if we needed to stay in basic hostels. I appreciated the family's generosity to invite us into their home, but I felt upset that it seemed our host saw us as rich westerners that he could take for a ride. So, when he invited us to spend Christmas with his extended family, adding that we would need to make a financial contribution, we made our excuses and moved into a hotel.

Fortunately, he didn't seem to realise he had upset us. We didn't want to fall out with him as he had been friendly and helpful during our stay; this was a small thing and we could write off the experience as a lesson learnt. Anyway, it was Christmas, a time for goodwill and cheer, and we switched our focus to the next day's media interviews at the embassy.

To the chagrin of Paddy, I had decorated our bikes with tinsel and Santa hats, and had learnt the phrase for 'Merry Christmas', so we could say *Feliz Navidad* to the camera; the journalists loved both. We started with a television interview in the lobby of the embassy with an excited reporter who asked Paddy easy questions while I smiled dumbly. One female journalist was more interested in the state of our relationship, and we answered her questions with bemused glances at each other – it felt a little personal to be sharing with a national newspaper.

Our story got picked up across various Ecuadorian media and even featured in a centre page, colour spread in a national newspaper's weekend supplement. Joel stumbled across it reading the newspaper and told us he almost choked on his sandwich when he saw it. We also did a piece to camera for the embassy website; sitting in our sweat-stained T-shirts and Lycra shorts, we talked about the trip and how we were excited that the Olympics would be taking place in our home city. It was a fun, bizarre day and the embassy staff were lovely, they even took us out for a meal once the media circus had departed.

We told them how surprised we were to see the close connection between Ecuador and the United States, with the imported produce, the use of the dollar, yellow taxis, and even the same restaurants. So, we were amazed when they told us that actually, under Correa, Ecuador had adopted a hostile stance towards the US and had closer links to Hugo Chávez in Venezuela. The president had refused to sign free-trade agreements with the USA, or to renew a lease on the Manta military base which the Americans had occupied for anti-drug operations, rent free, for ten years. It was a sign of things to come; in June 2012, the Australian, Julian Assange, who the British government wanted to extradite to Sweden on sexual assault charges, was awarded asylum by Ecuador in its London Embassy. The founder of the Wikileaks site had released online secret files that implicated the US government in many ways, and the Ecuadorians seem pleased to support him in spite of pressure from the US government. It was fascinating to learn about these official policies as they seemed at odds with what we saw around the country.

By the time we wheeled our bikes out of the embassy, we were exhausted, and checked into a hotel where we would be spending Christmas.

Diary, 25 December 2011 *- Christmas Day! We felt a bit homesick this morning when we Skyped our families who were all very merry, had shared presents and were about to eat. It was a bit sad to miss out – we hadn't done gifts, but Paddy had bought bucks fizz and croissants for breakfast, which was a real treat. We walked into the ex-pat area about midday as we thought things might be going on, but it was quiet. The Irish pub was open though and there were lots of friendly drinkers.*

They were doing a traditional Christmas lunch, so we hung about, chatted to some of the regulars who live in Quito – they were really friendly and welcoming, but there were some interesting characters who looked like they might not be allowed back into their own countries! We played pool and drank Black Russians like we would back home with my family. It worked out well and was lots of fun. We have a seven am start tomorrow morning though, and I'm wishing I hadn't drunk quite so much. We could have another day off, but if we want to celebrate New Year in Colombia we have some cycling to do!

Soon after leaving Quito, we were back on winding mountain roads and our Christmas lunch was soon burnt off. I used the excuse of reaching the 11,000 kilometre point of the trip to open the fruity Christmas panettone I was carrying. We reckoned we were approximately halfway around South America now, and 20 kilometres further on we reached another milestone when we crossed the Equator into the northern half of the globe. We recorded the moment with photographs of us sitting in different hemispheres and filmed a video message explaining we would cross back into the southern hemisphere when we reached the Amazon River in Brazil.

In addition to the usual traffic, we now shared the road with Lycra-clad cyclists who whizzed past us on light aluminium bikes. High in the mountains, we pedalled under avenues of arched trees, past fields of cud-chewing cows and wooden, Swiss-style huts, that conjured up memories of holidays in the Alps. The landscape consisted of dark green verdant valleys that were peppered with crystal-blue lakes and lofty volcanoes, the peaks of which disappeared into wispy, soft cloud.

Yet, the views changed depending on the altitude, and after coasting downhill to the small riverside town of El Juncal, it felt as if we had arrived in Africa rather than South America. The population of this grey, dusty town was predominantly Afro-Ecuadorian – it was unlike anywhere we had been in Ecuador so far. Most of the community were the descendants of slaves who arrived in Ecuador in the early 16th century to work the local cotton and sugar cane fields. Now, running parallel to the fast flowing Río Chota, the town's main street of crumbling concrete shops and houses symbolised how El Juncal was one of the most disadvantaged places in Ecuador.

El Juncal was humid and sticky and my legs came under attack from clouds of flies that tracked us as we crossed the bridge on our way out of town. The river was banked by steep, bare cliffs, and we spent the morning climbing up hairpin bends cut into the rock face. We were officially still on the Pan American Highway, but it felt like a minor countryside road as we passed through tiny villages and hamlets.

We were near to the border with Colombia now, but there was no let-up in the winding of the mountain road as we got closer to the border town of Tulcan. We pedalled through hilly, lush green valleys, at times feeling as if we were riding through an English country park as we rolled up and down grassy knolls, past mossy rocks and bubbling streams. The remote countryside was quiet and beautiful, but with few main roads the terrain was inaccessible, and it was easy to see why this area might be a favourite hiding spot for Colombian guerrillas.

Nearby, in 2008, Colombian armed forces had launched an attack on *Fuerzas Armadas Revolucionarias de Colombia* (FARC) guerrillas in a camp just inside Ecuador. 21 guerrillas were killed, including one of the FARC's senior figures, Raúl Reyes. Ecuador was furious that Colombia launched a military operation inside its borders, while Colombia accused Ecuador of not doing enough to combat these groups, and the incident led to a breakdown in relations between the two governments.

It was unnerving all this had taken place so close to the border crossing where we were now headed, but in spite of everything we knew about the country's troubles with drug trafficking and guerrillas, we were excited to be entering Colombia. Every cyclist we had met who had ridden through the country was really positive about their time there. Plus, I had fallen for the slogan on the Colombian Tourist Board billboard poster that I used to ride past each morning in London – "Colombia: the only risk is wanting to stay."

Now, so close to the area where FARC guerrillas hid and with a police helicopter buzzing over our heads, I began to wonder if it really was such a good idea to ride through one of the most dangerous countries in the world.

10. Colombia

“See how thick they are?” Richard asked, as he pointed through a hole in the wire fence at the bare walls of his neighbour’s unfinished house.

“They’re rocket-proof, that’s why. The guy never finished it because he was put in prison. The owner of the house on the other side of us, he was shot dead. They were both drug mafia.”

Richard was a distant cousin of Paddy’s, an Australian who emigrated to Colombia on marrying his Colombian wife, Patty. He and Paddy had never met before, but after emails from family, it had been arranged we would spend a few days with him while we passed through the humid city of Cali. Richard ran a student exchange programme, developing links with universities internationally to take South American students. He and Patty lived with their daughter Nicole in a beautiful home on the outskirts of Cali, where like long-lost friends, the family welcomed us. Showering off the day’s grime, I felt a sense of relief to have a few days off with real home comforts.

In the overflowing supermarket, Richard laughed as I struggled to choose from the mind-boggling assortment of products available, and he took control, throwing wedges of brie and bottles of red wine into the basket. It was a long time since we had seen such a variety of food and I didn’t know where to start. The cheese and wine formed part of the grand spread laid along the long veranda table that evening, where we tucked into a Mediterranean-style buffet, watching lightning rip through the distant night sky. The storm clung tightly to the mountains, rain pounding down on the already-sodden roads along which we had ridden to Cali.

“Did you have any problems getting here?” Patty asked, “The road from Ecuador used to be the most dangerous in Colombia for kidnappings and attacks. It’s better now, the guerrillas have been pushed back into the mountains. Still, we often hear helicopters flying overhead – it’s the army going to hunt them out.”

"Back in 1999," Richard added, "one of the guerrilla groups burst into the church that we passed on the way to the supermarket. The congregation was in the middle of a Sunday service and the church was packed. The guerrillas rounded everybody up, including the priest and took over 100 people hostage in the mountains. That's what Colombia used to be like. There was something like 3,500 kidnappings a year."

We had entered Colombia via the chaotic border town of Ipiales, the day before New Year's Eve, when people were preparing to welcome 2012. Limp papier mâché figures, like scarecrows, hung from balconies and perched on wooden stools along the pavement, watching soon-to-be revellers rushing about with heavy holiday luggage and bags of shopping.

The New Year's *Carnaval* began the next morning, led by muscular young men parading along the street in elaborate drag; some wearing teeny-tiny dresses that clung to their masculine curves, while others twirled along the high street in sumptuous flamenco dresses, heavy with ruffles of black and violet. One man dramatically gave birth as he marched, running into a portable hospital carried by his helpers, where he quickly delivered a new-born baby doll to the delight of the crowd. We were confused as to what this all signified, but the cheering and loud music was infectious, and we joined the locals applauding from the pavement. A loud roar went up when a young man dressed in luminous pink tights and with balloons strategically placed as breasts, rushed over to us and pulled Paddy onto the street. Applauded by the watching crowds, he entered into the spirit, dancing a shuffle as locals photographed the strange spectacle of a tall, bearded foreigner salsa dancing with a man in drag.

Next, there followed an elaborate parade of papier mâché characters. Bob Marley, dreadlocks and all, carried his guitar with him, while a smiling Lionel Messi glided down the street with a football at his feet. There were proud-looking policemen, jugglers and even the Flintstones made an appearance – their life-size papier mâché car rolling slowly along. Some figures were so big that they were preceded by men with long sticks of bamboo, who raised overheard electricity lines so the procession could pass safely underneath.

The smaller papier mâché characters scattered around town were known as *Mr Old Year*, and were destined to be incinerated as revellers waved goodbye to 2011. Some people had stuffed their figures with fireworks for added effect, which is how, later that afternoon, we found ourselves running through Ipiales as rockets shot sideways across the pavement. Merry revellers packed the streets carrying crates of beer and soon-to-be-burnt effigies over their shoulders. Considering this was the atmosphere in the middle of the afternoon, we had great expectations for midnight.

Strangely, however, by ten pm the entire town was deserted. A few hours earlier crowds had blocked the streets, but now a heavy blanket of smoke hung over the town, which resembled a recently-bombed war zone. We carried on to the main square, past a papier mâché policeman smouldering on the pavement. Earlier we had seen a stage being set up, but now it was empty; we weren't quite sure what was going on.

> ***Diary, 1 January 2012*** *- At our hotel, the receptionist told us most people had gone home to dance. This was disappointing news – there would be no public midnight celebration. Ten minutes later, however, we were relieved we'd come back as there was a power cut across the entire town and all the lights went out. The hotel's generator kicked in after a while, and we celebrated at midnight in the room with a rendition of 'Old Lang Syne' – a reminder of New Years with friends. It was a damp squib compared to some we have celebrated at home, but one we will remember!*
>
> *So that's the end of 2011. It's been a good year, and quite incredible to think back on the trip so far, but there's so much ahead in 2012.*

Our new year began with a peaceful day on the road, as most people slept off hangovers. We were cycling through the Colombian Massif, a mountainous knot from where the Andes fan out in three ranges that spread northwards through the country. The shape of the mountains resembled steep-sided Toblerone cones squashed up close together, creating short jagged peaks everywhere I looked. Colombia's 'most dangerous road', a narrow stretch of the Pan American Highway, had been dug into the luxuriant green mountainside, winding its way northwards around the slopes.

It was a quick ride down to 1,800 metres, where we refuelled on eggs and coffee courtesy of a friendly café owner in a small riverside village. Another 50 metres lower, the descent stopped at a straight metal bridge crossing a wide river. On both sides were soldiers who gave big thumbs up as we passed. They were there to secure the bridge, and others along the route, from guerrilla assaults. I was reassured by their presence. It meant the road, and most likely us, were under close surveillance, and I pedalled on giving no thought to the reason why all this security was needed.

We saw cyclists everywhere now. Not touring cyclists; the stream of people riding southwards from Alaska to Ushuaia that we had seen in Bolivia and Peru had long since dried up, as people hurried to reach Argentina before winter. Instead, the road was dominated by locals out on bikes enjoying Colombia's second favourite sport – football being the first. There were Lycra-clad road riders who raced up and down the mountains, and then there were those who took to the saddle for their daily tasks. The mountains didn't perturb the Colombians, not even the cheery 70-year old we passed cycling slowly uphill in his wellies.

From the bridge we climbed up to 3,100 metres, and earned ourselves a smooth afternoon descent into the city of Pasto, where people were excitedly celebrating the *Carnaval de Negros y Blancos*. Traditionally, on 5 January each year, Colombian black slaves were allowed to hold parties; to show they approved, the masters painted their faces black and, in appreciation, the slaves painted their faces white the following day. It was a tradition enthusiastically upheld over several days each year.

Colombia was a major player in the South American slave trade, the Caribbean coastal city of Cartagena de Indias being the landing point for many Africans who were forcibly transported across the Atlantic. The slaves were put to work in a variety of tasks, including as blacksmiths, domestic workers, gold miners and sugar cane workers. Slavery was finally abolished in 1852, over 20 years after Colombia became an independent state.

Today's revellers used shaving foam or flour, and instead of painting themselves they targeted oblivious passers-by, we realised, as somebody ran up to Paddy and sprayed foam into his eyes. At first we were annoyed, but we noticed everybody was covered in foam and they all seemed to find it hilarious. We couldn't quite work out why it was so funny, and when a group of teenagers arrived with bags of flour to throw about, we decided to escape the mayhem.

Heavy grey clouds loaded the sky the next morning as we climbed out of Pasto. We were accompanied by six teenagers on a day trip to thermal baths about 25 kilometres away. They were in good spirits and rode with us as we tackled the steep slope, asking us questions about the trip. We lost them when the heavens opened; devoid of waterproofs, they stopped to shelter under the wide leaves of the roadside foliage, and waved cheerfully as we continued on.

On our second ascent of the day, we were accompanied by two small boys in worn out T-shirts, baggy shorts and sandals, who followed us out of their village. They had an endless list of questions, including about which football teams we supported, and they roared with laughter when I responded with my grammatically-confused Spanish. Unlike adults, they had no inhibitions about correcting my pronunciation, and delivered an impromptu Spanish lesson as we climbed.

In the mountains, days on the road were usually long. We would spend at least eight hours in the saddle, plus time for breaks, and we could be out for up to 12 hours. Usually something made the day memorable; we might meet somebody interesting, or ride through an area of spectacular beauty. At other times, nothing would happen and we would ride head down with little to stimulate our minds.

But sometimes we would have an amazing day, when we would climb into bed struggling to believe how far we had come or what we had seen. It would feel as if we had fitted a whole week into the space of just ten hours, and we would struggle to recount everything that had happened. The day after my impromptu Spanish lesson was one such time.

We had spent the night in a £6-per-night petrol station room on the outskirts of a village that resembled the Caribbean. It was hot and the local people looked African with their dark skin and glossy chestnut eyes; the descendants of Colombia's slaves who once worked in the local sugar cane fields. Breakfast was in one of the village's rickety wooden huts where we devoured plates of rice, eggs, potato and fried plantain. It was a poor area yet people were incredibly cheerful and, as we rode along the hot valley, small children waved excitedly from outside mud huts.

From the valley we climbed up to the agriculture centre of El Bordo, tackling a set of switchbacks cut into the side of a hill. The gradient was gentle and we were shaded from the sun by heavy foliage, but Paddy still decided to truck-surf on a lorry that spluttered and gasped as it crawled uphill, not helped by the weight of a cyclist hanging off the back. For me, relief came in the form of juicy, fresh oranges that, halfway up the hill, a man on a motorbike pulled over to give me.

From mid-level El Bordo, we continued to climb along a road where the rituals of *Carnaval de Negros y Blancos* were in full swing, and I got sprayed several times by passengers leaning out of buses. It also seemed to be water throwing day, as a cluster of small children ran out of their homes and chucked buckets of icy water at me. Initially, I laughed – it was hot and they had cooled me down. The higher we climbed, though, the colder the air became and the damp shirt clung uncomfortably to my skin. When I thought it was safe to do so, I changed T-shirts, only to find a waiting mob of kids at the next village, buckets ready. I pleaded with them to let me pass; a begging expression on my face as I repeated over and over, "Por favor, no, por favour!"

Fantastically it worked, and instead they targeted Paddy who was trying to avoid detection by clinging onto the back of yet another truck. The driver, keen to shake him off, pointed him out to the kids, who attacked him with louds screams of delight. It was nothing personal; anybody travelling along the road was a potential victim, and we watched them throw water into open car windows, the unsuspecting drivers swerving across the road as the cold water landed in their laps.

As we rode higher we could see clouds mustering in the sky, growing gradually greyer until they opened in a sprinkling of rain. We sought shelter under the wide leaves of a tree, copying the technique of the teenagers we had ridden out of Pasto with. Next to us, on a wooden perch, sat a beautiful red macaw parrot, his wings tipped with blue, green and yellow feathers.

He seemed unperturbed by the weather, and continued to suck the mango in his talons, but as the rain grew heavier, his owner appeared to rescue him. She pointed us in the direction of a football pitch further down the street, where we ran to take cover. Our arrival failed to distract the penalty shootout that was taking place under the high corrugated iron roof; the group of young boys and teenagers were absorbed in the competition. They were playing on a surface of large, concrete tiles, shooting towards medium-size goalposts, the metal of which sported chips from where powerful shots had narrowly missed the target.

Along each length of the pitch were two levels of bleachers made from bricks, which is where I sat to watch the match Paddy was invited to join, once the older boys won the shootout. Nobody queried who these two foreign cyclists were – they were more interested in persuading Paddy to be their goalkeeper, as his huge frame filled most of the goal.

When the rain finally eased off, the game broke up. The boys returned to their chores, and we to the road, conscious there was still ten kilometres to cover before nightfall. Camping was out of the question in this area; the road was cut sharply into the side of the mountain, with no level ground to pitch a tent. Regardless, landslides were common, and we knew our flimsy tent would stand no chance against a collapsing mountainside. We had seen several resulting rock falls, from where heavy rain had saturated the ground, but not yet an Andean storm in full fury; that was about to change.

The sky was dark grey and low over the mountains as we pulled away from the football pitch. We hoped to cover the final section quickly, to reach the top of the pass before dark, where we had been told there was a petrol station with rooms. The road was steep, but we were making steady progress, as we spun the wheels in our low 'granny' gears. As we plodded on, it was impossible not to notice black clouds slowly drifting ahead, until they formed a thick blanket that blocked out any sunlight that might have penetrated through. Soon, the rain returned. At first it was soft, and we hardly noticed it fall onto our waterproof jackets, but it quickly grew to the force of a power shower on full as it battered the tarmac. The weight of the flow was so strong that it muffled the roaring thunder that boomed overhead.

Still, we pushed on, unsure what else to do until we could find somewhere safe to stop. Silver lightning shot repeatedly through the sky, illuminating the mountain valley that was under the control of the storm. Crashing down the mountainside, we could see powerful waterfalls that a few minutes earlier had been just minor trickles. Water gushed off the hillside, torrents running to join the flooded drainage channels at the side of the road before pouring onto the highway, which now resembled a fast-flowing stream.

As the water flowed down the road, it brought with it tumbling rocks and stones that rolled hastily downhill. We swerved to avoid debris as we fought against the flow, pushing in higher gears to compete with the forces working against us. Riding uphill against the force of the water was a surreal and terrifying sensation, and I kept my eyes fixed on the road in front of me.

Briefly, we stopped under the narrow shelter of a thatched-roofed house, wondering what we should do. On the face of it, the option to stay still was the most sensible, but we were still getting soaked as the rain lashed sideways, so we decided to push on. Drivers had pulled up to let the storm pass, the road was quiet, and we figured it was safer to continue riding when we had more space, rather than waiting until the traffic set off again. Plus, there was no sign of the storm abating, and if we had to cycle in the storm, I preferred to do so before nightfall.

It took another hour to reach the top of the pass, without any let-up in the conditions. Each time the lightning lit the sky, I looked upwards to see how much further we had to ride, until finally it was over, and we pulled into the muddy forecourt of the petrol station. It had been one hell of a day; from tropical heat down on the valley floor, to a ferocious Andean storm. When at last we huddled in bed in the dingy petrol station, we could still hear the rain lashing down, and I fell asleep to the sound of a gale swirling around the building.

Diary, 6 January 2012 *- It was still raining as we left, and the weather stayed miserable all day. Apparently, this is the dry season, but it's been raining every day for four months solid. The road showed signs of it; in places one lane was lower than* *the other where the earth had slipped away. Elsewhere, there were landslides and in some place the holding walls were bulging with the weight of the soaked earth behind.*

We stopped for breakfast up the first climb of the day and sat next to a guy whose truck had come off the road the night before. He was OK, but we passed his truck which was on its side and hanging over the grass verge, with long traffic jams on either side, as drivers were having to squeeze past it.

Instead of the long climbs that we had become accustomed to, the terrain had transformed into short rolling hills. Late one afternoon, I pulled over to refuel on some crackers, when, head deep inside my pannier, I heard a Gallic "'ello" from over my shoulder. I looked up to see a grinning Joel behind me. The three of us rode together into Popayan, our camaraderie resumed when we stopped to help fix Joel's puncture, even though it made us sitting ducks for revellers who squirted foam from their car windows. We fared no better inside the city, whose cobbled streets were confusing to navigate and, lost, we repeatedly rode past party goers who targeted us with delight. By the time we finally found our hostel, we were covered in a sticky layer of foam, water and flour.

Our ghost-like appearance was apt, for we were now in the 'white city' of Popayan, famous for its impressive white colonial buildings bordering the central square. It was difficult to believe, but in 1983 an earthquake destroyed much of the peaceful spot, where we sat slurping the flesh of juicy mangoes. Yet, even harder to imagine was how at times during the last few decades, this quiet, relaxed city, which was now a tourist venue, had been cut off from the rest of Colombia by fighting between guerrillas, paramilitaries and the Army.

The country's problems began in 1948 when, after the assassination of the Liberal Party leader, a civil war between Conservatives and Liberals broke out. The period was known as *La Violencia,* because of the extreme murders, rapes, torture and gruesome mutilations that were carried out by the different sides. Over 200,000 people died during the violence that lasted until the 1960s. In the 1970s and 1980s, disillusioned with the leadership of the Liberal Party, several Marxist guerrilla movements sprang up, demanding improvements for Colombia's rural poor, and using rural warfare and tactics similar to those of the civil war.

The FARC was one of the oldest and largest of the rebel movements, funding its activities through drug trafficking, kidnapping, extortion, and an unofficial 'tax' it levied in the countryside for 'protection' and social services. By the late 1990s-early 2000s, FARC at the peak of its strength, had significantly expanded its territory across Colombia. The Colombian Government attempted peace negotiations without success, but in May 2002, the hard-liner Álvaro Uribe was elected president. Uribe's father had been murdered by the FARC, and he was determined to destroy the guerrillas. There was significant movement when, in 2008, the leader of the FARC died and a number of senior rebels surrendered. Then, in July that year, government forces infiltrated the FARC, freeing 15 hostages, including the former presidential candidate, Ingrid Betancourt, whose six year imprisonment in the jungle had drawn international condemnation.

By the time we entered Colombia, guerrilla groups across the country had been significantly weakened, but not defeated. The FARC was still active in the area around Popayan. In June 2011, it exploded a car bomb in the city injuring 17 people, and just three days before we arrived there, guerrillas destroyed three homes and damaged 30 when they launched an early morning raid on the town of El Tambo, 28 kilometres away. I was oblivious to events like these and under the illusion that things were more secure than they actually were. Had I known guerrillas were active in the area, I would have felt much less confident about being there.

As it was, my most pressing concern was the terrain. I was incredulous that on the day we left Popayan, although we dropped 1,300 metres overall, we climbed 1,000 in the process. I was very much looking forward to a few days break in Cali.

Joel, in the meantime, was heading north towards Medellin. On our last evening together for a while, we booked into a roadside lodge, where we shared cold beers on the terrace. A local, seeing us, came over to ask if we liked mangoes. The man was delighted when we said yes and rushed off to collect a huge pole, with which he started poking hanging fruit on a nearby tree, delivering us a complementary fresh supply that would last several days. Later that evening, it looked as if we would be eating mangoes for dinner, when our recently-temperamental stove finally gave up the will to live, nearly taking the lodge down with it.

> ***Paddy:*** *The temperature extremes and heavy use on the trip so far, had taken its toll on the stove components, particularly the o-ring seals, which prevented leaks where the pump and bottle met. The stove, an MSR Whisperlite, had performed well up until recently, and I had become complacent about firing it up, particularly when hungry, and I tended to sometimes over-pressurise the fuel bottle.*
>
> *The room we were in was completely wooden apart from the concrete floor. When I pressurised the bottle the first time, I pumped it too high and some fuel spilt on the floor. I decided I would clean it up once the stove was going as it didn't look too much, and Laura was waiting with the pan of water for the pasta. So, I moved the stove slightly to the side and started again.*
>
> *This time the flow was good, the fuel came down the line as it should, and I leant in with the gas lighter as normal. I didn't even get close before the whole thing bloomed into a fireball that leapt out and lit the fuel I had spilt on the floor. A line of fire raced across the room, stopping just centimetres before the curtains of our wooden, box room.*
>
> *It all happened so quickly that neither of us had time to react. When it stopped, I turned around to see Laura with a look of panic on her face, still holding the pan of water. We both knew that if the fire had reached the curtains, it would have moved onto the wood very quickly.*
>
> *We borrowed Joel's stove to finish dinner, and we never used the Whisperlite again, replacing it in Cali. It was a great piece of kit, but it required regular maintenance and it preferred good quality fuel, neither of which we were good at providing while in South America.*

The next morning, we said goodbye to Joel and headed towards Cali. We were out of the mountains now, riding across the hot, open plain of the Valle del Cauca. The sun beat strongly down on the fields, and we stopped for a drink at a row of stalls built from thick poles of sugar cane. We settled in the shadiest booth we could find, where the stallholder pulled cold bottles of Coca-Cola out of an ice bucket, droplets of water sliding down the glass bottles as we glugged away.

The pit-stop was strategically placed to capture the custom of drivers made to stop at the army checkpoint, a few metres along. Dressed in full camouflage uniform, with heavy round helmets and high webbing belts containing extra ammunition, the soldiers carried loaded automatic machine guns slung around their chests. One wandered over towards us, and I shuffled nervously in my chair wondering what he wanted. Stopping outside, he pointed the barrel of his gun towards our bikes.

"¿Donde van ustedes?" he asked.

"Cali," I answered, "pero, nuestro destino final es Rio de Janeiro."

This had him interested, and his rifle dropped to his side as he beckoned his friend over. Relieved that the tense atmosphere had disappeared, I pulled out our 'magic letter' from my handlebar bag to show them the route we had taken around South America. Together, they read the explanation about our trip, smiling and laughing, and in pidgin Spanish, I answered their questions about our adventure. After finishing a second bottle of soda, we waved goodbye to the soldiers, leaving them to guard the highway into Cali, the city once home to the notorious drug cartel, 'Cali's Gentlemen'.

Coca leaves have been grown in the Andes for centuries, to be chewed or brewed as tea to provide energy and combat the symptoms of altitude. In its natural form, the leaf is a mild stimulant on the level of coffee, but in the mid-1800s a German chemist extracted cocaine from the coca leaf, beginning a global infatuation with this powerful drug.

In the 1970s and 1980s cocaine was a fashionable drug in cities like New York and London, and Colombian drug traffickers, who were already involved in the marijuana trade, identified a new market to exploit. Lawlessness in rural areas, caused by the growth of guerrilla groups, encouraged an environment where illegal processing and exporting of cocaine could take place, away from prying eyes. Processing labs were built in jungle areas that were difficult for the police to penetrate, and where workers would convert coca leaves from Peru, Bolivia and Colombia into cocaine. The drugs were smuggled into the US in the spare tyres of small planes and even by submarine. Rapidly, Colombia became the world's largest exporter of cocaine.

Drug production was run out of two of Colombia's largest cities, Cali and Medellin, where rival drug cartels ruled. In Medellin, the cartel was run by the infamous Pablo Escobar, and by the 1980s, it was estimated 80 per cent of all cocaine imported into the US came from that city alone, making the drug lords insanely rich. In 1989 *Forbes* magazine listed Escobar as one of the richest men in the world, with an estimated wealth of US$3 billion. He worked hard to grow a 'Robin Hood' image, giving money to the poor for social projects, but at the same time he ruled with violence. His policy was one of *plata o plomo*, silver or lead.

By the late 1980s the cartels were waging war on the state, in an attempt to intimidate the government into legalising cocaine, and rejecting US demands for the extradition of drug traffickers. They organised bombings, assassinations and kidnappings. Escobar and the Medellin Cartel were thought to be responsible for the murder of hundreds of government officials, police, lawyers, judges, journalists and innocent civilians.

'Cali's Gentlemen' were so called because the founding members came from a higher level of society than the usual drug trafficker. In the past they had operated second to the Medellin Cartel, but as the government focused on destroying Escobar and his allies, the 'Gentlemen' dominated more of the drug trade. In December 1993, after years of evading the police, Pablo Escobar was discovered hiding in an apartment in Medellin. He was flushed out and killed on a rooftop overlooking the city.

The death of Escobar led to the dismantling of the Medellin Cartel and the rise of the Cali group, until its leaders were also captured and imprisoned in 1995. After the fall of the cartels, smaller organisations took over, allowing cocaine production to continue, but at reduced levels. US sponsored campaigns targeting the drug trade, including spraying coca fields with weed-killer, helped reduce production. In 2000, the UN estimated Colombia grew 74 per cent of the world's coca leaves; in 2011 that was down to 42 per cent, and the next year Colombia was overtaken as the largest producer of cocaine by Peru and Bolivia.

Aside from the rocket-proof walls of Richard's neighbour's house, we saw little of the impact the drug trade had on Cali. Instead we discovered a calm, thriving city, with new shopping malls where we treated ourselves to new T-shirts. In a bike shop packed with light high-end road bikes, we handed over our Thorns to the experienced mechanics who got to work giving the bikes a long overdue service, in preparation for taking on the toughest road of the trip so far; *La Linea.*

Colombian road cyclists are some of the best in the world, competing in events like the Tour de France. One of the reasons they make great climbers is they have some of the world's toughest mountain roads as their training ground. *La Linea* was considered one of the most challenging paved roads in the world, peaking at 3,287 metres high. From Cali, at 1,000 metres in altitude, we would ride up gradients that, for much of the route, ranged between nine and 16 per cent.

Richard, who knew the road well, offered to drive us to the top. He was an adventurer himself, having disappeared into the Amazon Rainforest when he first visited South America, much to the concern of his family, to whom he had neglected to mention his plans. We felt we couldn't accept his kind offer, however; this was a challenge we needed to do ourselves, something which Richard could understand.

We covered 100 kilometres the first day out of Cali, riding along the valley floor mostly. It was hot and sticky, and we stopped regularly for cold grape juice, until we began climbing up towards the town of Calarca. During the afternoon we gained about 500 metres of altitude, the landscape gradually becoming mountainous and the air cooler. As we approached Calarca, I heard somebody shout as they passed on the other side of the road, and I turned around to see what was going on. Paddy was also distracted by the noise, which had come from a speaker on the back of a van, and had turned around himself. Facing the opposite direction, he didn't realise I had slowed down, and he ploughed into the back of my bike with a heavy thud.

My bike jolted forwards, while Paddy swerved across the road. His handlebars led the bike in one direction, while he flew off the saddle horizontally in the other, landing heavily on a narrow grass verge, grazing his arms. But he was lucky; it could have been far more serious. Much of the afternoon, we had been riding along the edge of steep precipices – if the collision had happened just ten minutes earlier, Paddy would have fallen off the side of the mountain.

The next morning we set off early for the big climb. There were 25 kilometres to the top, which we hoped to reach by lunch.

> ***Diary, 14 January 2012*** *- It started off alright and I was quite enjoying it. We spotted a few local cyclists hanging on to trucks and tried to do the same. Paddy was good at it, but I was useless. I struggle to get up the speed to get on, and if I do, then I wobble all over with the weight of the bike through my arms. I did try at some road works, but I let go as I was nervous that I might get pulled under the wheels. The road got steep anyway, so there was no way that I would have been able to hold on – it would have pulled my arm out of the socket!*
>
> *About 15 kilometres along they had started to build a tunnel, but it wasn't open yet. As we neared the top the gradient got really steep and difficult. At about seven kilometres to go, the road got bad with landslides, road works and grit, and the hard shoulder disappeared. I ended up panicking in sections as I couldn't get over the gradients without wobbling, and there were so many vehicles going past.*
>
> *I'd stopped to let traffic go when a small truck with two guys in stopped and offered me a lift. I jumped straight in. It was really quick to the top as I was practically there, but it was a relief not to cycle as the road was busy, steep and narrow. When I got to the top, Paddy was waiting, looking perplexed as I offloaded the bike. With raised eyebrows, he asked if he should worry about my willingness to get in a truck with strangers in Colombia. Mmmm..... That's a good point, it never occurred to me that they could be kidnappers, they looked so friendly!*

With the wind gusting around the mountain top, it was freezing cold, and we hurried into the small café there. Richard had told us about this place, insisting that we sample its speciality, *aguapanela con queso*. We were sceptical; it was made from *Panela*, unrefined cane sugar, dissolved in hot water with a lump of soft white cheese thrown in. There was nothing else on offer, however, and famished, we ordered two bowls. The cheese was supposed to melt, but mine sunk to the bottom, where it sat in an unappetising-looking block. The sugar water, however, tasted like treacle toffee and I gulped that down greedily.

I spent the break talking about how hard the ride up had been, and watching Paddy roll his eyes at my complaining, but when we got outside I spotted that my back tyre was flat. I thoroughly enjoyed watching him fix the puncture as punishment for his cynicism. Heading down the other side of the mountain, we passed work underway on the new tunnel and a highway. 50 metre-high concrete columns, which would support the new road, reached out of the tiny villages. It appeared the new route would sit high in the sky as it reached up to the tunnel. *La Linea* would certainly be more fun to cycle when the work was finished and the road was less busy.

We spent the night in Cajamarca, a narrow town serving the passing traffic, with electric church bells that rang every 30 minutes. It was a grating noise that woke us at 5.30 am and encouraged us to hit the road early. Later that day, in a flat valley where locals were out for a Sunday cycle along dedicated cycle lanes, we stopped to celebrate reaching 12,000 kilometres for the trip. There had been some long days in the mountains since we marked 11,000 back in Ecuador, and it felt like a hard earned thousand kilometres. So when we arrived in the capital, Bogota, a few days later, I was relieved to have another few days off.

We rode into the city along the *Ciclovía,* one of the largest networks of cycle lanes in the world, with over 300 kilometres of bike paths around the capital. Separated from the busy traffic, they were impressive, and far better than anything in London, taking us straight to our art-deco hotel. Parts of the city looked dirty and edgy, and we obeyed advice to avoid certain areas, sticking to the historical centre. It felt safer there, thanks largely to the heavy peppering of police around the Plaza de Bolivar. The large, rectangular plaza housed grand buildings from across four centuries, including the modern Palacio de Justicia on the north side of the square.

The Palacio had been recently reconstructed, after the original was damaged in 1985, during a siege by the M19 group. The guerrillas had issued demands for the then-President, Belisario Betancurhad, to stand trial, and had destroyed files of Colombians under threat of extradition to the US. In response, the Army stormed the Palacio. More than 100 people were killed in the raid, including 12 Supreme Court justices, and a fire ravaged the building for two days.

One morning, we took a cable car to the top of the rocky outcrop that overlooks the city, *Cerro de Moserrate*. Below, we could see the expanse of the metropolis sprawling out across the high plain. Over eight million people reside in Bogota, and like in many South American cities, a large proportion of residents live in poverty. The city had a tough feel to it, as if it was still struggling to find its feet after decades of violence. As if to demonstrate that, a debate was raging about gun control. The city's mayor, Gustavo Petro, a former guerrilla, had suggested a ban on people bringing guns into public places. The reaction had been mixed, with many arguing it wouldn't work. Petro had countered that with 1,600 homicides in Bogota in 2011, 60 per cent of which involved firearms, the ban could make a difference.

I liked Bogota, yet I didn't fall in love with the city. There were some nice artistic areas to explore, a selection of restaurants to eat in, and attractions like the gold museum, which contained floors of artefacts from pre-Hispanic societies, but after a couple of days wandering around, I had started to grow bored. The overcast weather didn't help, and after our admin was sorted, I was happy to move on again. It was a sentiment that proved short lived, when I remembered I didn't like cycling in the mountains.

Diary, 23 January 2012 - *A really tough day, it feels like it's been so hard ever since we left Bogota. I spent most of the morning in tears from physical and mental exhaustion. My hormones were playing up too, which didn't help. I got a lot of odd looks from people as we cycled along. I turned into somewhat of a robot on the bike – just keeping pedalling and not thinking about distance or speed.*

The road was endlessly undulating and really hard work. We climbed 400 metres coming up through just one town. God knows what we did throughout the whole day. We finally reached the town of San Gil about six pm after seven and a half hours in the saddle and 101 kilometres in the hills – a killer.

Although I could always moan about riding in the hills, this was something different; I was really struggling. We had been in the Andes since August, it was now January, and my body had had enough of seemingly-endless climbing. It was the lowest point of the trip for me. I was finding it virtually impossible to derive any fun from the riding, which had become a chore. I was annoyed that we had planned the wedding, because if not, we could take a holiday, but it was too late now to change our plans.

From the town of San Gil, we followed a river upstream along a gentle gradient. The road was busy with trucks overtaking on the narrow road, leaving us squashed into the drainage channel to cycle. Paddy was in front, climbing at his own pace, when two kilometres from the top of the pass, I saw him stop and start chatting to a guy at the side of the road. When I caught him up, he introduced me to Alberto, a coffee grower who lived just off the main road.

***Diary, 26 January 2012** - Alberto invited us in for lemonade which we readily accepted. He was a short man with pale brown skin about the same colour as Paddy with his tan, and is a former policeman. He lives with his father and mother. She looked just like Alberto, but with shoulder-length white hair, and she was a fabulous host. She made us a huge lunch and offered us a bedroom for the night. When I offered to help, she gave me big hugs, although, come to think about it, I may have got my grammar wrong and asked her to help me!*

Alberto showed us around his plot of coffee plants. It was fascinating to see the buds growing on them and the white seeds that come out. They look like coffee beans but need to be dried and roasted to get the brown colour. I'd never seen it before. We worked out that he must make about £9,000 a year from his crop – which seemed decent given it wasn't a huge farm by any means. They were both incredibly friendly. We took a photograph with them and promised to email it to Alberto's nephew who has an email address.

Alberto's was not the only farm in the area. The Colombian Andes provided perfect conditions for growing coffee beans around Medellin and Bogota, where beans were grown by families on small landholdings. They were handpicked and dried on the terraces of farmhouses or, not sensibly, on the hard shoulder of the road, which we sometimes didn't notice until we had ridden through the crop. Then they would be taken to local farming associations who sold the beans to the national association for worldwide distribution. This was how Alberto was able to secure a fair price for his coffee.

At the top of the pass the views were other worldly. The road wound down a deep gorge, which on our side was packed with verdant emerald-green vegetation, while across the river the slopes were completely barren. The riverbed, far below, was a sandy snake that wriggled along the valley, past a dinosaur-themed water park, where adults and children shrieked as they slid down giant slides. We quickly agreed that we should join them, which brought a premature end to the cycling.

The next morning we covered ground quickly, reaching the hectic, sprawling city of Bucaramanga by lunchtime, from where we began our very final climb above 3,000 metres. The road out of town was full of potholes and rubbish, to the joy of dogs and vultures that fought for scraps. It was formed of endless hairpin bends, but the gradient wasn't too steep and we made steady progress, and by four pm had cycled 14 kilometres and were feeling rather pleased with ourselves. Then a policeman flagged us down and our fun was swiftly brought to an end.

The police officer was friendly, but he wasn't happy we were on the road so late in the day, and wanted to know where we planned to spend the evening. We explained we hoped to camp, or if there was accommodation, we would stay there. He shook his head sternly; there were no hotels, he said, and he could not allow us to camp along the road. "OK," we thought, "but what about the campsite that we could see further up the road, just over his shoulder?" It was closed, apparently. He would not entertain the idea of us pitching our tent behind the small police station, or asking the woman in the shop where we had bought drinks, if we could stay there.

Stuck for ideas, we asked what he suggested we do, and he motioned for us to stand still while he went to resolve the problem. His solution was to stand in the middle of the road the next time a huge lorry chugged up the hill, flagging down the worried-looking driver and making him take us to the top of the pass. Frustratingly, the driver agreed without protest, and we were forced to go along with the plan, thanking the policeman who had only made the arrangements kindly.

We dumped our bikes in the empty hold of the truck and crammed inside the cab with the driver and his young son. They were driving from Cali where they had been to make a delivery, and were now heading home. The driver was friendly, but he spoke fast Spanish and we struggled to understand each other over the roar of the truck's engine, as it fought to conquer the steep gradients near the top. Instead, we spent most of the ride up to *La Laguna* in silence, me looking out across the lush green valley, regretting the lost opportunity to ride the final high pass of the trip.

The next day was easy, thanks to our lift, and we spent the morning coasting down towards the city of Pamplona, just 35 kilometres away. We reached the ridge overlooking the city just before midday and, with time on our side, stopped for coffee in a café where we got chatting to the owner and his friend. They were fascinated by our trip and insisted on treating us to the coffee.

Theirs summed up the welcome we had received from most Colombians. The tourism agency was right; our biggest problem in the country was that we would happily have stayed longer. The country had some truly jaw-dropping scenery that was markedly different to that of other Andean countries. Yet, it was the people of Colombia that I remember most warmly. The welcome they gave us stretched right to the border, when on our last day in the country, we were escorted into our final Colombian town by the Cucuta Cycling Club.

> ***Diary, 29 January 2012** - Today it was all about leisurely Sunday cycling. The route from Pamplona to Cucuta was totally downhill and flat – my kind of cycling for a change! About 25 kilometres away from Cucuta, I turned around to see where Paddy was, and he was riding in the middle of a peloton of about 20 road cyclists. They were from Cucuta Cycling Club and two of them stayed back with us, even treating us to a Coca-Cola in a bakery, and guiding us to a hotel in town. More*

friendly people in Colombia!

According to the United Nations, we had just ridden through one of the most dangerous countries in the world – it had felt anything but. Obviously, the drug trade and guerrilla movements were ongoing, but we had seen next to nothing of this, only precautions to keep people safe. If time had allowed, we would have diverted our route to stay longer, but we were already at the border.

Anyway, if dangerous countries were my thing, I wasn't to be disappointed for long. Our next port of call was Hugo Chávez's Venezuela, a country that in 2010 the United Nations awarded the dubious title of being one of the most murderous in the world. On the British High Commission website, a thick red line ran along the length of the border between Colombia and Venezuela – a no-go zone for British citizens.

I, however, had developed an 'I laugh in the face of danger' approach after our time in Colombia. I was thoroughly excited about exploring Venezuela, on the promise of 'lost world' scenery and flat roads that the cycle club assured me were in excellent condition. Not many backpackers travelled to the country, and I was buoyed by the idea of getting away from the usual traveller routes. The country promised adventure, in which I was keen to indulge.

11. Venezuela

I feel as if I am competing in the Tour de France. Cars and vans are parked along the road, their passengers lined up on the opposite side clapping wildly and cheering as I puff past on my way up the mountain. They are shouting out words of encouragement and drivers are beeping passionately on their horns. Their watching eyes and enthusiasm keeps me going: "I can do this," I tell myself. "Don't stop yet."

Further down the mountain, Joel is behind; also being urged on by the crowd, he is gaining ground on us. He is encouraged by progress reports from the spectators, and he knows our exact position on the mountainous route long before he sees us and begins his final assault on our lead. The crowd is loving the spectacle, and the higher we climb the greater the applause; they have been waiting for us.

This is how we were welcomed into Venezuela, one of the most dangerous countries in the world.

There had been a landslide at the bottom of the mountain road, near the immigration post, and the cheering passengers were waiting for it to be cleared. Many of the drivers were Colombians who had popped into Venezuela for cheap fuel. We provided a novel distraction while they waited – not many tourists visited the country anymore, especially on heavily laden bicycles. It was a memorable way to end our final climb in the Andes.

We were immediately struck by how different things felt in Venezuela compared to elsewhere in South America. People drove huge 1970s American gas-guzzlers – the kind of cars in movies like *Starsky and Hutch*. Thanks to the huge oil reserves under Lake Maracaibo in the north of the country, petrol was dirt cheap in Venezuela, a litre costing less than the same volume of milk. Lots of the cars looked fairly battered, with faded paint work and headlights hanging limply out of their sockets. There was a shortage of spare parts for these old beasts, so ingenious mechanics made do with whatever came to hand to keep them on the road. Unusually, these second hand cars could be more expensive than new ones from abroad. The demand was due to a shortage of imported vehicles – people could wait years for their order to be fulfilled – but also, with sky-high inflation rates, Venezuelans were better off investing in cars than leaving money in the bank.

Considering their worth, the cars were driven without much care, drivers cutting each other up and stopping unexpectedly as we made our way into the city of San Cristobal. From our map, we expected a small town, so we were surprised to find ourselves riding along a six lane highway, the city's main shopping street, pedalling manically to keep up with the traffic. Some of the drivers were on their way to San Cristobal's many drive-thrus, from fast-food restaurants, banks and pharmacies, to doughnut shops.

To escape the mayhem, we pulled into the first hotel we saw, a heavily guarded building where we locked the bikes inside our room while we went out for dinner. Strangely, the entire town now seemed deserted. Shops and restaurants were closed with heavy shutters over their fronts and the roads had quietened to a level that we could cross the six lane high street without breaking into a jog. Finally, we found an empty bar in an underground concrete shopping centre where we ordered food. Ordering drinks was a little more complicated.

"Yo quiero agua con gas, por favour."

"¿Que?" he replied.

"Agua con gas." I repeated, turning to Joel who had far superior Spanish than me, to check I was pronouncing it right.

The waiter looked at me annoyed and to Joel said, "¿Ella está tomando el pelo?"

Joel looked as perplexed as me and reassured the waiter that no, I wasn't taking the piss. I genuinely wanted a sparkling water.

'Water with gas' is the literal translation of 'agua con gas', so perhaps the waiter thought I was asking for water with petrol in. I thought, maybe the name might have changed. A soft drink, *gaseosa* in other Spanish speaking South American countries, was called *refresco* in Venezuela, but I couldn't see any sparkling water anywhere in the drinks cabinet to check. We wouldn't see any bottles during our time in the country, just one of many items like milk, bread and toilet paper that we often struggled to find.

We asked the bar manager why everywhere was closed and he told us for security reasons people didn't go outside in the dark, and advised us to do the same. With his warning echoing in our ears, we headed back after our meal. On our way out of the shopping centre, I motioned for the guys to stop. A strange creature was crawling down a flight of concrete steps towards us. Covered in coarse, long blonde hair it was hunched over like an old woman, and had two sharp ivory claws protruding from its hands and feet. Paddy was unimpressed and dismissed it as a dog, at which Joel and I looked at him bemused; it was a sloth.

Remarkably, it made its way over towards us and as it got closer, we could see its jet black eyes and nose. When Joel stroked it gently on the head it smiled serenely. Sloths normally live in trees in the Amazon Rainforest, moving to the ground at night to eat or defecate. How he had ended up in this concrete mall I didn't know, but we left him to his night's work as we headed home to obey the city's unofficial curfew.

Wednesday 1 February 2012 was memorable for being the day we left the Andes behind. It was hard to believe we arrived in the mountains just after our engagement, and now, all those months later, were leaving on our way to get married. The mountains had provided great challenges and memories, but I was happy at the prospect of some flat cycling.

The first day on the plain, we stopped for lunch in a roadside café with pink walls and sticky plastic tables. We collapsed into our chairs, quickly finishing the first jug of *papelon y limon* – sugar water with lime – that the server had instinctively brought us; it was hot outside and we were thirsty. The meal was topped off with sugared coffee in espresso-size glass cups. It was so sweet that the first time I tried it I winced from the sugar hit, but I was quickly won over.

Like most things in Venezuela, the set *almuerzo* wasn't particularly cheap, and it bit into our reserves of *Bolivars* that were rapidly diminishing. Getting cash was a complicated process here. President Hugo Chávez had fixed the national currency against the US dollar at an artificially high rate, in an attempt to control inflation and shelter domestic industries. In February 2012, the official rate was approximately 4.3BsF to $1 (US), which is what we would have got if we exchanged our dollars at a bank.

However, there was a thriving black market for dollars, the rate of which was about 8.5BsF to $1. The difference meant that if we ordered a set lunch that cost 50BsF it would translate to $11.50 at the official rate, or $5.90 on the black market. We had managed to change some money at the better rate at the Colombian border, but we had underestimated how expensive things were in Venezuela and our cash was quickly running out.

Having been advised the best people to exchange dollars with were businessmen, after eating we asked the café owner if he might be interested in buying some from us. He eyed us nervously, muttering that he might, at which point he disappeared into his house behind the café. His other customers had fallen silent, listening to our conversation and they stayed that way until the owner's wife came out to confirm he didn't have any money to exchange.

It was then we realised we had made a major faux pas. Changing money on the black market was illegal and we had just asked this guy to break the law in the middle of his busy café, where anybody might have been listening. We felt terrible about putting him in that position and stupid for being so naive. Quickly, we made our way out of the restaurant under the gaze of the watching customers.

Outside, as we prepared to leave, a couple jumped into a silver pickup parked next to the bikes. Leaning out of the window, after checking that nobody else was around, the guy whispered to us that there was a shopkeeper in a town further along the road and he suspected that he would be able to help. This was great news and we set off in the direction of Abejales realising that it was obviously the 'done thing', but very hush-hush.

It was a good call, the businessman was keen to exchange our dollars. The rate wasn't as good as we had received in Colombia, but he had us over a barrel and we were desperate to complete the transaction – otherwise, it was going to be prohibitively expensive to stay in Venezuela for long. While Paddy was inside changing over our dollars, I was surprised by a journalist who pulled over on a red motorbike to ask what we were doing.

Fortunately, he was referring to our bikes rather than the illegal money exchange going on inside. He was a local reporter for the region's radio station and he pulled a voice recorder out of his bag for an impromptu interview that he promised to air later that evening.

We said goodbye to Joel the next day. Our routes, which had followed a similar path since Lima, were different now. He was heading east, deep into cowboy country in the tropical grassy plains of Los Llanos, before heading towards the Caribbean coast and back to Colombia, from where he hoped to catch a boat to Panama. We, on the other hand, were riding directly northwards towards Caracas for our flight to Barbados, and once we returned would continue west on our circuit around South America. There was still a chance our paths may cross again in a few weeks, so it was a quiet goodbye for the time being.

It was hot out on the plain but we pushed out the kilometres far easier than in the mountains. The scenery was lush and green, even the small hills we passed were coated in bushy trees. Palm trees reached tall towards the sky and cattle grazed happily in the rich grassy fields that lined the roadside. The road was in fairly good condition and traffic not too busy, which allowed me to concentrate on the important job of spotting the tropical road kill before I rode through gruesome piles of blood and bones smeared on the hard shoulder. I was used to seeing dead dogs, but Venezuelan drivers hit much more than the odd mutt. There were squashed snakes of considerable length, caimans, tortoises, and the worst; horses. Riding into the wind, we would smell the stench of a rotting horse long before we would see it and I would hold my nose as I approached. It was a truly horrible sight, partly because they all seemed to die with their eyes open, and try as I might, I couldn't stop myself staring at their distressed glare as I rode past.

One day, I spotted a tortoise slowly ambling across the hard shoulder in the direction of the highway and just managed to stop before I hit it. Paddy rescued the confused animal, placing him into the long grass where he hid inside his shell before wandering back towards the fields. For his efforts, Paddy got covered in tortoise pee. In the knowledge that there was a wide variety of fauna hiding in the long grass at the side of the road, I developed an aversion to nipping into cover for a quick wee. The idea of being bitten on the ass by a snake or caiman did not appeal.

We were heading towards the region's capital, Barinas, once home to President Chávez. It was useful hearing about the omnipresent president and the political situation in Venezuela from our Couchsurfing hosts, José and Patricia, because I was finding it difficult to understand the country's complicated history and how things worked now he was in power. It was all about oil, they said.

Venezuela's huge oil reserves were discovered in the early 1900s and the country rapidly became one of the largest producers in the world, neglecting old industries like farming and ranching until, by the 1970s, it was completely reliant on oil. The money chiefly benefited Venezuela's rich, and by the 1980s 50 per cent of Venezuelans were living in poverty. In 1992 a group of army officers, led by Chávez, attempted a coup against President Pérez. Although they failed to overthrow the government and were imprisoned, Chávez's speech conceding defeat was broadcast on television and won him nationwide recognition. In 1998, after his release from prison, he won the presidency with 56 per cent of the vote.

Chávez promised radical change and the creation of a 'new democracy'. At first his reforms were cautious, but after a series of attempts to remove him from power in the early 2000s, Chávez became more radicalised about his socialist aims. He brought in advisers from Cuba, and opened new healthcare facilities stocked with Cuban doctors and dentists sent by Fidel Castro in return for subsidised Venezuelan oil.

By 2006, oil accounted for 92 per cent of Venezuela's total exports; the money was used to fund social programmes for Chávez's poor supporters. Growing public spending caused inflation to rise to 30 per cent, which hit wages and savings. José told us that nearby the government had built a neighbourhood of houses for people from the slums of Caracas. If they wanted anything, he said, like wood for the property, they only had to ask and the government would give it to them. This policy, he believed, had created a generation who expected hand-outs from the state. With an air of exasperation, he said many people in the housing development complained they didn't have jobs now they had moved out of the capital, and they wanted the government to find them work.

One of the greatest concerns for people when they talked about everyday life under Chávez was the security issue. José was particularly concerned about us going into the capital, Caracas. Dubbed the 'murder capital of the world', the city witnessed an average of one murder every hour. We had planned to cycle there, but he put us off the idea with a description of crazy drivers and highway robbers. The streets, he said, were roamed by gangs and organised crime groups who robbed, murdered and kidnapped people. He wasn't telling us anything we hadn't heard before, but hearing it from a proud Venezuelan, who looked at us with genuine concern, made me sit up and take notice.

Still, we needed to get to Caracas, as we had arranged to leave our bikes at the British High Commission office in the capital while we were away. The Ecuador office had put us in touch with their colleagues in Caracas who were keen to do some media work with us around the Olympics. Only, a few days after posting on our website about riding across the Colombian border, we received a strongly worded email informing us they would not be able to work with us. It seemed the border area was deemed an extremely dangerous 'red zone', and we had gone against official advice which they could not be seen to condone. It was a shame that they felt that way, but we appreciated they had to stick to their rules, and at least they would still store our bikes.

José was a huge help in organising transport to Caracas from a town a few hours' drive away. He found a guy who was willing to take us for £50 which seemed reasonable and would avoid us having to navigate around central Caracas. While José was busy organising the lift, Patricia hooked us up with a neighbour to exchange dollars with. It was all very clandestine. The woman we met was acting as a go-between for the actual buyer, and we sat in her lounge counting out bills agreeing not to mention this to anybody.

After a few days with our fantastic hosts José and Patricia, we set out to cover the 80 kilometres to Guanare where, looking confused in the central square, we were rescued by Alvaro and his girlfriend Claudia. Alvaro's first concern was what we were doing cycling through Venezuela – it was far too dangerous, he said. Over coffee we tried to explain that everybody we had met so far had been lovely, but they looked at us sceptically. However, they only confirmed our experiences when they invited us to dinner and offered us a bed at Claudia's home.

We hadn't been in the house long, when Claudia's mum lifted up her T-shirt to show us her abdomen and chest that were tightly bound in bandages after recent breast enhancement surgery. Plastic surgery was common in Venezuela, and a major industry. This was the country with the world's most beautiful women, apparently. It was a claim based on the three 'Miss Venezuelas' who were crowned 'Miss Universe' in international beauty pageants of the 1970s and 1980s. The way Claudia's mum gingerly walked, it looked a painful process to join the ranks of the most beautiful.

The next morning, Alvaro took us for breakfast. His family owned a local cattle farm and, in a lowered voice, he told us how Chávez's socialist policies had affected the area. It was impossible to find milk, he said, because farmland had been nationalised, divided up and handed to poor peasants who had no idea how to farm. According to him, some landowners had stopped bothering to farm because the produce was worthless and the businesses could be taken away at any time.

Alvaro had chosen his favourite café for breakfast, a small diner that specialised in *arepas*, small corn cakes stuffed with a choice of ingredients. He treated us to the traditional breakfast *arepa perico* which was filled with scrambled egg, onion and tomato. It was good, but I wasn't overly surprised; Venezuela had served up my favourite food of the trip so far and the *arepas* were no exception.

I was also partial to an *empanada* – thin, corn, deep-fried pasties oozing with cheese or stuffed with beef or chicken. They were great hot or cold, and if we passed an *empanada* stall we would buy a bag's worth to eat throughout the day. My favourite Venezuelan dish, however, was a gigantic corn pancake, the size of a larger dinner plate, a *cachapa*. Shallow fried to a light golden brown, it was spread with a generous layer of butter and topped with a flat round of white cheese the same size as the pancake itself. It was unhealthy, but oh so delicious. I could just about manage one in a sitting, but we watched locals tucking into fully loaded *cachapas* plus huge plates of barbecued meat. With food like this and the attitude of driving everywhere, it was no wonder we saw so many overweight Venezuelans.

We waved goodbye to Alvaro, whose parting words were to be careful on the road towards Valencia. Although I appreciated there was a genuine threat, I was starting to find the constant security warnings irritating.

> ***Diary, 7 February 2012*** - *We got stopped at one point today by a guy in army uniform. He wanted to take us in his pickup to Valencia as he said the road was in a poor condition and full of 'bad people'. He actually picked my bike up and made as if to put it into the back of his pickup. Paddy fortunately was on the ball and pulled out the map. Once he showed the officer our route and explained our trip he let us cycle on.*
>
> *It was an odd one. He wasn't threatening, but he wasn't friendly either, so it was hard to read the situation. On the whole, everybody along the route was friendly with lots of waving and hoots from drivers. But the paranoia after all these warnings meant I spent most of the day waiting for somebody to jump out of the grass to get us.*

We had cycled over 13,000 kilometres around South America now. I was much more confident than I had been when we left Rio de Janeiro about many elements of the trip, security included, but there was something about the warnings we heard in Venezuela that made me concerned. One of the most recurrent warnings was about the local police force. We were told never to show them our passports, as they would make up some reason for our paperwork being wrong and demand a fee before we could get them back. It was something we heard over and over, and we were taking the threat seriously.

> ***Paddy:*** *We had decided to ride straight through the police checkpoints, to remove any chance of having to converse with the police. Each time we approached one, we rode close together wearing our sunglasses and put our iPods in our ears, so it looked like we couldn't hear them if they tried to call us back. At the first checkpoints in Venezuela things had gone well, with the officers not paying any attention as we passed*

by.

One day, however, Laura was about 50 metres ahead of me, rolling downhill fast, and we both spotted the checkpoint too late to prepare our usual routine. One officer was stood behind a lorry that had been stopped in a lay-by. He only noticed Laura as she whizzed past him, and he rushed towards the road shouting for her to come back. She just kept going.

By now, I was only ten seconds away, and the policeman noticing me approaching, moved into the road, waving frantically for me to stop. There were only two officers in total and they seemed to have no vehicle, so I decided to just go for it. He was blowing like crazy on his whistle the closer I got, but I just waved nonchalantly at him as I passed and kept pedalling hard. I didn't dare look back.

The funny thing was, a few weeks later, we did stop at a checkpoint and the officers were lovely. We'd been riding all day and hadn't seen anywhere for a drink. There was a small hut selling cold soda next to this checkpoint, and we were so thirsty that we decided to risk stopping. The police just wanted to know where we were going and to have their photos taken with us. After that, we always stopped at checkpoints without any problems.

Riding into the city of Valencia was little fun. The road was narrow and badly surfaced, with long grooves where heavy trucks had ground into the tarmac, but that was better than when it turned into a three-lane motorway with no hard shoulder. At least the drivers gave us plenty of space, and even stopped to let us pass at junctions.

The following morning we took a bus to Las Trincheras thermal springs on the outskirts of the city, where we spent the day soaking in the warm water. I could feel my muscles relaxing with the heat and I smothered my face in mud from the bottom of the pools. We got chatting to a blonde woman, seemingly the only other westerner at the baths, who was Dutch but had married a Venezuelan. She was surprised to see us as she said tourists rarely visited anymore. In 2009 there were only 600,000 foreign visitors to Venezuela and less than half of those came on holiday. The downward spiral of tourists was not helped by events like the 2011 murder of a British tourist on the holiday island of Margarita. It was a shame as the country had an awful lot to offer.

Jackie agreed to exchange some dollars with us, and we met her later that evening to do a swap. She had parked away from any street lights and we exchanged envelopes of money in her car, counting out piles of cash away from the windows in case anybody passed by. It was a relief to have met her as we were running short and starting to worry that we may have to take some cash out of an ATM at the official rate, something we really didn't want to do. In one supermarket, we had seen a box of muesli that cost an astronomical $20 at the official rate. We would never have spent that much, but things were extremely expensive here and we needed to avoid paying official prices.

We were spending the weekend in Venezuela's third largest city, Valencia, at the home of our Couchsurfing host, Eisen, an architect about the same age as us. A keen cyclist, Eisen took time off to show us around the city and we learnt lots during our stay, including our favourite word of the trip *chevre*, the best translation of which would be *cool*, but it had far more kudos than that. Karmela, his Jekyll and Hyde Siamese cat was *chevre* and she knew it. She was quite happy to let me spend half an hour stroking her, but as soon as she was finished she would let me know by clawing at my arms. She was intrigued by our bikes and they fast became her climbing frame.

For breakfast Eisen cooked *arepas*, teaching me how to heat them on a flat griddle to get them perfectly golden brown, and he brewed fresh coffee that was so strong I was still shaking an hour later. In the evening we joined his friends in a bar, loud music blaring from the speakers which made it even harder to keep up with their fast Venezuelan Spanish. They were all young professionals, working hard despite the challenges laid down by the socialist government. One woman, a teacher who worked at a private school, said she would prefer to work for the state because the salaries were better, but there were more teachers than jobs and once somebody had one of those coveted positions they rarely left.

There were murmurs of carrying on the night at a house party, until somebody remembered that the stores weren't selling alcohol that evening. The next day there were to be national elections to decide who would represent the opposition in the presidential election in October. Most of the people around the table were not Chávez supporters, but they weren't going to vote. They explained the government took a list of everybody who voted, and people feared that if their name appeared it could lead to repercussions.

The next morning, groggy from too much beer, we were frustrated to receive a text from the driver who was taking us to Caracas. He had upped his quote hugely, leaving us no choice but to decline and come up with another way of getting to the city. We rattled through a list of elaborate, expensive and stressful-sounding plans, until it occurred to us that perhaps Eisen wouldn't mind looking after the bikes. Before the trip, I could never have imagined leaving them with a stranger I had met through the internet only a few days earlier, but I was much more relaxed now.

Eisen was fine with our new plan, and we left Valencia the next morning, leaving Karmela to enjoy her climbing frame a little longer. We were carrying just one pannier each, as we had very little that would be of use in Barbados, and our families had been tasked with bringing out clothes to replace our grease and sweat stained garments. There were still a few days before our flight, so we decided to start the holiday with a few days relaxing along the Caribbean Sea in the resort of Puerto Colombia.

The long bus journey, up a winding mountain road and through thick jungle, was well worth it when we saw the white beach framed with palm trees and with warm waves crashing onto the shore. At last, I was on holiday. We ate *arepas* in bed, crashed out on sun loungers, and frolicked in the aggressive sea which tore off my bikini the first time I jumped in. It was warm, it was relaxing and it felt wonderful.

As we headed back from the beach, we stopped in surprise when we spotted a sunburnt Joel walking towards us. After weeks in the heart of Los Llanos, where he had ridden with cowboys and slept in ranches, he had made it to the Caribbean coast. He joined us for dinner on a balcony overlooking the sea, our last meal together. It was a long time since we had met along the hideous highway leaving Lima, and we were glad to have had his company.

We stayed with many people who became friends during the few days we spent together, but before long we would move on. Facebook and email were fantastic ways to keep in touch with them, but it was brilliant to have somebody, like Joel, who we met up with every few weeks. We shared stories from the road, asked each other advice, and Joel's company broke up the monotony of it being just me and Paddy all the time – or in Joel's case, it was a change to the solitude. He was great company and it was sad to say goodbye after so long. Our final view of Joel was of him crawling up the mountain road out of Puerto Colombia, while our taxi zoomed past on our way to Caracas. The taxi driver beeped frantically at him; Joel smiled and waved as we disappeared around the corner.

The drive to Caracas took several hours, the traffic was hectic, with people beeping constantly and pushing in front of each other. As we reached the outskirts of the city, we could see slums lining the hillsides, reminiscent of Rio de Janeiro's *favelas*. It would have been a fascinating city to explore, but now was not the time – we were off to get married, something that struck us both as being slightly bizarre.

After all the worrying about delays because of broken spokes, illness and dogged tiredness in the mountains, we had made it on time for our flight. From Caracas, the plane followed the Andes until they disappeared under the Caribbean Sea before resurfacing as small peaks on the island of Trinidad and Tobago. After spending so long in the mountain range, it felt good to see where they finally ended, but there was little time to dwell on the Andes – we were heading north towards Barbados and our wedding.

12. Barbados

Our wedding party was comprised of our parents, siblings, their partners and Paddy's one year old niece, Abi, who, unsurprisingly, didn't recognise us after so long. The 12 of us were staying in a modern villa in the seaside resort of Holetown, just back from the beach where people lounged on the white sand and ate fried fish in wooden huts.

Arriving on an expensive holiday island was a bit of a culture shock for us, as was being in the prolonged company of other people for the first time in ages. The personal jokes that we had developed along the road, didn't go down well in civilised company. "Yeah, but your face!" was our favourite comeback whenever accused of having done something wrong – we had picked it up from an episode of *Scrubs*. We probably said it to each other 20 times a day, and it would send us into fits of childish giggles each time, but we had to tone it down in front of our families who were looking at us as if we had gone mad.

In the days leading up to the wedding we explored the island's beaches, enjoyed low-key hen and stag dos, and travelled with the wedding planner to organise the marriage license. It would be a very relaxed, simple day and there was not too much to arrange, which was good as it came around very quickly.

Diary, 21 February 2012 - *Wedding day!!! It felt very strange sleeping alone last night. I think that's only the second time I've not slept in the same bed with Paddy since we left for South America. It was quite a chilled morning; I spent it trying not to bump into him, although I later learned he'd gone jet skiing with Ed – of course!*

The hairdresser arrived at 10.00, and the photographer at 12.30, but nobody was ready for her. I'd been trying to hurry everybody up all morning, but they were all chilling out, eating pizza in their scruffs. Dad did the photos and then jumped in the shower to get ready properly!

I was happy with the dress. It fitted well and hid my suntan marks, and I felt quite pretty with my hair done and make-up on – a transformation from this time last week. Abi looked cute as flower girl, but it was all a bit scary for her and she needed help walking down the 'aisle'. The ceremony was in the garden, in front of a pergola. The wedding planner had decorated it nicely and made a tiny aisle with the chairs.

The ceremony absolutely flew by. Ginnie and Mike both did great readings and then there were the vows – all in all it took about 20 minutes. Paddy looked very smart in his suit and the hairdresser had done an amazing job of taming his hair. I really enjoyed the ceremony, we were both relaxed, it didn't feel scary at all – I'm not quite sure it felt real either though!

Our wedding cake was chocolate. The photographer asked us to feed it to each other, but Paddy just shoved it in my face, which made us laugh, but she looked at bit horrified. I'm not sure she got many romantic shots of us. She took us down to the beach, which felt very odd as it was packed with people sunbathing and they all watched us posing. My dress got soaked as I ended up in the sea, and when she asked us to run down the beach for a photo we set off at a competitive sprint, which in hindsight, I'm not sure was what she was looking for.

After photos, we ditched the wedding clothes and headed off to Bridgetown for a catamaran cruise. It was absolutely fantastic. The boat and the crew were lovely and very generous with the rum punches. We sailed out along the coast and they handed us snorkels to swim with Hawksbill turtles. They were amazing creatures, so calm and relaxed swimming around us, strong and fearless. It was a special moment and I think everybody was quite taken by it. My hair was ruined as a result, but it was worth it. It was dark by the time we got back to the harbour, the boat was playing out music and we were dancing on the net at the front of the catamaran like lunatics.

A quick change back at the villa and then time for dinner on the terrace. We'd organised a chef to come in and do the catering and it was absolutely magnificent. They'd found Chilean wine for us. On the tables, we'd put a few silly games which everybody got into the spirit of – it was quite a drunken evening.

It was a great day, I really enjoyed it. I'm so glad we did it this way rather than a big white wedding at home, which I wouldn't have enjoyed. It feels rather surreal to be married. We both agree that it won't really change much as how can you get closer than spending 24/7 together. Great to have it all official though.

Paddy: *It was a perfect day! As a groom, I couldn't have been luckier – I was marrying the girl I love, we were holding the wedding where we wanted, how we wanted and it was a stress-free day. The fact that I only had to wear a suit for an hour, got to swim with turtles and watched the sun set while drinking rum cocktails, made it all pretty cool too! Of course, like Laura, it felt strange not being able to share it with our friends and extended families, but then everything about our way of life was unusual now. At least having our close families with us brought some reality to the situation.*

I slept pretty poorly the night before, yet I think the nerves would have been worse if we'd had the wedding back home. Having spent all of the time together doing a lifestyle that we both loved, getting married seemed the most natural thing to do. I was surprised how well I handled it, and as Laura will testify, I was probably more nervous when we moved in together a couple of years before!

Two days after the wedding it was time to head back to Venezuela. Paddy had promised me a trip to Angel Falls as a honeymoon, which sounded lovely, but he was making me cycle nearly 700 kilometres first. On the final afternoon, I caught our mums in the kitchen sniffling at the thought of us leaving. There was not much I could say to comfort them, other than pointing out that we were on the home straight and would be home before August, which wasn't too far away.

At the airport, it was back to being just the two of us. Strangely, I was quite relieved to be heading back to South America and the simplicity of life on the road. Barbados was a beautiful place, but it was expensive and showy, and we were used to living off a tiny budget and wearing tatty clothes.

I was delighted that we had chosen to get married on the island though. I had always imagined having a simple ceremony, one that I could enjoy, rather than worrying about minutia, like whether the bridesmaids' dresses matched the invitations. We had definitely achieved that. It had also been far cheaper than organising a traditional wedding back home, plus everybody had got a holiday in the sun. I felt a little sad that our friends and extended families couldn't join us, but we were planning a party when we returned home which we were calling our 'wedding reception', so there would be time for a knees-up then.

For now we were heading back to Caracas, wondering if, after a week of over-indulgence, we would struggle to get back on the bikes.

13. Venezuela – la segunda parte

Karmela wasn't pleased to lose her climbing frame. She showed her displeasure by scratching my arms before skulking off, at which point we hurriedly carried the bikes out of the flat before she could strike again. Eisen guided us out of town along Valencia's hectic streets, taking selfies of the three of us riding, until we said goodbye at the south side of Lago de Valencia.

In the heat of the day the blue water looked inviting, but the half-submerged electricity pylons and litter bobbing on the surface suggested it wasn't the cleanest lake. Alone again, the wedding slipped to the back of my mind, and my thoughts returned to life on the road as I forced my stiff legs to work. A steep hill as we turned away from the lake felt like a mountain; it would take a few days for my body to catch up with my mind.

Little had changed in Venezuela. The constant security advice continued, people hanging out of their car windows to issue warnings as they passed. By the afternoon the insistent threats had begun to grate on my nerves, when we were adopted by an old man on a push bike, carrying a machete. He was heading in the same direction as us and talked incessantly in fast Spanish that I struggled to understand. I recognised he was saying there were dangerous people on the road, but I couldn't work out if he was declaring he would protect us with his machete, or that he planned to kill us with it. Fortunately, neither scenario came to fruition.

In Villa de Cura we checked into a motel, flopping on the bed after our first day back in the saddle. We spent a quiet evening watching episodes of *Downton Abbey* that we had copied onto our battered laptop in Barbados. There were other treats we'd picked up too, including open-toe sandals, which like the shoes we had sent home, had cleats on the bottom to clip into pedals. With no more need for socks, our feet felt happier under the hot, tropical sun, although they did develop stripy suntan marks which looked ridiculous.

The next morning we woke to the news that President Chávez had flown to Cuba for treatment on the cancer that, in 2011, he had announced he was fighting. Later in the year he was due to stand for re-election and I hoped his current trip was not serious, as I could imagine the country shutting down if news of his death came through. It was impossible to overstate how large a figure Chávez was in Venezuela. Pictures of him in his ubiquitous red shirt, a closed fist raised in the socialist salute, were plastered all over roadside billboards, promoting his links with local politicians, who garnered support through their connection with *El Commandante*. He spoke to the nation through speeches that lasted up to eight hours, on his weekly television programme *Aló Presidente!* If Chávez was to die, nobody knew how the country would react, and I did not fancy being there to find out.

We were back on the flat plain now. Our route was taking us due east for the first time on the trip. Soon we would arrive in the *Gran Sabana*, the area that inspired Conan Doyle's Victorian-era novel, *The Lost World*, about a land where dinosaurs, isolated for millions of years, roamed on table top mountains. We were now off the traditional South American tourist trail, heading to parts of the continent that few foreigners visited, and we were excited about what we might find.

We pushed on towards the 'lost world', navigating a narrow highway along which vehicles zoomed. Venezuela was reputed to have some of the best roads in South America, but we only saw a network of potholed, crumbling highways. The roads were in a shocking condition: hard shoulders had disintegrated, trucks bounced through cavernous holes in the tarmac, and heavy traffic formed long snakes of vehicles on single lane highways. Around South America, road workers were a common sight, clearing the roadside and filling in potholes; in Venezuela, we could count on one hand the number we saw. Toll booths lay disused, their raised barriers letting traffic pass freely. It was another of Chávez's socialist policies that seemed to be doing the country more harm than good.

Head down as I battled into a ferocious wind, I tried to weave around potholes and road kill that littered the hard shoulder. The tropical heat sapped our energy and warmed our water bottles. We took it in turns to ride in front, sharing the work of cycling into the gusts, and enjoying the time sheltering at the back. The road was pancake-flat, but our highest speed was 15 kilometres per hour as the wind strove to blow us backwards. Drivers gave us as much space as they could, but the hard shoulder had crumbled into the dusty verge, and often vehicles brushed past with only centimetres to spare. It was gritted teeth time. The distance between places where we could buy cold drinks and food was huge. One day we finally found lunch at four pm, and were still riding as the sun disappeared, leaving behind a pitch black sky, lit only by the glaring headlights of speeding trucks.

I was riding in front. Paddy's front light had broken and we were forced to rely on the dim beam of mine to brighten up obstacles ahead. It provided just enough warning for me to swerve in time to avoid countless potholes and one squashed dead dog. Paddy, behind me and dazzled by my rear lights, had little view of anything other than my bike, and followed my moves with blind trust. As I scanned the road, I became aware of a whooshing noise around my head; a cloud of bats had flown out of the bushes, only narrowly missing me as they went.

In the morning I refused to continue riding along the highway. The day before had been miserable and at times terrifying. I insisted we look at the map and find another route towards Ciudad Bolivar; fortunately, Paddy didn't need convincing. We chose a road that meandered north-eastwards. It was a longer route, still along a tarmac highway, but by avoiding large conurbations we guessed the traffic would be lighter.

We were right; the road was much quieter, plus it was lined by hedges that buffered the worst of the wind. We were deep in agricultural country, where sleepy cattle grazed in the hilly terrain. In a small town called Aragua de Barcelona we stopped for lunch. After a morning in the hills we were shattered, but a quiet meal was out of the question, as people approached us with questions and suggestions about routes for the next few days. It was nice to meet people who weren't obsessed with warning us about security. After a long lunch the idea of powering out more kilometres didn't appeal, so we called it a day and headed in search of a room.

We were aided by a young woman called Maria who took control of the situation when she spotted us riding past her home. She was slim, with olive skin and long dark hair, smart and bubbly, hosting her own slot on the town's radio station. Her proposal was that she would find us somewhere to stay, if we agreed to appear on her show that evening. Laughing nervously, we pointed out that our Spanish was not really up to a live interview, but she wouldn't take no for an answer, and we found ourselves signed up for our first ever live radio appearance.

There were no hotels in town, but Maria knew people who had spare rooms, and we followed her around as she made enquiries. Everywhere we walked, people shook our hands and took photos with us; we were minor celebrities even before the interview. The radio station was homed in a small office just off the main square, with one production booth, and a slightly larger room, where we sat around a circular table equipped with three microphones on stands. We had agreed that Paddy would do the talking, and he sat nervously biting his nails under a giant poster of Chávez and a portrait of the South American liberator, Simón Bolívar. Maria asked him questions about the trip, nodding encouragingly as he slowly formed sentences in reply.

She seemed delighted to have landed the scoop of the foreign cyclists and thanked us warmly when she dropped us at our lodge. It was a basic establishment, consisting of concrete boxes for rooms fitted with concrete bed stands on which lay a thin, uncomfortable mattress. The landlady had paid us little attention earlier in the day, but she was suddenly interested after listening to the radio and kept us chatting for a while, until we made our excuses and snuck off to our room. While I took a cold bucket shower in the corner, Paddy killed the fat cockroaches that had been jumping around our bed. After a long but fascinating day we huddled into our sleeping bag liners, too exhausted to worry about the roaches we hadn't caught.

In the morning we bought breakfast from a woman on the outskirts of town, who had just fired up her stove improvised from an old oil barrel. She specialised in *empanadas*, and we drank strong shots of sweet coffee while she rolled out the dough for the pastries, stuffing them with white cheese before tossing them into the boiling oil. We ate the first batch hot and oozing straight out of the barrel. Mine were good, but Paddy's had added protein in the form of a cluster of deep-fried ants stuck to the pastry. They must have wandered, unnoticed, across the *empanada* seconds before it was tossed into the oil. Paddy had eaten half of them before I could point out what he was doing.

The *empanadas* fuelled us to reach the agricultural hub of El Tigre by late afternoon. On the outskirts of town we pulled into a quiet service station to top up on petrol for the stove. It was the first time we had needed to in Venezuela, and we were wondering how much it might cost.

> ***Paddy:*** *Our fuel bottles usually lasted for a month between replenishing and it was time to see how much a refill in Venezuela might cost us. Over the previous days, we had passed several stations with long queues of motorists waiting for a fuel tanker to arrive. Even though Venezuela had huge oil reserves, it didn't mean petrol was always available.*
>
> *While I stood straddling my bike at the pump, I handed the attendant our two metal fuel bottles to fill up. He looked perplexed at having to provide such a miniscule amount, but nevertheless pointed at the two grades of gasoline, asking which I'd prefer. The higher quality was still much cheaper than anything we could get back home, so I went for that. It's likely that this fuel was Brazilian, because even though there are huge reserves in the country, Venezuela struggles to refine it properly to international standards. Thus, strangely, we saw tankers from Brazil bringing higher grade fuel that state-owned stations would sell at a loss.*
>
> *Eisen had told us motorbikes often don't pay for fuel if petrol pump attendants don't have small change. Therefore, we weren't too surprised when the attendant waved his hand nonchalantly when I asked how much it was for the two litres. It felt strange cycling away without paying.*

From El Tigre to Ciudad Bolivar it was a long, empty stretch of road and we had loaded the bikes up by six am, in the hope that with an early start we would miss the worst of the day's heat. On the outskirts of town, we stopped at a row of wooden shacks that served workers from the oil factory opposite, and ordered 20 *empanadas*, which would be breakfast, lunch and dinner for the day.

It was a Sunday and the traffic was light as we made our way through low, dense shrub-land. The road was deserted and there were no villages or services. When we reached 14,000 kilometres for the trip, we stopped only briefly to mark the occasion; it was too hot to hang around for long and we were running out of water. What we did have had heated to an unpalatable temperature, and I could only manage to gulp it when really desperate. We had expected the road to be quiet, but had assumed there would at least be somewhere to top up on fluids. The only thing I could think about was cold water, which made my mouth feel even drier and my tongue stick to the roof of my mouth.

I thought at first it was a mirage, the way the shiny silver roof sparkled in the sun. As we grew closer though, I realised we had at last found civilisation – a modern factory with large metal sheds. Our pace quickened at the prospect we might find water. The gates were locked, but our banging brought the caretaker running to investigate the noise. On seeing our heavily laden bikes, he welcomed us warmly, introducing himself as Orlando. Opening the small door in the gate, he invited Paddy to fill up the bottles with water so cold that it scorched my throat on the way down.

As we drank, Orlando talked about Chávez, exclaiming how wonderful he was and explaining the socialist principles of the factory. He was the very first openly Chávez supporter we had met in the whole of Venezuela. Wearing a faded election-time T-shirt with the president's name blazoned across his chest, his appearance was different to the middle-class opposition supporters we had met elsewhere. It was not an inaccurate generalisation that political support in the country was strongly influenced by social standing and personal wealth, with Venezuela's poor forming the base of Chávez's support.

Not long after leaving Orlando, Ciudad Bolivar appeared in the distance. It was a small city on the other side of the wide Río Orinoco, which Paddy informed me we needed to cycle across. I looked at him as if he was mad; I could see the high suspension bridge that he was suggesting we ride over. The Angostura Bridge, so called because of the original name of the city (which is where the herbal, alcoholic bitters, Angostura Bitters were first produced), spanned 700 metres between the two banks, rising high above the water to let ships pass underneath.

After receiving a pep talk from Paddy, his argument being that I had no choice, I rode onto the bridge. Climbing slowly up the ramp, I stuck close to the guardrails to avoid the traffic that continued at speed, oblivious they were driving over a huge drop. I tried not to look at the brown water below, but the inside lane of the bridge was a metal grate, which offered a clear view. When I finally reached the top, I freewheeled down as fast as felt safe, trying to ignore the many missing guardrails.

We followed the river eastwards into the city. The Orinoco was first spotted by Europeans in 1498, when Christopher Columbus, on his third voyage to the Americas, spotted fresh water flowing into the seas around Trinidad and Tobago. He realised there must be land, *tierra firme*, from the direction of the flow, and a year later, his friend Amerigo Vespucci led an expedition to explore the Orinoco Delta and the Venezuelan coast. It was he who gave his name to the Americas.

Our hostel was just off the historical square, down a side road where houses were painted in vibrant pastel shades. On our first evening there, the cook made a meal for the handful of guests. The hostel was almost empty – the owner explained that in recent years tourism had dropped off by 60 per cent. Security concerns were part of the reason, but also the fixed dollar rate made Venezuela expensive for travellers.

To get around the problem of the exchange, we transferred money into the owner's European Paypal account, including enough to purchase some Bolivars. It was a complicated transaction, but it was the only way of organising things thanks to government financial policies, and it enabled the lodge to stay in business. Relieved to have found a way around the money issues, we headed off on our honeymoon to the world's highest single-drop waterfall; Angel Falls.

The 979 metre-high waterfall was named after the American aviator Jimmie Angel, who in 1933, became the first person to fly over the falls. Its water poured from the top of the Auyantepui table-top mountain in the middle of dense, isolated jungle. To reach it would take us several days and require various means of transport.

We began with an early morning flight out of Ciudad Bolivar's airport to the lagoon-side village of Canaima. Our small Cessna plane was loaded with boxes of fruit and vegetables, and I squeezed sideways into the back seat, resting my feet on a box of bananas. We flew high above the jungle canopy, a patchwork of trees scrunched together like broccoli florets, broken by the occasional burst of pink flowers or parrots flying between branches. As we grew closer to Canaima table-top mountains, *tepui* began to appear on the horizon – flat-top mounds with straight, tall sides.

Much of the flora and fauna on top of these mountains was different to that at the bottom of the steep slopes, and some species were unique to the *tepui,* because the high eco-system had existed without interference for hundreds of thousands of years. This was why Conan Doyle nicknamed the area 'the Lost World'. We banked sharply right as we approached Canaima, the pilot swinging the small plane towards the runway. Situated on a palm tree-lined lagoon that boasted numerous flowing waterfalls, Canaima was an attraction in itself and we spent an evening in the village sat by the waterside, listening to the sounds of the jungle and gazing up at a clear, star-filled sky.

Early the next day, we took our places in a narrow canoe-shaped boat. It was powered by a motor, or by oar when the water level was low. The bumpy journey upriver took five hours, weaving around rocks and rapids. I passed the time watching bright coloured birds hopping between branches, but our view into the forest was limited, the thick foliage blocking out the light. When our boat finally pulled up against the shore though, we had an opportunity to discover what lay beyond the riverbank.

Following a narrow track, we began the hour-long hike up to the base of the falls. It was hot and humid under trees that grew thin and tall towards the light. The ground was soft with a blanket of leaves, and we scrambled over slippery rocks, streams and fallen branches as we made our way up the steep climb. At last, the forest opened and we found ourselves in a clearing of gigantic boulders, at the base of the magnificent falls.

It was the dry season and the flow of water over the cliff was a thin stream, but it still created an impressive spray that reached our vantage point. Behind the falls we could see the worn face of the cliff, rubbed to shades of yellow and red by the water. At the base of the falls lay a pile of rocks that had fallen to form a channel down which the cascade ran. Streaming over three small waterfalls, the water collected in a shallow rock pool, before continuing on towards the river along which we had journeyed. With the low flow of water it was possible to swim in the pool, and stripping down to my bikini, I slid into the ice cold water. It was hard to get a perspective of how high the falls were. It was like looking up at a skyscraper, not being able to see the top and bottom at the same time, and feeling as if I might fall backwards as I leant to view the peak. Resting against a slippery rock, I savoured swimming underneath the world's highest waterfall, in the middle of a lost world.

From Ciudad Bolivar, we continued south towards the eastern side of the *Gran Sabana*, following the Orinoco towards Ciudad Guyana where we were staying with our host, Gabriel, who we had contacted through Warmshowers – a website similar to Couchsurfing, but specifically for cyclists. Gabriel was a keen rider, he had taken his bike to France the year before on a solo journey around the country. He lived with his wife, Elba, who welcomed us with delicious, healthy meals, far removed from traditional Venezuelan dishes.

Gabriel had a friend, Luis, who was a presenter on a state-wide radio programme called *Pata y Pedal* that specialised in sports and adventure topics, and he was keen we should appear on the show. We were happy to take part, but were still nervous about speaking live on radio, and I half hoped the show wouldn't be able to fit us in.

> ***Diary, 11 March 2012*** - *The show was in full swing when we turned up at the station, but Gabriel was insistent we would get on. They said they could squeeze us in for a three minute slot, but we ended up on air for about 15. It was quite a professional set-up, much more so that the local station in the village the other day, and it was very lively. It was led by Luis and his female co-presenter who were both excitable and funny – with lots of whooping, whistling and laughing.*
>
> *I could follow most of what was being said, but fortunately they stuck to asking Paddy questions, after Gabriel had introduced*

us and our trip. They made Paddy read out a slogan about the radio station to use for a jingle – he did it really well. I can't imagine just turning up to a radio station, like 5 Live or Talk Sport back home, and insisting they put some foreign cyclists on air – it would never happen. It's great how friendly and open to things people are here.

Gabriel rode along with us the next morning as we continued towards the *Gran Sabana*. My bike was heavy with food for the next week on the road, so I was delighted when Gabriel asked if he could try it out. He rode it for the final 20 kilometres, huffing up the hills, while I raced along on his light aluminium mountain bike. I had forgotten how little effort was needed on a normal bike.

As we got close to Upata, a friend of Gabriel's pulled over on a motorbike, and invited us to stay at his home on the outskirts of town and we headed there after waving Gabriel off. The compound was an odd place, a huge area of ground next to a small hill. There was a large woodshed and about ten little cottages, which had once been accommodation for his *posada,* but now lay closed and dilapidated. He told us one day government officials turned up and told him he could not open because of an electricity pylon close to the site. He was unable to pay for the relevant paperwork, and his business had closed. The plot was rapidly going to ruin. A few chickens pecked around between the disused cottages, and he lived alone in a larger building with just the basic home comforts. He showed us into one of the decaying *posada* rooms that still had a working toilet, and we brushed away the worst of the dirt to lay down our tarp and roll mats for a bed for the night.

The next day, we marked ten months on the road. We were far fitter than when we started, covering 125 kilometres in spite of a strong wind and rolling hills, which would have been inconceivable when we left Rio de Janeiro. As we continued southwards we were getting closer to the border with Brazil, which we needed to cross to get into Guyana. Venezuela was in dispute with neighbouring Guyana over a mineral rich area of jungle they both claimed, and consequently, there was no open border crossing between the two.

We stopped for a day's rest at a campsite along the Río Cuyuni, on the outskirts of El Dorado. The camp was managed by a German called Gerard, who we had contacted through Warmshowers. We set up our tent close to the riverbank while we waited for him to appear, away from the monkey tied by rope to the main table in the camp. He was continually wrapping his lead around the table leg, and we would try and untangle him while keeping enough distance in case he should attack. At one point he dived under the table, hiding from a giant eagle eyeing him up for dinner from one of the trees.

Gerard appeared later that evening with bottles of good wine that we sat together enjoying. He had been on his own cycle adventure in South America, but had stopped at the camp one day and, years later still hadn't moved on. He was a nice guy and a real talker, so it was late when we finally got to sleep, wondering what state we would wake up in after too much wine.

> ***Diary, 14 March 2012*** *- The plan was to do some stuff with Gerard, but he never appeared. We had a nice and interesting day, nonetheless. Late morning, a guy called Reuben offered to drive us into town, which was good as we needed drinking water. It was a fascinating place – small and dirty, but thriving from local gold mines. There were prostitutes everywhere and a generally dodgy feeling – I was glad we went in with a local.*
>
> *We went down to the harbour where there were lots of wooden boats being filled up with oil and other supplies. People go off deep into the jungle along the river in search of gold. It looked a hard life. The river they were searching was thick brown, but Reuben said 20 years ago it was bright blue. It's changed with all the mining, which churns up the riverbed, and is apparently full of mercury and other bad stuff now.*
>
> *From there, we went to pick up cement he had on order from the government – apparently there are no other suppliers of it. He was on the list for 15 bags, but was only given ten as the army turned up to take their unwritten share. He was annoyed, but resigned to it, as it happened all the time.*
>
> *Next, we went to pick up wood. He hadn't told us about all these errands when he offered us a lift, but we weren't in a position to refuse him as we had no other way to get back. We headed down the main road, then off a dirt track that disappeared into the trees and gradually disintegrated where*

heavy rainfall had rutted the ground. As he was driving, he was telling us how it is illegal to cut trees down in the forest without a permit, but it was the only way for people to get the supplies they needed for their businesses.

We pulled up outside a well-hidden shack in the middle of the forest. A woman came out and two raggedly-dressed children followed her. The husband had already cut down the wood for Reuben, and we found it hidden in a clearing in the forest, in case the police should turn up. It was thick forest around three sides of the house, but a huge area had been cut down and recently burnt as well.

Paddy had to help load the wood into the truck – it was becoming clear why Reuben had invited us along on the ride! On the way back we had to pass a police checkpoint, which he seemed nervous about. I think he hoped we would act as a decoy, and that the police would be more interested in us than what was in the back of the truck, but in the end we were just waved through. What a complicated, pain in the arse, way of living and running a business.

By sunset, soldiers had arrived in the campsite to take up their nightly position along the banks of the river. The Cuyuni flows from Venezuela to neighbouring Guyana and is a highway for the smuggling of gasoline. We initially thought the soldiers were on guard to stop the illegal night time smuggling, but that was naive. This point was just one of several along the river where boat crews had to stop and pay a 'passage fee', which the soldiers collected for their commanders, and most likely the owner of the campsite. They all carried machine guns, but there seemed little chance of a firefight; the situation was seemingly accepted by everybody involved in the illicit trade.

The next morning we left, crossing the river by an ornate iron suspension bridge that was designed by Gustave Eiffel, the architect behind the Eiffel Tower. The bridge was in a poor state of repair, and had been replaced with a concrete plank that ran parallel to the Frenchman's design. We chose to ride across Eiffel's bridge, the wooden slats shaking under the weight of our bikes, as we made our way past grass growing through the wood and thick vines climbing up the iron supports.

For long stretches of the day we were surrounded by thick

jungle, silent apart from birdsong. Many villages along this road were known by their position on the road, rather than by name, and we finished the evening at Kilometre 88. In the distance we could make out the mountains of the *Gran Sabana* disappearing into the clouds, which was where, in the morning, we were headed.

The ride up to the *Gran Sabana* was steep, rising 1,440 metres in 35 kilometres, through thick rainforest. It was incredibly hot and we stripped off our tops, sweat running down our backs. I looked a sight in my cycle sandals with stripy, sun-tanned feet, Lycra shorts which were see-through where the sun had faded the fabric, a sports bra encrusted with sweat after months of daily use, frayed cycle mittens, and a red buff wrapped around my head to keep the sweat off my face. I didn't care, I was desperate to keep cool.

I pulled my T-shirt back on before the police checkpoint at the top. The relaxed officers welcomed us warmly, beckoning us under the shade of their hut and handing us mugs of sweet coffee that replaced some of the energy we had lost during the climb. They were interested in the route we were taking, laughing as we explained we were heading into Guyana, which they thought was far away.

Tearing ourselves away from the police officers' hospitality, we rode out of the rainforest onto a wide, expansive plain – a grand savannah; it was suddenly clear how the area got its name. The grasslands stretched out in front of us as far as our eyes could see, and the low sky seemed to go on forever. It was the first time since the Atacama Desert in Chile we had been in such utter wilderness.

We camped for the night on the sandy shores of a shallow river, our green tent blending perfectly with the spiky bushes that lined the water's edge. The sunset that night was special, hues of red and gold warming the sky, but there was little time to enjoy the view – I was busy fending off a swarm of black, biting flies.

> ***Diary, 16 March 2012** - They attacked me on the arse when I went to the loo. As if it wasn't difficult enough having my time of the month when wild camping, I lost the use of one hand which was solely dedicated to swatting the little bastards to stop them biting my sensitive areas. So I'm in a grump. Also,*

Paddy left me to set up camp so he could go and bathe in the river. By the time he got back the flies had descended, and I was left to use baby wipes.

He's been obsessed with the river all day – wanting to camp by it and drink the water. He just collected two bottles, and when I suggested he put water treatment tablets in, he got all grouchy about it. We might be high up, but it doesn't mean some animal hasn't died upstream and leaked bacteria and whatnot into it.

The next morning, my hormonal grump had passed, and we set off to enjoy some of the most beautiful riding of the trip. Helped by a favourable wind, we flew along the empty road that was in excellent condition. The scenery was mind-boggling: huge plains of stubby grass and short bushes that rolled over gentle hills; wide rivers and trickling streams; and, distant table-top mountains, clouds hovering overhead like tablecloths. It all felt incredibly big and people-less.

Several times, we stopped to explore waterfalls that peppered the landscape, all unique in character, and conveniently joined by the main road. My favourite was the Quebrada de Jaspe, a tiger-red rock waterfall in the middle of a forest. We left our bikes leaning against a curio hut in the car park, unable to push them up to the waterfall. I was only mildly concerned about leaving them unattended as we disappeared into the thick trees; there was something about this part of Venezuela that felt safe. This waterfall was especially beautiful because the smooth red rock, with its marbled finish, formed not only the drop over which the water flowed, but the riverbed that meandered off through the forest.

I was so glad we had come to this part of South America. People who had cycled the west coast of the continent had told us we were missing out by not visiting the south of Chile. Yet, the landscape on offer in Venezuela was breath-taking, different to anything I have ever seen, and almost void of people. We had this amazing place to ourselves as we rode along; I would not have missed it for anything.

It took us three days to ride across the *Gran Sabana,* to the small town of Santa Elena on the Brazilian border. We had arranged to camp in the garden of a tour operator called Andreas, who ran a *casa de ciclistas*. He already had guests, two German carpenters on a three year journey around the world.

They were following the medieval tradition of the *journeyman* – tradesmen, who after learning their craft set out to practise their new skills. With only a small sum of money, they must spend their *journeyman years* at least 50 kilometres away from home, and when they return must not have accumulated wealth. The Germans were working at places like Andreas' in return for food and lodgings. In the evening, they went to the pub dressed in the traditional *journeyman* uniform: black bell-bottom trousers, tight waistcoats with shiny buttons on the front, and wide brimmed hats. I had never heard of this tradition, and at first thought they were pulling our legs, but they talked passionately about the experience and took it incredibly seriously.

I woke early the next morning; 5.40 am seemed to have become my natural wake up time. We spent the day preparing to ride into Brazil. It felt strange to be leaving Venezuela after so long. We had arrived from Colombia as boyfriend and girlfriend, and were departing as husband and wife. Our time in this country had at times been difficult – the endless security warnings, fear of bad things happening and complications with accessing money, had been wearing. However, my overriding memory of Venezuela is of the people we met, more so even than the breath-taking scenery.

It was hard to believe, but Venezuela was our last Spanish-speaking country of the trip. In Brazil we would need Portuguese, in Guyana English, then Dutch in Suriname, and French in French Guiana. My Spanish had improved significantly over the past few months, and although I wasn't at the stage of conducting live radio interviews, like Paddy, I could manage basic conversations and understood more than I could speak. It would be a shame to stop now, but the prospect of speaking English with locals was one I was looking forward to.

We headed to the border past queues of Brazilian drivers stocking up on cheap Venezuelan fuel. It was a similar scene to when we entered from Colombia all those weeks ago, only this time nobody clapped us as we rode past.

14. Brazil – a segunda vez

Soon after the border, we stopped for a drink and were quickly reminded how difficult Portuguese was to understand. To me, it sounded like Russian, and while people seemed to comprehend our Spanish, we couldn't work out what they were saying. The drunk driver with slurred speech, who stopped us as we rode away from the border, was even more incomprehensible.

We had dropped down from the *Gran Sabana* to an altitude of 200 metres, onto a pancake-flat plain that baked under the sun. The long, straight road was surrounded by short shrubs and the occasional palm tree, with lakes and stubby hills in the distance. It took 115 kilometres of riding before we reached the first village after the border, a small collection of buildings where we thirstily glugged bottles of our favourite Brazilian soda, *Guanabara*.

It felt unreal to be back in Brazil after so long. Heading towards Rorima State's capital, Boa Vista, we were at the most northerly part of the country, far away from the white beaches of Rio de Janeiro. The closest Brazilian city was Manaus, an 11 hour drive south through the Amazon Rainforest.

Our first night back was spent baking in the tent on the sandy foreground of a gas station. We crawled inside only when our eyes could no longer stay open, reluctant to enter the oven that our canvas home had become in the tropical heat. After a miserable night tossing and turning, we hit the road early to make the most of the cool morning air.

It was a day of riding across continual savannah, and we sought refuge from the heat and wind at each roadside stall we came across, but there weren't many. At lunch, I discovered the delicious Venezuelan food we had grown so fond of was now a thing of the past; we were back in meat-eating Brazil, and the only vegetarian options were slabs of hard cheese. I fed bits to the two tiny Siamese kittens that were charging around the café. They were adorable, and I offered to steal one, if Paddy would like. Unfortunately, he declined which left me still needing a gift for his birthday the next day.

On the outskirts of Boa Vista, along a dusty section of road, we reached the 15,000 kilometre mark for the trip. We celebrated by smashing green coconuts with machetes to get to the juice inside. The woman who owned the stall was in hysterics as she watched Paddy swing and miss, sending the coconut crashing from the chopping block more than once. But the effort was worth it, the cold liquid fuelling us along to the centre of town.

> ***Diary, 22 March 2012*** *- Paddy is 30! While he went for a shower, I put out the cards people had given me in Barbados and blew up the balloons. I gave him a Portuguese phrase book, a Brazil guide and Portuguese audio lessons. After a typical Brazilian buffet breakfast that he loved, we spent the morning Skyping home.*
>
> *Boa Vista is quite modern, it's also VERY hot, and we were sweating like crazy looking for a restaurant along the riverfront that was recommended in our guidebook, but it didn't exist. So, we ended up in a 'por kilo' restaurant, which was less nice but Paddy enjoyed it.*
>
> *We found a pair of sunglasses that fitted Paddy's huge head, and I bought them as a present – amazingly my card worked as I haven't used it all trip! We spent the afternoon chilling by the pool with beers. To be in the water and cool was absolutely wonderful. It was a nice day and I think Paddy enjoyed it. It was hard to get him out of the pool, even when bats were swooping down to take a drink!*

The next morning, we hit the road, stopping for drinks whenever we could. Most of the roadside stalls principally sold alcohol, and we watched one guy down a triple shot of rum and then climb into the cab of his truck with a beer. At lunchtime we stopped at a place that only sold beer, but the couple who ran it let us use their table to cook our noodles. Although it was basic, their place was immaculate, and the two children who hid shyly behind their parents were adorable. We gave them Paddy's leftover birthday balloons, which they excitedly blew up, the little girl clinging to her mother's skirt. I would happily have stayed to play with the kids all afternoon, but we needed to push on if we were to reach

Guyana the next day.

We stopped 40 kilometres before the border, camping outside a bar where the village's teenagers were playing a football match. Barefoot in the sand, they kicked a small ball at a goal just 30 centimetres wide. If that was how Brazilian footballers learnt their trade, it was no wonder they were so good.

The next morning, we reached the river that forms the border with Guyana. It had been only a short spell in Brazil, but before too long we would return and start making our way towards Rio de Janeiro. First we would ride through the Guianas, the three smallest territories in the whole of South America, comprised of Guyana (formerly British Guyana), Suriname (previously Dutch Guyana) and French Guiana (a department of France).

I promised myself that over the next few weeks I would commit to learning Portuguese in preparation for arriving back in Brazil, but of course, that would not happen. I had underestimated how, with over 80 per cent of the area covered in thick forest, rather than listening to language tapes, I would spend my time on the lookout for crouching jaguars and jumping snakes.

15. Guyana

It was the most complicated bridge I had ever seen. The modern, concrete structure criss-crossed over itself until we found ourselves riding on the left hand side of the road for the first time in South America. We were now in Guyana, once a British colony, and little seemed to have changed since colonial times.

Immigration was in a one-storey, white-brick building with a red tiled roof. Inside, smartly-dressed government workers sat behind wide desks. I was excited to be in a country with strong links to home, particularly about having the same language, but the customs officer had little interest in the connection, brusquely informing me he would issue us a two-week visa, instead of the three months we expected. There was no explanation for his decision, and he only relented after I had given a day-by-day breakdown of how long it would take to ride across Guyana.

The Guianas were a bit of a mystery to us. Our guidebook included only a tiny chapter on the three territories, and my history book on Latin America didn't mention them. Prior to looking at a map of the continent, I hadn't even known the Guianas existed. The most we had discovered about Guyana was that it was where Demerara sugar came from, and that the singer Leona Lewis and cricketer Mark Ramprakash were both of Guyanese descent. Then there was the infamous incident of 1978; the Jonestown Massacre.

Back in 1976, an American cult, the Peoples Temple led by the Reverend Jim Jones, moved from the US to settle in the Guyanese jungle. Hidden away from the world, Jones' several hundred followers worked long shifts in the fields and listened to rambling sermons by the Reverend. Accommodation was in communal dorms and punishments were handed out to anybody not working hard enough, including hanging disobedient children inside a well. Gradually, Jones' behaviour became more erratic and he made the community practise mass suicides, telling his followers the time would come for them to all die. Many began to distrust the Reverend, but deep in the jungle, far away from any roads, chance of escape was limited.

In November 1978, the American Congressman, Leo Ryan, flew with a television crew to visit the community. On his second day, he was approached by several members of the Temple who wanted to leave. Jones gave them permission, and the group set off in a truck towards the airstrip where planes were waiting to fly them to Georgetown. It was an ambush. Jones sent armed men to attack the delegation, killing Ryan and members of the camera crew. Back at base, Temple members were urged to commit 'revolutionary suicide'. Poison was squirted into the mouths of men, women and children, while Jones died from a gunshot wound to the head. 918 people died deep in the Guyanese jungle, a third of whom were children. Only a handful of Temple members escaped.

It was Guyana's darkest moment, yet few of Jones' victims had been Guyanese. It seemed the incident belonged more to America's history rather than Guyana's, and the more I got to know the country, the harder I would find it to connect the two. Yet, Guyana had its own complicated past and things were rarely straightforward in this fascinating place.

From immigration, we rode the few kilometres into the border town of Lethem. Home to only 12,000 people and named after Sir Gordon James Lethem who was the British Governor during the 1940s, it was a peculiar little place. Spread out across a wide plain, it had a Caribbean feel thanks to the casual manner of the inhabitants; a middle-of-nowhere sensation, because the buildings were so spread out; and a ranch-feel with dusty ground sectored off by flimsy wooden fences and cowboys on horseback. Huge warehouses packed with Chinese goods lined the main street, selling to Brazilians who, unsure of which side of the road to drive on, headed straight down the middle.

We had arranged to stay in the garden of the Outdoor Shop, owned by Warmshowers hosts, Joe and Christine. They weren't in town, but had asked their neighbour, Rebecca, to show us to a locked cottage where we could camp on the porch. The shop had glass-top counters, stocked with fishing tackle, head torches, stoves and hunting knives. It was more ordered than the Chinese-run warehouses in the centre of town, which were stuffed with cheap T-shirts, kitchen utensils, hats and other items. The *Savanna Inn* sold food, including cans of baked beans and bars of Dairy Milk chocolate. We were amazed to see favourites from home, and enjoyed an oddly-concocted dinner that night, swinging from our new hammocks as we ate.

After several hot and sticky nights in the tent, we had decided to buy hammocks. Rebecca helped us tie the ropes and mosquito net to the hammock, a far more complicated procedure than we had imagined. She also demonstrated the best position for a good sleep; the trick was to sleep diagonally rather than lying in it like a banana. They took a bit of getting used to, but were far more comfortable than the tent and I slept deeply that night, rocking between the posts of the porch.

The next morning we called in at Rebecca's house to say thank you for her help, and she gave us directions to her mother's ranch where we could stay that night. We headed out of town in high spirits, or at least that was until we reached the end of the tarmac. The next stretch of our route was along *The Trail*; 460 kilometres of red dirt across the Rupununi Savannah and through thick jungle.

Diary, 25 March 2012 - *I'm writing in a hammock on a ranch in the middle of the Guyanese Savannah. Today we covered 85 kilometres along a tough dirt road, thick with red sand. In parts it was fine to cycle on, but in others it was painful, especially on the boobs when I was bouncing over stones and washboard. We could have covered more, but the wind was strongly against us, and I found myself being blown sideways to where the sand gathers at the side of the road.*

The savannah was quite monotonous, it's just miles and miles of grass with short bushes and the odd tree. But, towards the end of the day a set of hills came into view which looked spectacular after the barren savannah. We were relieved to see them as Rebecca's mother's ranch was there. It took forever to reach the hills, we were only moving at ten kilometres per hour, and the sun was setting by the time we finally stopped.

The ranch is large and full of animals. There are huge fields fenced off from the road with worn wooden posts, and in the middle of them is a cluster of outhouses and huts where people live and work. They are protected from the wind by palm trees and other bushes that have been planted around the perimeter. To get to the buildings, we had to weave our way through stubborn-looking cows and sheep.

We met Rebecca's mum this evening. It felt like meeting the Queen. One of her staff brought us over to her cottage that was far away from the farm workers' huts, and we were made to wait on the doorstep until she would receive us. People here speak very slowly and don't say much, which makes me nervous and I start to blabber. We only spoke briefly to her and thanked her for letting us stay, and then we were dismissed.

There are lots of farm workers, who have all been very friendly. One older guy helped us set up our hammocks in the round shelter. It has a thick pole in the middle which one rope gets tied to, then the other end goes around a pole on the outside of the shelter. It has a thatched roof, low brick walls and a concrete floor that I keep banging when I sit on the hammock – I've misjudged the height, but I'm too lazy to change it.

We washed in a creek just off the main road, where the old man told us go to. When the coast was clear, we stripped off and jumped into the water with our bars of soap. There were bats circling overhead and I was praying there weren't caimans. I'm not sure how clean I am, the water was quite brown.

A girl made food for us. Unfortunately, it was meat, so Paddy enjoyed double portions, while I nibbled on dry cassava bread – not the best thing I've ever eaten. It's not even nine pm, and I'm exhausted. Swinging in a hammock isn't helping my eyes stay open.

The ranch's cockerel started crowing at three am. At least there was an outstanding view to wake up to: the sight of the rising sun as it appeared from behind the hills. The old farm worker watched as we cooked porridge on our stove. I think he thought we were slightly mad, and he waved us off with a bemused grin as we headed back to the bumpy road.

The morning passed quietly, the road hugged the hills and we stopped only briefly to fix a puncture on Paddy's back tyre. There was no traffic, so we just sat down in the middle of the trail to repair it. While we were busy working, we were approached by a man on a bicycle who had ridden over from the small cluster of houses we could see along the road. He introduced himself as the chief of the village, and pointed out a cluster of people by the roadside. They were waiting for a minibus, he explained, to take them to Georgetown. Nobody knew if one might come today, or if there would be room, if not they would try again tomorrow.

Before lunchtime, the road began to weave through the hills past the village of Annai. It was rare a vehicle passed us, we were more likely to be held up by a herd of cows. Slowly, the bush at the side of the road thickened, until the savannah disappeared and the road cut through thick jungle. Lush green trees and bushes grew on either side of the narrow red trail that was pitted with water-logged holes, where rain had poured off overhanging branches. The trees shaded us from the sun, while the damp forest air was cooling, and clouds hung low and grey compared to the hot, clear skies of the savannah. The quietness was broken only by the cries of monkeys playing deep inside the tree cover, and squawking red macaws performing acrobatic moves overhead.

Thick jungle covered huge swathes of Guyana, hosting one of the most diverse ecosystems in the world. Scientists still discovered new species of flora and fauna, but my thoughts were dominated by the forest's most ferocious resident; the jaguar. Smaller only than lions and tigers, these huge cats looked similar to leopards with golden spotted coats. They thrived in rainforests where they stalked and ambushed their prey, killing them with a bite through the skull. According to locals, the forest was packed with jaguars.

I was terrified by the thought of being eaten by a big cat. Every time we stopped, I insisted Paddy and I sat facing, so we had a 360 degree view of our position. When I told Madonna about my fear, she laughed. I shouldn't be scared of jaguars, she said. Instead, she warned me to take care of snakes that she said snuck up on people. Her positive spin on jaguars did nothing to calm me; now I had two animals to watch out for.

Madonna was the owner of the rest stop outside the village of Sumara, and she was sleeping in a hammock inside the shop when we arrived. She was very chatty, explaining we should set up camp in the carousel-shaped structure similar to the one we had used on the ranch. Across the grass, where I carefully looked out for snakes, there was a small wooden cubicle with a long-drop toilet, and behind the house an open air shower. We raided her shop for goodies, and ate crisps for dinner, swinging in our hammocks as we watched a thunderous downpour unleash itself on the jungle.

It was still raining when we woke up the next morning. The hammock stop was now full of snoring Brazilians, who I vaguely remembered arriving during the night; I was finding it easy to sleep in the hammock, more so than Paddy, who hadn't mastered lying sideways. Madonna joined us under the edge of the canopy, sighing as she looked up at the grey sky and saying that it looked set in for the day. I would have preferred to wait and see if the rain stopped, but we had 80 kilometres to cover that day.

The rain had turned the red dirt trail to slush, but the middle of the road was firm enough to hold our weight. After nine kilometres we came to the gates of the Iwokrama Forest, where a warden searched our bikes for a serial number and took our details in case we got eaten by a tiger, the boss-man explained. I used up a lot of energy that day looking for jaguars, or *tigers* as they are known locally, and every rustle in a bush set my heart beating like crazy. I decided if I saw one, I would use the method for coming across a lion – to stand still and look big, rather than run. Of course, we didn't see any. The forest wardens were probably taking names to stop illegal mining in the forest – they were having a laugh with us, but I was too worked up to get the joke.

As we rode away from the wardens' station, the trees grew taller and the light dimmer. At first we made good progress, but as the terrain became hilly, the trail began to deteriorate. Small potholes turned into pits several metres long covering the width of the road. They were full of water and the bottom consisted of sticky red mud and stones. We had no option but to wade straight through, the red mud squelching out of our sandals and caking our legs.

At times we were forced to push uphill, unable to ride along the slippery surface in our low gears. The last few kilometres to the river were the worst. Heavy trucks belonging to mining companies had churned the road into sticky mud that covered the bikes. It collected under the brake pads, making it impossible to move the wheels without clearing the mud guards every 100 metres.

It was a relief when we at last reached the wide river, one of over 1,500 in Guyana. It was this watery connection that gave the country its name, *Guyana* being an interpretation of the Amerindian word meaning 'land of many waters'. The way across was by an hourly ferry, which took ten minutes to reach the village of Kurupukari, our next rest stop.

Trevor was the first person to speak to us when we walked into the bar. Eyeing our mud splattered bodies, he said, "I have a truck and go to Georgetown tomorrow. I have space, you'll come with me." He laughed when we made to decline his offer, and pointed at the sky that loomed ominously black over our heads. The north stretch of road was even worse, he said, and he'd only just got through in his Bedford truck.

It wasn't the thought of getting dirty that made me capitulate; it was calculating how many times I would have to clear my brakes of mud over the next 100 kilometres, and how long it would take to cover the distance. We had little option but to accept his offer, or else we would be stuck in the jungle with the jaguars.

> ***Diary, 28 March 2012** - I was asleep by 8.30, but woke throughout the night with new people turning up with music blaring out. I convinced myself at one point that a jaguar would come and get me in my hammock, but I finally fell back to a heavy sleep until 5.40 when it got light.*
>
> *We loaded up the Bedford and set off about eight am, behind lots of combis and trucks as everybody travels in a convoy in case of trouble. The road wasn't too bad and would have been nice to ride, but in places it was thick mud and huge puddles that we would have struggled to get through. It was hilly too; there would have been lots of pushing. No way could we have covered 100 kilometres in a day.*
>
> *The road closes at certain times of the year because it becomes impassable, and Trevor thought that would happen very soon. At one point we had to pull a couple of combis and trucks out of the mud. They were stuck so fast that we broke a couple of tow ropes. At one point, they adopted a strategy of raising the*

dumper on the back of the Bedford, Trevor had forgotten our bikes were in the back, and we stopped him just before they slid out.

Trevor was saying he normally rides over the bumps in the road, he had a sprung seat, but he was taking it slower because we were there. We never would have guessed; it was the most bouncy journey that I've ever taken – I kept slipping down into the foot-well. I tried speaking to Trevor, but the noise of the truck made it difficult, plus even though we both speak English, we couldn't understand each other. He speaks Caribbean English, and I could only make out a handful of words. In the end, we gave up on the chat.

We didn't spot any jaguars, but I saw what Madonna meant about them not being the biggest concern. We were going quite fast along the road, when Trevor slowed down – it looked like a fat tree had fallen across the road. Only, when we got closer, it was actually a silvery green snake with a red underbelly, and it was absolutely huge.

The road must have been at least four metres wide, and it took up most of it. It didn't get out of the way as we approached, instead it decided to attack us. It coiled itself up, like something in a cartoon and then launched itself. Its head actually reached the cab window and I looked it straight in the eyes, before it got sucked underneath the truck. Not even Trevor was laughing. He said that breed was deadly venomous, that it jumped up to bite its enemy in the face. He gave us some lessons about what to do if we encountered a snake, but mostly his advice was to avoid them.

Not long after, we arrived at the pit stop at Mabura Hill. In the morning, we'd contemplated riding from here if the road looked good, but after the incident with the snake, there was no way we were getting out. Instead, I gorged on the food there. I had a huge plate of macaroni cheese and a bar of Dairy Milk, Paddy had a spicy curry. I think Guyana may challenge Venezuela in the food stakes.

At the service station, we got chatting to a Canadian woman who was looking to invest in the local mining industry. With a wealth of natural resources, Guyana principally mines bauxite, gold and diamonds. The Canadian was interested in gold mining, an industry split between large companies with permits to exploit the land, and small-scale illegal searchers who disappear into the jungle in search of riches. I could sense she felt there was money to be made in Guyana, but I wasn't quite sure how international developers would help lift poor Guyanese people out of poverty.

Mining trucks had churned up the road after Mabura Hill, and we bounced along in the Bedford for several hours until we finally reached smooth tarmac in the industrial town of Linden. As we unloaded our bikes, a skinny, dark-skinned guy approached us. He introduced himself as Nigel, a competitive road cyclist. After examining our bikes and asking countless questions about the Rohloff hub, he invited us to stay at his mother's house that overlooked the main T-junction in town. It was a kind offer, but I was exhausted and wasn't in the mood for company. Plus, there was something about him, the way he launched at us before Trevor had even left, that made me a bit wary.

> ***Paddy:*** *We had got used to accepting offers to stay with strangers we met randomly, so I didn't think too much of it, or that Laura would mind. Nigel led us across the main road to his mother's stilted house, which he lived underneath in a small, dusty workshop. The place was packed with bikes and parts, and there was little room to sit, let alone hang our hammocks.*
>
> *The only option was to pitch our tent in the garden, which was over-looked from the busy road. I began to think something might not be quite right when Nigel showed us his shower – a hose in the garden. His mum was in the house, but it seemed Nigel wasn't allowed inside.*
>
> *This included not being able to use the bathroom, and he suggested I use a bucket and that Laura could walk down the road to a restaurant. At this point, there was no ignoring the look on Laura's face, and when we had a few minutes to ourselves I discovered how strongly she wanted to leave. Because it was my fault we were in this situation, apparently, I was left to make the excuses.*
>
> *Nigel was OK about the decision and took us to a motel. It was one of the seediest places we'd stayed. The walls were black and red, and the toilet in our room was as high as a bar stool, sectioned off by a plastic shower curtain. When we got there*

he tried charging a finder's fee, which really annoyed me. I said we would pay him in the morning but we left at the crack of dawn to avoid him. I had to admit Laura's first impressions had been right.

From Linden, we made our way over sand dunes towards the home of our Warmshowers hosts, Joe and Christine. They lived along a sandy track, sandwiched between a motorsport track and the international airport. In several hectares of land, their beautiful house was surprisingly quiet considering the location. We were greeted by a huddle of dogs, puppies and cats that bounded excitedly towards us. Joe and Christine weren't home yet, but their staff showed us to the wooden tower where we were to stay. The large white guesthouse was raised on wooden stilts above a communal living area. There were two floors of accommodation and a viewing platform from where we could see for kilometres around.

The puppies had followed us to the tower and we were playing with them when Joe and Christine appeared later that afternoon. They had travelled from Georgetown to welcome us, bringing a feast of Chinese food to share. We were joined at dinner by Birdman, a black pet bird that Joe had rescued as a tiny chick. He was small enough to fit into Joe's palm, his favourite spot when he wasn't chipping at people's feet with his yellow beak. The couple were obviously animal lovers; their main business was a busy pet shop in Georgetown and they also had a property in Brazil, they explained, in case the situation in Guyana grew unstable.

Guyana had a complicated and at times turbulent past. Around a third of the population was descended from African slaves brought to the country by the Dutch who ruled the country before Britain. Half of the country was descended from Indian agricultural workers, who arrived under the British after the abolition of slavery. Persistent tension between these two groups fuelled political instability, and the two main parties, which were ethnically-based, had a hostile relationship.

The country had gone to the polls in November 2011, electing Donald Ramotar of the People's Progressive Party/Civic as president. It was his party's fifth straight victory, although it lost its parliamentary majority for the first time in 19 years. There were concerns that if the opposition parties formed a bloc against the government it could lead to tensions within the country, which is why people who had the means to do so made contingency plans.

We were the only guests in the tower, because soon after building the lodge, Guyana's economy had faltered and Joe and Christine had never opened it to the public. In the absence of paying guests, an unwelcome character had set up home in our room. When I saw it first, I was sat underneath the mosquito net writing my diary and it took a while to grasp what it was. I watched as the furry dark legs crept slowly out from the gap above the doorframe. Fat and hairy with white tips, the limbs kept appearing, bringing with them a round, heavy body, and then even more legs, until it stood clinging to the wall in full glory; a tarantula.

I was a little taken aback to find a poisonous spider in our bedroom and had no idea what to do. My first thought was to stay calm; I knew not all tarantulas had a deadly bite, it depended on their coloured markings, only I couldn't remember if black was good or bad. We contemplated running to get Joe, but we didn't want to look like neurotic wimps, so we tucked ourselves inside the mosquito net, hoping it would protect us if the spider decided to attack.

I slept lightly; stirring every time the net touched my skin. As it was, when we woke, the giant spider had moved very little, keeping to the edges of the room, where it seemed happy to observe us. Still, we were unsure of its long term intentions towards us, and took to ducking and running through the door while it sat above. When we mentioned it to Joe, he casually said the spider lived there. He did offer to kill it with a broom, but that seemed mean. We were the ones trespassing on its territory and I would have felt terrible about taking its life. So, for our remaining time in the tower, we continued to live peacefully side-by-side, with us watching its movements with great diligence.

After a few days, we said goodbye to Joe, Christine, Birdman and the puppies, and headed back to the highway for the 50 kilometre ride into the capital, Georgetown. The busy, bumpy road followed the Demerara River into town, a wide brown expanse of water, controlled by sluice gates to prevent flooding. It was around the plains of the river that Guyana's sugar industry thrived, producing the world renowned Demerara sugar.

In the 1700s Europe developed a sweet tooth, and the Dutch set about turning Guyana's northern shores into a hub of sugar production. The coastline was lined with fields growing sugar cane – for every kilometre of which there were 95 kilometres of drainage canals that had been dug by African slaves. Today the country still produced sugar, accounting for almost 30 per cent of its total exports.

We stopped for something to eat on the outskirts of town: roti and egg balls – boiled eggs wrapped in cassava and deep-fried, with a hint of spice. When I returned from buying seconds, I found Paddy ensconced in fixing the puncture of a teenage boy. A group of older men had gathered around, scolding the kid for not fixing it himself and an uncomfortable atmosphere was brewing, with everybody in the crowd having an opinion. A man in a wheelchair joined the group. His argument was unconnected to the puncture, he was insisting I give him my cycle gloves. If he had been slightly nicer I might have considered it, but he was aggressive and rude, and I actually wanted to tell him to get lost. I was glad when Paddy finished and we could continue on towards 'Town', as Georgetown was known.

We rode in from the south of the city, through a scene reminiscent of the *Little House on the Prairie* books. Around the central market were saw mills where men loaded planks into horse-drawn carts. Almost all of the buildings were built from wood, including the grand St George's Cathedral with its tall spire. Outside a yellow and red hall sat a plump statue of the British monarch, Queen Victoria, while 1950s rock and roll music blared out of the diner close to our guesthouse.

Decorated in chintz and with the boiling-meat smell of a nursing home, the guesthouse prided itself on being 'the friendliest in town'. Our room was up a creaky staircase, with flowery curtains that fluttered in the breeze from the open windows, lace doilies and a small brass-knobbed bed. Everything about Georgetown felt as if time had stood still since independence.

The Dutch were the first to colonise the area, establishing themselves in Demerara in 1752. In 1814, the British purchased the colony and the capital was renamed Georgetown in honour of the British monarch, King George III. Guyana became an independent republic in 1970. The country is a member of the British Commonwealth, perhaps explaining why strong links remained. Many of the streets had names that wouldn't have been out of place in London, like Waterloo Street, Regent Street and Sussex Street. My favourite connection, however, was the food. In a supermarket we found more baked beans and other favourites from home, including a huge bar of Dairy Milk that quickly melted in the heat of the afternoon.

Some areas of the city were no-go areas for security reasons, particularly the market. The seafront also had an edgy feel to it and there was no pristine white beach here. We had reached the Atlantic, but unlike in Rio de Janeiro, this stretch of ocean was murky brown and choppy, churned up by rivers flowing into the sea. A Dutch-built seawall held the water back from the city, which at high tide rose one and a half metres above Georgetown's streets. From it, narrow concrete platforms protruded out into the sea, and we wandered out to where the waves lapped at our feet. Staring out towards the ocean, we didn't notice another couple walk out behind us, trapping us at the end.

Fortunately, there was no need to worry, they were a Guyanese couple who now lived in Canada and were home visiting family. Their story was typical of the exodus of educated Guyanese. Over 90 per cent of tertiary graduates headed abroad for better employment possibilities and to escape the security situation in the country. They were a lovely couple and clearly missed their home country, but had no plans to return, having built a quality of life in Canada they could never achieve in Guyana.

We continued to explore Georgetown's maze of streets that baked under the hot Sunday sun. The city was quiet aside from the occasional cheers of cricketers. Guyana competes as part of the West Indies, and it was clear that the game was taken seriously around the city. In a stadium a match was underway, but likewise, on every small scrap of land, men and young boys were conducting their own fiercely fought contests. It was fascinating to see that in South America, the game of cricket was so loved.

*Notice: No school on Tuesday – K*ite flying at the national park.

The handwritten sign on a blackboard outside a school, made us chuckle. It summed up everything about Town, a city that seemed glued to the past. From the centre we rode out towards the coastal road, overtaking horse-drawn carts as we went. The route to Suriname was one long road, and every inch of the single-lane highway had been built on. It was packed with shops and cafés serving hot, spicy meals that had us stopping continually to taste them while we still had the chance.

On our second day along the road, a heavy rainstorm delayed us and we took shelter under the porch of a roadside stall, where we were astonished to witness a tractor pulling a house on the back of a trailer. It was a one-storey wooden structure, with large windows on all sides, out of which hung small children. The movers had literally picked up the entire thing to move it.

The highway was amusing for us to cycle along, as the small villages squished up against each other were named after British cities and towns. I spent five minutes riding through Manchester, and came out the other side in Liverpool. We had almost cycled the entire length of England by the time we ran into Daryl Dorsett.

Daryl was a Rastafarian with long, greying dreadlocks, a raucous laugh and a complicated, fist-bumping handshake. We had stopped in front of his house when my cleat stuck in the pedal, leaving me unable to detach myself without taking off my sandal. Apparently, this was man's work, and the guys set about banging and whacking the shoe with a collection of tools. After an hour of watching their over-complicated solutions, I couldn't bite my tongue any longer, and suggested they turn a screwdriver under the cleat; it came away at the first attempt.

Daryl invited us into his home, a two-storey structure with balconies, and a garden packed with fruit trees. In the shady kitchen, Daryl introduced us to his mother, whom he said had been to London.

"Really," I asked her, "how did you like it?"

"I didn't," she replied. "I don't like England."

She was so rude, it was actually funny. Her manner was similar to many Guyanese we had met. While the majority of people were warm and welcoming, a few, like her, were so grumpy and forthright that they were awfully rude. Having met enough people like her to know it was nothing personal, we laughed about her manners when we rode on.

Our final stopping point in Guyana was the border town of Corriverton, a busy settlement along the Courantyne River. We took the last opportunity to stock up on our British favourites, loading our bags with Cadbury Creme Eggs and Tullock wafer bars, hoping they wouldn't melt in the heat. I had loved our time in Guyana. It was a fascinating country, completely unlike anywhere I had been before. With connections to Britain, the Caribbean and the Netherlands, it was a hodgepodge of these cultures, with the added mix of descendants from Africa, India and China. The people were warm and fun to chat to, even the grumpy ones, and the food was amazing – Venezuela had almost been knocked into second position on the 'best food of South America league'.

Yet, the scenery was the knockout thing in Guyana. Our time riding *The Trail* from Lethem to Linden, across the savannah and into the forest, was special. It was a place few tourists ever get to visit, and I hoped the foreign mining investors wouldn't ruin it for the future.

On our final morning in Guyana, we were on the road before six am to reach the ferry port in plenty of time for the daily crossing. It was only 13 kilometres from Corriverton and we made good time, but the guards were already closing the gates as we rode up, and we just snuck in before they attached the padlock. It was the Thursday before Easter and the ferry would be closed after today, hence the long queue for the nine am crossing.

> ***Diary, 5 April 2012*** *- The whole thing was a real drag. The guys who worked there were like prison guards, walking around with sunglasses on and barking orders at people. The power had gone to their heads. We made good targets and were constantly being told to "move here" or "don't do that", even though everybody else was doing the same. That over-zealous authority drives me crazy.*
>
> *We finally made it through customs and then sat, hiding from the rain, while we waited for the boat which was an hour late. It was midday by the time we finally got off the ferry into Suriname – our 12th country of the trip!*

16. Suriname

Running along a wide canal, the road was pancake-flat, but that was where the similarities with Suriname's old colonial power ended. There were no fields of tulips one might find on the outskirts of Amsterdam, just thick, bushy jungle under a clear blue sky. Exotic birdsong accompanied us as we pedalled along perfectly smooth tarmac towards the coastal town of Nieuw Nickerie, 40 kilometres north of the border.

Canals were prevalent in town, too. A wide stretch of water, packed with pink water lilies and lined by white-trunked palm trees, divided Westkanaalstraat from Oostkanaalstraat in the centre of town. Dutch was still the official language of Suriname, and we found it impossible to understand in the family-run supermarket we stopped at. The owners were Chinese, members of a thriving Asian community descended from workers the Dutch brought to Suriname from India, Indonesia and China.

The first people to colonise the territory, however, were the British. In fact, the country's name was originally *Surreyham*, after the Earl of Surrey who created a settlement along the coast. The Dutch came to control the territory in 1667, when they struck a deal with the British to exchange it for a piece of land they called New Amsterdam on the east coast of North America; an area that would become New York City, renamed in honour of the-then Duke of York.

It was a complicated history for the smallest country in the whole of South America. Most of the half a million population lived along the coast, as much of the interior was covered in impenetrable forest. We would be riding eastwards across the country, following the principal highway to the capital Paramaribo and then towards the border with French Guiana.

Perhaps the term 'highway' is a little grand, it was a rough stretch of single-lane tarmac that meandered through swampy areas. Snakes and caimans that had dared leave the watery channels lay squashed on the roadside, flattened by heavy farming vehicles. In places the jungle encased the road, while sometimes we cycled along flat, wide plains cleared for farming. As we pedalled past watery rice paddies and packed banana plantations, only rarely would we find ourselves away from a perfectly square-sided canal; the Dutch had built waterways all over the landscape.

On our second morning in Suriname, we met two white, dreadlocked cyclists, heavily laden with bags bungeed to their racks, and one carried a guitar as if it were a rucksack. In flip flops and baggy shorts, they were riding single-speed city bikes; the kind you might expect to find in Amsterdam. The two Frenchmen had picked up their rides in Paramaribo after crossing over from French Guiana. Only a few days into their trip, they were taking things slowly, with no real destination in mind. I hadn't expected to see cycle tourists in this part of South America, although with their laid-back approach, they were more drifting along by bike, rather than cycle touring.

The day was turning out to be one of unexpected sights, when soon after, we rode into the village of Totness, an old Scottish settlement. From 1799 to 1816, Britain temporarily regained control of Suriname, and in a bid to prevent French Guiana from expanding, Scottish farmers were recruited to settle along the coast. They worked on clearing the land for farming and cotton production, helped by African slaves. Few white descendants of the Scottish immigrants survive as most died of diseases like typhus and yellow fever. However, Scottish names live on in the ancestors of children that land owners produced with their slaves.

> ***Diary, 7 April 2012*** - *We were aiming for the village of Jenny, but we must have cycled through as we never found it. Instead, we came to a bridge with an army camp on the other side. We asked if we could put our hammocks up in the base, but the commander said he couldn't let us. He was very nice about it, and pointed us in the direction of a police station in the nearby village.*
>
> *The police officer wasn't having any of it, even though there was a huge garden out back. He sent us to a hammock spot in the central plaza that was packed with people, all with bags of stuff. They were waiting for a riverboat crossing, but nobody knew when it would arrive. I refused to stay there – it*

really didn't feel safe. I wouldn't have slept, as I could imagine waking up in the morning and finding all our bags had been taken. Paddy was really pissed off with me, but I didn't have a good feeling about the place and stood my ground.

We carried on in stony silence. The problem was the next village was absolutely miles away, and it was starting to get dark. There weren't any spots along the side of the road to camp, and we didn't know what we were going to do. About two kilometres along, we passed a half-built house where a group of people was waving from the balcony. We waved back and carried on, but then I realised they had lots of green space and outbuildings, so we turned around and asked if we could put our hammocks up there. The guy looked pretty surprised, but he called his boss, who said it was fine.

They were a nice crowd. Anail and his wife worked there, helping build the camp for tourists who wanted to take trips into the jungle. Their fathers were both there. They were of Indian descent and spoke Hindi, which I understood even less than Dutch, but we managed to communicate with hand gestures and bits of English.

We'd asked to stay in one of the outbuildings, but they insisted we stay with them in the vast room of the main house, which was newly-finished and built on stilts. They helped hang our hammocks up from the roof and cooked dinner for us as well. The fathers didn't stay over, as they were going fishing. I wasn't quite sure of the exact plan as they had drunk a lot of rum. We all went to bed about nine. I was absolutely shattered after covering 157 kilometres.

The sound of falling rain on the corrugated iron roof woke us early. Anail was up too and we headed off soon after, leaving him to his work. We grabbed breakfast at a roadside roti stall in a small village after an hour on the road. The *Sandjana Rotie Stall* was a small, corrugated iron hut in the front garden of a family home. When we rang the bell, a teenage boy came rushing out to serve us the daily special of roti with curry sauce, which was spicy, hot and delicious.

Paddy's stomach was not keen on spicy breakfasts, we discovered, when he suddenly disappeared into the bushes.

As soon as he was out of view, I was approached by an Afro-Surinamese man on a motorbike who invited me to come home with him, telling me quite graphically what he thought of white women and what he intended to do with me. I was immensely relieved when Paddy stumbled out of the bushes and the guy shot off.

A few hours later we reached a very quiet Paramaribo – the city had closed for Easter. In a bar, we bumped into Joe and Christine who were enjoying a weekend away with friends and they suggested we take a wander around the historical part of town. Most of Paramaribo's buildings were wooden, painted in fresh white and pastel shades, yet down by the riverfront, at the end of a tree-shaded path, sat the old colonial complex containing the round, pale red-bricked Fort Zeelandia. Built by the British in the mid-1600s, it was taken over by the Dutch where it sat uneventfully until independence in 1975. Soon after, it staged one of Suriname's most notorious moments in history.

In 1980, a group of army sergeants launched a military coup against the sitting government. The country fell under control of one of the coup leaders, Desiré Bouterse, who based his headquarters at Fort Zeelandia. His military dictatorship banned other political parties, imposed curfews and restricted the press. In 1982, 15 members of the opposition – a group of journalists, lawyers and university teachers - were taken to the fort and murdered by the army.

There was no mention of the killings as we wandered around the fort. Today tourists were encouraged to clamber over the ramparts and dine in the fancy restaurant. We opted not to eat there, and headed instead to a roti restaurant. It was hard to decipher the Dutch menu, but I took a punt on *patat veg*, and was rewarded with a huge plate of potato curry, buttery green beans, a curried egg and a floury roti. There wasn't much I missed from home, but I craved curry, so this was heaven.

I made Paddy stop there again the next morning, so I could pig out one last time before we left Paramaribo. Easter was over and the city was slowly returning to normal. We had managed to get a new cleat for my sandal from a bike shop in town, and fuelled up on roti, we were ready to hit the road again. The problem was we had different ideas about how to do that.

Paddy wanted to ride over the massive bridge that crossed the Suriname River. The structure was high enough for ships to pass through and over 1,500 metres long, and after seeing the erratic driving on the way into Paramaribo, there was no way I was going to repeat that experience a hundred metres above water. Instead, we agreed to take a water taxi across the choppy brown river.

Our driver, eager for the fare, hurried over as we approached the riverside. A long row of boats was waiting for passengers, the flow of which was lighter since the bridge opened in 2000. He and Paddy carried the bikes into the low wooden boat with ease, and we settled down under the canvas roof for the easy ten minute journey to the other side.

If we had turned left at the riverbank, we would have reached the old plantations where Dutch masters put slaves to work producing cotton, sugar, coffee and cocoa. Instead, we turned right, picking up the hideous highway towards Moengo. In patches it was brand new, but mainly it was bumpy tarmac or mashed up dirt and we bounced along, our cycle computers ticking over to 16,000 kilometres in the process.

We were riding through thick forest and could only see into the trees where people had cleared them to build small wooden houses. The closer we got towards Moengo, the more the appearance of the villagers changed from Indian to Afro-Surinamese and people seemed poorer. As we approached the bauxite mining town, passengers started hanging out of cars asking us for money. I took an instant dislike to the town, it felt unsafe and scary, the atmosphere was tense and I could see people watching us closely as we passed.

Paddy: *Unlike normal towns, Moengo seemed to have no centre to it, there was just the occasional shop and residential streets. It had an army-town feel to it with everyone moving about purposefully as the sun set. We stood out a lot, and I could tell that Laura was quite nervous about all the attention we were getting, especially as it was taking a long time to find somewhere to stay.*

At first we got directed to the police station round the back of a bank, but we couldn't find it anywhere, and were beginning to think that people were messing us about. As darkness fell, we met a restaurant owner who said her uncle had a vacant place.

The price was far more than we wanted to pay, but even I was beginning to get a bit concerned and with the language issue, we had little choice but to go for it. The apartment was the top floor of a house, with locks on all the doors and windows, and as soon as the owner left, we shut ourselves inside. It really was a strange place.

Moengo had a violent history. In 1986, a bank-raid there by one of Bouterse's former bodyguards, Ronnie Brunswijk, kick-started a six year war against the government. Brunswijk formed an army of guerrilla fighters known as the Jungle Commando, fighting for land rights in eastern Suriname, where many descendants of slaves now lived, as well as for control over the lucrative trade in cocaine.

The government took a hard line against the guerrillas, burning villages, water pipelines, power lines, schools and businesses. The terrible state of the road, which was also destroyed by government forces, was just one example of how the area had not recovered from the conflict. The government, now led by Bouterse who was elected president of Suriname in 2010, had not yet repaired the damage its forces caused.

We left Moengo early, keen to escape the eerie town. As the morning progressed, we found ourselves climbing until we were overlooking the jungle. The scene was of tightly-packed trees with a steamy mist rising off the tops, and in the distance the small border town of Albina. We had spent only a week in Suriname, a tiny country, thick with forest and a complicated history. In Paramaribo, I had felt safe, but at other times I hadn't felt comfortable on the road.

I wasn't too disappointed to be leaving, but I would miss the curries. The thought of swapping spicy food for French meals was not appealing, as I knew as a vegetarian I would struggle. At least French Guiana should have cheese and red wine, and if I had to survive on that then I couldn't be too sad.

Our taxi driver picked us up from the quayside at the back of the immigration office, helping carry our heavy bikes into the narrow wooden boat. Paddy and I huddled together under the canvas roof – it was bucketing down and the crossing was choppy, but within ten minutes the engine shuddered to a halt and the driver beckoned us forward. We stepped into the light and looked at each other in surprise as our eyes settled on a bright blue sign with a circle of yellow stars.

"Welcome to the European Union," it exclaimed.

Somehow during the ten minute boat ride, we had journeyed from South America into Europe. The Guianas were about to get even more fascinating.

17. French Guiana

It was appallingly hot, for they had shut the port-holes. Through the glass you could see the bush. So we were in the Maroni. The water was muddy. Untouched virgin forest, green and impressive. Disturbed by the ship's sirens, birds rose and flew across the sky. We went very slowly, and that allowed us to pay close attention to the thick, dark-green, overflowing vegetation.

We saw the first wooden houses, with the corrugated iron roofs. Black men and women stood at their doors, watching the ship go by. They were quite used to seeing it unload its human cargo, and so they never bothered to wave as it passed. Three blasts on the siren and the churning of the propeller told us that we were there, and then the engines stopped entirely. Not a sound: you could have heard the buzzing of a fly. (Papillon, Henri Charrière)

The Saint Laurent du Moroni of 1933, where Papillon disembarked to begin a life sentence for murder, was not that dissimilar to where the water taxi dropped us. The vegetation was thick and green still, but now groomed where it encroached onto roads or pathways. Tropical birds continued to fly overhead and the population remained predominantly French Creole. Even now it wasn't a noisy, bustling place, but the persistent rain may have had something to do with that.

France was our 13th country of the trip, or at least its overseas department, French Guiana, was. One sixth the size of *L'Hexagone*, it was a territory of thick, impenetrable forest and rivers; *l'enfer vert*, the green hell, as the earliest settlers used to call it. The French had tried to build a colony in the area as early as 1613, but wave after wave of settlers succumbed to disease, until there was success and African slaves began work on the land. Hot, humid, plagued with mosquitos and disease, it was a harsh place to live, perhaps why enemies of the French Revolution were banished there. It was later, however, that the department became an official penitentiary colony, when in 1850, with France's prisons overflowing with opponents of Louis-Napoléon, an order was signed to send prisoners to French Guiana.

Saint Laurent du Moroni was the first place that convicts arrived, marched into the *Camp de Transportation*. It, like many of the buildings in the town, was built from bricks made by the convicts, one of the menial jobs to which they were put to work. Between 1858 and 1946, over 67,000 prisoners passed through the camp's gates, serving sentences for violent and other serious crimes. Many would never see home again.

On our day off in Saint Laurent du Moroni, we wandered around the camp, gazing in amazement at the concrete barrack blocks into which 3,000 convicts were crammed at a time. There were tiny individual cells with iron bolts to which the convicts were locked at night, and the old tribunal room, where convicts who committed further crimes or made attempts at escape were sentenced to months or even years of solitary confinement. At the end of the central, sandy courtyard, past the rickety football posts, was the place where the camp's guillotine had once sat. Last used in 1942, the method of execution was quintessentially French. Now, the camp's baby pink walls had faded and the paint was peeling, mould grew freely and vegetation sprung off the rooftops, from where the corrugated iron had long since disappeared. It was a sullen place, but in its heyday, packed with convicts in striped uniforms and straw hats, it must have been an even more depressing sight.

Today it was a tourist attraction, one of the few reasons why sightseers might come to the department. Most visitors, like our Couchsurfing hosts Vanessa and Bruno, were from mainland France and were there for work. They were both teachers at the local lycée and told us because wages were higher than at home, many young teachers came to French Guiana to make money and live somewhere different for a few years.

The relationship with the department was complicated. Local teachers didn't receive the same wages, which caused animosity between staff. There was a need for teachers from France though, as there were so many children in French Guiana. Vanessa explained the same benefits were on offer in Saint Laurent du Moroni as in Toulouse, for example. For every child, parents received a monthly payment from the state, which encouraged people to have large families. She said most parents spent the money on expensive goods like televisions, which explained the nice cars parked outside worn out shacks on our way to Vanessa's house.

She lived in a one-storey concrete block, off the road heading out of town and surrounded by thick jungle. There was a damp feel to the house, the heavy, moist air having permeated into everything. The nicest place was the veranda, where we sat enjoying cheese and red wine from the mammoth Carrefour supermarket in town. It wasn't the French way to pig out on cheese before dinner and Bruno looked confused by our eating habits, even when we explained that it had been months since we had enjoyed luxuries like these and we were too excited to wait.

We had used our credit card to pay for the treats, but when we tried to withdraw some Euros from an ATM, we found it no longer worked. A call to the bank revealed they had been flagged as fraudulent payments because the system thought we were in mainland France, rather than South America as we had informed them. It took a while to convince them there was a French department on the continent, but at last they conceded and we could continue shopping.

The Carrefour was amazing; it was as if the supermarket had been picked up from the outskirts of Paris and dropped into the South American jungle. The shelves were stocked with warm baguettes, *croissants*, ripe cheeses, meaty casseroles, fresh vegetables and rows of red wines. Nearly everything on sale had been imported from France, hence expensive Euro price tags.

Paddy's panniers were stuffed with *pain au chocolat* which fuelled him as we headed towards the coastal resort of Plage les Hattes. We bought cold bottles of Orangina from the *8* à *huit* convenience store in the village of Awala-Yalimapo, a few kilometres before the beach, and Paddy munched away happily on a hot *croque-monsieur* that oozed melted cheese.

Plage les Hattes was a windy section of coastline close to the border with Suriname. There was little to see here during the day, and we spent the afternoon swinging in our hammocks outside the deserted youth hostel. The reason we had made the journey was to meet the giant night time visitors who had patrolled these shores for thousands of years.

The giant leatherback turtle is the largest living turtle in the world. They hatch on beaches, before scurrying down to the water where they remain for the rest of their lives. Only females return to the land to lay their eggs, normally on the beach where they hatched, which is what we were there to see.

> ***Diary, 14 April 2012*** *- We found a turtle almost straight away. We were both a bit shocked as it was huge, about two metres long and very wide. She looked prehistoric, with a tear-drop shaped body that was black with white patches – almost like a huge mussel shell. She'd just started to dig her hole and we sat and watched for a couple of hours as she laid her eggs and covered them back up.*
>
> *There were hundreds of eggs. They were white gloopy things, a bit bigger than a golf ball. I think they lay so many, because the chances every one hatches is slim, and because not all baby turtles survive. She looked exhausted by the end. It was an amazing thing to witness, a real feat of nature. It's incredible to think the same thing has been happening on these beaches for thousands of years.*

It took two days to ride from the beach to the town of Kourou. We spent most of the time cycling through thick rainforest, with little to see aside from a wall of green on either side of the road. Palm trees poked out above the treeline and every now and then the forest would clear to reveal swampy pools and wide rivers. There were only a few villages along the route, all with 8 à huit stores.

Kourou itself held little attraction. It was a haphazard town on a flat plain, but we stopped to explore as it was the home of French Guiana's top tourist attractions. The first on our list was the Centre Spatial Guyanais (CSG), the French and European spaceport, from where over half of the world's commercial satellites are launched. It was built in French Guiana as, being near the equator, satellites have a shorter distance to cover into space and are propelled by the spin of the Earth. Operational since 1968, it employs many people in Kourou, including our Couchsurfing host's housemate.

Like Vanessa in Saint Laurent, Vincent was a teacher, but his housemate was a tour guide at the space centre. It was clear this guy wasn't pleased about us sleeping in the lounge; he put in an extra stint of television-watching to delay us getting to bed and we could hear him complaining to his girlfriend about us. Feeling a little uncomfortable, we told Vincent we would look for somewhere else, but he was insistent we stay. The guy's behaviour had irritated him and the other housemates, who went out of their way to make us feel welcome.

All young French mainlanders, they were working in French Guiana in various occupations. They told us few employees at the spaceport were local; aside from some cleaners, it was mainly staffed by Europeans. We took a tour of the centre, fortunately with a friendly French woman rather than the grumpy housemate. The visit started with a bus trip around the complex where we saw the railways which transport the huge rocket launchers and the buildings that store them. Everything was on a gigantic scale, towering high above the surrounding jungle.

Back at Vincent's, we asked him to clarify a few of the things we'd heard on the tour. The guide spoke in French, and having studied it to A-level standard, I could follow most of what she was saying, but not everything. My biggest problem with the language, however, was that I had completely lost the ability to speak it – everything came out in Spanish. Now I spoke two languages badly.

The next morning we were up early to catch a catamaran across to the Îles du Salut, the Salvation Islands. There was little hope of escape for the convicts who arrived on the three small islands when French Guiana was a penal colony. The smallest, Diable, was once a leper colony and used to imprison political prisoners, including Captain Alfred Dreyfus. However, it was to Royale and St Joseph that most prisoners were sent.

The catamaran dropped us first at Royale. The captain was a friendly, chain-smoking Frenchman who found it amusing that I developed horrible sea sickness on the flat crossing. He helped me off the catamaran, pointing towards the main square, promising that I would soon feel better. Royale was the largest of the three islands and where the administrative buildings were, including housing for the prison wardens and their families. There was a hospital, church and an old red iron lighthouse. Many of the buildings had been repaired, but lots lay in ruins, green with moss and slowly being covered by thick bushes. The tidy central square was lush green with tall palm trees shading the grass, where *agouti* – large, gerbil-like, red-haired rodents – foraged for food.

The old barracks where the prisoners had slept had not been repaired. They looked cold and cramped, especially the single cells which were only just big enough for somebody of Paddy's height to lie down in. However, with the sun glistening off the Atlantic Ocean, the island seemed beautiful as we took in the views by the man-made pool.

The book *Papillon* by Henri Charrière was a huge success when it was released in 1969. In it Charrière talks about escaping from the islands, but it is unsure how much of his story was true, as it was extremely difficult to escape from Royale. The island had steep sides and was surrounded by choppy, shark-infested water. The sharks ate dead prisoners thrown into the ocean, and it was said they recognised the sound of the bell being rung before the bodies were thrown overboard, and would come rushing for free food.

In the afternoon, we visited Île Saint-Joseph, a smaller island where prisoners were kept in solitary confinement, made to live in silence and sometimes even darkness. The crumbling camp was high in the centre of the island, deep in the jungle, and had been cordoned off, but we climbed through the wooden fence to get a proper look. The walls, with their rusted iron window grates, were being taken over by the jungle. Some buildings had collapsed completely, while others grew trees out of their walls and floors. Rats hurried about, scuttling between fallen coconuts, some of which were sprouting into new trees themselves. The whole place look like it had been abandoned in a hurry, as if somebody was ashamed it ever existed.

The catamaran took longer on the way back, as we dodged a black raincloud hovering over the mainland, but we got soaked anyway, something that was becoming a regular occurrence in French

Guiana. We left Vincent's the next morning, our damp clothes stuffed into the top of the panniers. Vincent was a great host, but meeting new people was only one reason for Couchsurfing in French Guiana, the other was that accommodation was insanely expensive. One night, having found nowhere to camp, we ended up paying 45 Euros for a tiny room in a restaurant's garage, which was horrendously overpriced.

Jean's Couchsurfing profile said his house in Cayenne was not a hotel, but I wasn't so sure. He too was a teacher, but older than the other hosts we had met so far. When we arrived, he showed us into our own room – a real treat – and didn't seem at all insulted that the first thing I did was pass out in bed. I woke to find him and Paddy watching Chelsea versus Barcelona in the Champions League, with dinner cooking in the oven. It was a delicious cheese and potato dish, washed down with red wine and finished with local rum. Jean insisted that he wasn't very good at cooking for vegetarians, but I wasn't sure about that either.

In the morning he organised a walk with his friend Paula, among the mangrove swamps that sat behind the beach to the east of Cayenne. The mangroves were ever changing because of the drifting of the sand, and we followed the boardwalk through the spindly, winding roots that rose creepily out of the ground, until we returned to the wide white sand beach. From a distance, I thought it was a piece of driftwood that the dog was sniffing, but as we walked closer I realised it was in fact another giant leatherback turtle. I assumed it must be dead, as they normally nest during the night, but she was alive and hard at work. The deep tracks, where she had hauled herself to the top of the beach, were still visible, and in the daylight it was clear to see the monumental effort she was making to lay her eggs; amazing.

The wildlife here was certainly wild. One afternoon, while we were on Skype to Paddy's sister, I let out a scream that made her jump. Jean's fluffy white cat, that spent most of its time lazing in the sun, had flushed out a huge lizard from underneath a bookshelf, sending it scuttling towards my feet. Another day, we stopped for drinks in a café in the centre of Cayenne and decided to try the local cocktail, *Ti'Punch*, a mix of lime, sugarcane syrup and rum. Only, Paddy's sugarcane syrup arrived crawling with ants that were glugging greedily on the sweet nectar.

Paddy went inside to do our final shop in Carrefour, while I waited with the bikes, returning with so much food it only just fitted into our panniers. We were heading towards the border with Brazil; a 188 kilometre stretch we thought should take two days to ride, until that was we saw the hills.

***Paddy**: One night we stopped at a tiny auberge built in a clearing by a muddy river. The wooden hammock shelter was two metres off the ground to protect against animals and, from the looks of it, the frequently-flooded river. Inside the main building, a small restaurant served French cuisine that was out of place in the South American jungle, but perfectly in keeping with France's obsession with food.*

We had the place to ourselves. It was one of the most peaceful nights of the trip, swinging in our hammocks with the noises of the jungle occasionally interrupting the sound of water lapping against the river bank. The next morning, we spent ten minutes weaving through swarms of bright yellow butterflies, which was amazing. We were so lucky to be experiencing the rainforest by bike.

I was panting up the climbs, they were so steep and the bike was heavy with food and water, but I didn't mind too much, the scenery was spectacular. Sometimes the vegetation was too thick to see inside the forest, but when it opened up we could see the complex order that the trees and bushes had developed so they got the sunlight and nutrients they needed.

We spent the night camping in a dusty red-dirt clearing behind the road. This section of highway had been tarmacked within the last few years, and some cleared areas hadn't yet grown back, although saplings were pushing up through the ground. We were completely out of view from the road, surrounded on three sides by thick, quiet forest. Disappointingly, we couldn't find suitable trees to hang our hammocks, so we were back in the tent. Making the most of being in the middle of nowhere, we stripped off for a wet wipe wash. There was something exhilarating about standing in the rainforest completely naked. Nobody could see us apart from parrots flying overhead or perhaps a jaguar hidden in the trees.

Next morning, we were wrapped up again. A heavy mist had

settled over the rainforest, hiding our tent in the process. We returned to the road for the final 40 kilometres into the border town of Saint Georges, where it took a while to find the police station to collect our exit stamps, and longer still to argue we needed them. The officers insisted that as we were from the European Union we didn't need to be stamped in and out of France, but we pointed out that as we had an entrance stamp, we needed an exit one too, in case Brazilian immigration made any objections.

Before finding a water taxi to take us across the Oyapok River to the Brazilian town of Oiapoque, we stopped for a final Orangina. As we sat enjoying the cold orange soda in a shady square, we couldn't quite believe that our time in the Guianas was coming to an end. They had been fascinating, with incredible scenery from the flat savannah of Guyana to thick, swampy rainforest in French Guiana.

It was surprising how many similarities there were between the territories and their old colonial powers; I will never get over the surprise of seeing South Americans enthusiastically playing cricket. The food – varied and familiar – was my highlight of the Guianas. How I wished we could always enjoy Cadburys chocolate, baked beans, curry, red wine, smelly cheese and Orangina. The languages, the people, the histories of the places and the cultures, they were all so thoroughly un-South American. Yet, nestled into the top of the continent, with towns cut out of the jungle, I couldn't think of anywhere else in the world where they might fit.

French Guiana's eastern neighbour was Brazil. They obviously had a few neighbourly issues, as we watched a line of illegal Brazilian immigrants waiting in handcuffs at the quayside, under the supervision of a team of police officers. Most of them had come to French Guiana for illegal mining, and like many others that month, were being deported.

We had to wait until they had been whisked away in a water taxi before we could get in one ourselves. Soon a bridge was set to open that would link Brazil and France by road, but for now we had to travel upstream in a small wooden boat. Bouncing along the river it was hard to believe we were heading back to Brazil, and the last country of our trip around South America.

18. Brazil: the Amazon

Diary, 23 April 2012 *- It feels emotional to be back in Brazil after making our final border crossing of the trip. It's mad to think that in less than a year, we've cycled through every country in South America. Lots and lots of memories, and still a long way to go to Rio.*

However, our return to Brazil was, almost, disastrous. The heavens opened as our wooden boat pulled up to the high quayside in Oiapoque and the boat lurched in the choppy water, as we struggled to pull the bikes up steep, slippery steps. At one point my bike slipped and was only saved from disappearing into the river by Paddy, who lunged to grab it.

In many ways Oiapoque was like any other Brazilian settlement, despite being the most northern coastal town in the country, in a region dominated by the Amazon Rainforest. Producing more than 20 per cent of the world's oxygen, the rainforest is known as the 'lungs of the world'. It stretches across nine South American countries, but 60 per cent sits within Brazil. With this statistic in mind we were slightly confused, riding out of town, that there seemed to be little sign of any trees.

Instead, the road meandered past low green hills dotted with sad-looking tree stumps and grazing cows. Each year huge swathes of the Amazon Rainforest are destroyed by logging and for livestock pasture. In recent years, government programmes have helped decrease deforestation, with emphasis placed on protecting land owned by indigenous communities. There are over 400 indigenous groups living in the Amazon Rainforest, and we were pleased that when we passed a sign declaring *Terra Indígena Uaçá*, the rainforest returned with abundance.

With the forest came short, heavy downpours of rain that had us rushing for our waterproofs. A heavy mist sat on top of the trees, where the cold rain pounded down on the jungle. Slippery frogs littered the road and monkeys in search of shelter ran across the tarmac. During one particularly heavy deluge we hid in a wooden structure – something between a tree house and a guard post. It was part of a small community of wooden huts that seemed to have been abandoned.

For lunch we ate leftover pasta and soya chilli. It was a treat, as the next week we would be living off noodles. Our bags were full to bursting with them and our bikes were weighed down with extra water, which slowed us on the hilly road. We anticipated this stretch of the BR-156, to the town of Calçoene, would take several days, as most of it was not tarmacked. Indeed, halfway along a straight stretch of road and faraway from any settlement, the tarmac ended in a neat line and the potholed, bumpy and muddy dirt track began.

The state of the road was worse than we feared and the terrain grew steeper as we headed south over west-east trending hills, creating the illusion of riding over massive ripio. Our greatest annoyance was that at the bottom of every hill there were fragile wooden bridges, which we were forced to cross at walking pace to ensure we didn't slide off. It meant we couldn't gather any speed on the downhill to take into the next climb, which slowed our overall pace significantly.

Halfway up yet another long climb, we were stopped by a white man in a compact campervan. He was French, and was heading home to French Guiana after a two-year trip around South America. I asked if he was sad his adventure was coming to an end, but he said he was looking forward to getting home. It was encouraging to hear, as in spite of having a long way to go to Ipanema Beach, thoughts of the trip coming to an end had started to float around my mind. I was still enjoying life on the road and I didn't want it to finish but perhaps, like him, by the end I might feel differently.

The ochre-red road contrasted starkly with the deep greens of the thick rainforest. There were a few clearings where cattle grazed and small communities had built wooden homes, but we spent endless hours riding through deep forest. My time was spent watching for potholes and snakes, and scanning the vegetation for the rustle of a jaguar.

Our breaks were regular, often dictated by the need to remove or replace waterproofs. During one stop I forgot to put my gloves on when we moved off, realising ten minutes later when my sweaty hands starting rubbing on the handlebars. I could find only one glove in my handlebar bag; I must have dropped the other when we stopped, which was a real annoyance as we had just ridden down a huge, slippery hill. Over this kind of terrain the gloves were essential for impacting my hands, so we couldn't just forget about it. Gallantly, Paddy offered to go back, and he was halfway up the climb when a passing motorbike pulled sharply on the brakes and made a U-turn back to me.

From the way he was waving his hand wildly at me, my first thought was that the driver wanted to cause trouble, but then I realised he was wearing my glove. He had spotted it in the mud and picked it up for driving but when he saw us, he put two and two together. Kindly, he handed it back without fuss, before zooming off into the distance. It was a relief to have it back, and I was grateful for the honesty of the driver. It made me think back to Paraguay and whoever found our bag; I was still disappointed they hadn't handed it back.

Mid-afternoon, we passed the small village of Estrella, but pushed on as it was early. Throughout the day we had seen several roadside clearings suitable for camping, and we expected to find more. Only typically, they disappeared after Estrella and it was six pm by the time we finally found a place that would do the job. Pushing the bikes through high grass and muddy puddles, we settled in the clearing high above the road, hoping it wouldn't get waterlogged if, or more likely when, it rained.

As we expected, the heavens opened during the night and there was little let up throughout the next day. In the afternoon, the hills became ridiculously steep, and at times, we resorted to pushing up them. Some parts of the road were thick mud, which coated our bikes and caused the well-worn chains to repeatedly slip off. We gave up for the day at 4.30 pm, fed up with the slow and muddy progress. Camp for the night was in a gravel pit just off the road. It wasn't particularly well hidden, but we were too knackered to care by that point. I spent the evening lying on my front, trying to soothe my screaming behind that had developed a painful saddle rash in the damp conditions. It was an uncomfortable position as my Thermarest mattress had developed an alien air bubble I had to arch myself over. After almost a year on the road, it seemed our bodies and kit were beginning to wear.

I was also having problems with the cleats in my shoes, which stuck in my pedals if they got mud in them. I'd had a few close calls when struggling uphill on slippery slopes, only just managing to release my sandals before I came to a stop. It was only a matter of time until I got completely stuck.

> ***Paddy:*** *The road was in particularly bad shape that morning, rutted from the rain and heavy vehicles that used this section of the route. As I started another climb, weaving between puddles, I could see Laura ahead starting to slow down. Her shoulders were twisting to keep her balance, and her legs were pushing hard on the pedals to keep forward momentum.*
>
> *I could tell from her body language she wasn't going to make it to the top – she was sliding about in the mud and she never likes that, preferring to walk. But she was having trouble unclipping her feet from the pedals, she was squirming a lot and making hysterical squeals. Then, almost in slow motion, she fell sideways into a big puddle.*
>
> *When I reached her, she was still clipped into the pedals, unable to move. By the look I received, perhaps my first words to her weren't the best:*
>
> *"Damn, I wish I'd had the camera out!"*

In the afternoon we enjoyed short bursts of flat tarmac, but the road was mainly dirt as we turned east across savannah where the forest had been cleared. There was little else other than fields of grazing cattle until we reached Calçoene, a fishing town on the edge of a river where teenagers swam over a ferocious set of rapids. Observing them from the riverbank, we feasted on hot chips from a man who sliced and fried potatoes behind a wooden stall in the central square. Slurping from cold bottles of beer, we felt pretty pleased with ourselves for having made it.

Calçoene had the dubious title of being the wettest town in Brazil, and it lived up to its reputation, the rain continuing throughout our stay and for most of the 350 kilometres to Macapá. It was a flat, quiet stretch of road that saw us pass through the 17,000 kilometre point for the trip and fight off swarms of dragonflies. The most notable event was Paddy being propositioned by teenage boys on motorbikes who offered him a blow job. In shock, he exploded with a string of expletives that sent the guys running. Over the next few days we covered ground quickly, until finally, we were rewarded with one of the best views of the trip; our first glimpse of the Amazon River.

The sky was clear blue, but even under the sun the river flowed the colour of tea. At over 6,400 kilometres long, the Amazon is the second longest river in the world, starting at a glacial stream, 160 kilometres west of Lago Titicaca in Peru. The route we had ridden meant at some point we would have unknowingly crossed the tributary; traversing the river close to the Atlantic Ocean was going to be a bigger feat.

There were two ways to cross to the city of Belém; we could either fly or take a boat. Given the impracticalities and cost of flying, we opted to take to the water for a closer view of the river. Unfortunately, we had arrived in Macapá at the start of a public holiday and the city was closed, apart from the riverside stalls selling barbequed meat and cold beers. There was little option but to join the thronging crowds for an impromptu holiday.

Our break started off badly, as we hunted for something to eat. Vegetarian choices were limited, and Paddy was gentlemanly insisting he would wait until I was sorted. The problem was he gets grumpy when hungry, and the longer the search continued, the hungrier he got. We walked along the riverside not talking. We had only fallen out a handful of times on the trip – normally over something insignificant, like now – and were quick to resolve the issue. This time, the problem was solved by the discovery of a pizzeria selling strong *caipirinhas*.

The Amazon's riverfront provided a wonderful setting for sipping cocktails. The quayside was high above the exposed riverbed, where young boys played football and men flew huge kites. The riverside was dominated by the impressive Fortaleza de Säo José, a fort built in the late 1700s to defend the north side of the Amazon from potential French invaders. Today it was a popular tourist haunt for families and young couples, who enjoyed the fresh breeze blowing off the river.

The next day at lunch we watched a family set up plastic chairs, tables and a blazing BBQ. The father was in charge of the food, but he kept returning to our bar, where he had been for several hours by the looks of things. He hadn't paid us any attention, but when we attempted to leave, he refused to let us go, ordering more beers and playing the Beatles on the jukebox, singing along in a slurred accent. We couldn't escape.

After several more hours, by which point it was growing dark outside, we finally made our excuses successfully, but he had one more thing to show us. It turned out he owned a religious souvenir shop, where he picked out T-shirts and music he insisted we take away. I was given a purple '*I love Jesus*' T-shirt that had Paddy in fits of laughter, knowing how unlikely a statement that was for me.

On Tuesday, the hung-over city reopened for business and we purchased two tickets for a boat the next day. They cost £75 each, but we got an air-conditioned cabin for that. The cheaper option was to hang a hammock on the lower deck, but the extra charge for the bikes made the deluxe option only a few pounds more expensive in the end. We set off early to cover the 25 kilometres to the port of Santana, and in our hurry to make the boat, we missed the monument marking the point where our route traversed the equator. We were back in the southern hemisphere.

> ***Diary, 3-4 May 2012** - Boat day! We're on the Almirante do Mar. I'm really glad we have the suite. The lower hammock deck is crammed with people and luggage, there's no privacy and we could smell the communal toilet when we boarded. We'd have been stressed out about our bags all the time if we had to leave them there. As it is, we have a tiny wooden cabin on the middle deck with air con and our own bathroom, which is great. Food is available on the top deck; it isn't included, but we have enough so it's not a problem.*
>
> *We've spent a lot of time in the cabin actually, as there isn't lots of space to sit outside and it's been raining. It's hard to get my head around the fact we're going across a river rather than along it. It just goes on and on. We're cutting through the delta at the moment, so the channel's not very wide – although probably a normal river's width!*
>
> *There's lots of lush, low forest on each side, and every now and then a cluster of wooden huts appear. We keep seeing tiny*

children rowing wooden boats on their own. It's such a special sight to see how people live here in the middle of nowhere, and this bit is served by the ferry, so it's not even that remote in the scheme of things. It's dark now and there's nothing to see, although lightning did light up the sky quite dramatically earlier.

I slept well, but even when I woke up there was a lot of time left on the boat. It seems terrible to say, but it was a bit boring after a while. I couldn't travel as a backpacker anymore. I find little pleasure in sitting still watching the world pass by; my feet were itching to get going.

After 30 hours, the boat suddenly turned a bend in the river and this huge city with shiny glass skyscrapers appeared, climbing out of the forest – it was an awesome sight. We docked alongside another boat rather than the pier, so it was quite stressful getting the bags and bikes off as we had to carry them through the other boat. We couldn't carry everything in one go, so I stood with the bags, while Paddy went back for the bikes. The flow of people disembarking was so much that he had to climb over the roof of the other boat to get back to ours. Health and safety back home would have had a fit. But we made it intact – we crossed the Amazon!

We celebrated reaching Belém with beers by the old docks. Our accommodation was with a Couchsurfing host called Lysmar. He had kindly agreed to squeeze us into his small flat, which we promptly covered with laundry, washed in a machine for the first time in ages. We were taking a few days off to explore Belém, a city that grew during Brazil's rubber boom of the late 1800s, when the substance was extracted from local rubber trees.

Rubber and other materials would have passed through the riverside *Ver-o-Peso* market, built during colonial times. It was here that goods produced within the area were brought for weighing, to determine how much tax should be paid to the Portuguese crown. Now it was a thriving food, curio and witchcraft market, where stall holders sold concoctions including *Viagra Natural* in glass bottles.

We stuck with bottled beer instead, as we toured Lysmar's favourite drinking spots. In the converted dock down by the river, Paddy bought strong *caipirinhas* that got us so drunk we even joined in the dancing. The moves were a mix of traditional and modern pop, which looked fantastic when the Brazilians swayed their hips to the music, but less so when I attempted it, much to the amusement of the crowd.

On our final day in Belém, Lysmar took us back to the converted docks to work our way through a bar's beer menu. I was too slow for the waiter, who was constantly whisking away my glass before it was finished. When I insisted that I was fine drinking it slightly warmer, Lysmar and the waiter both looked at me in horror. Laughing, we explained that if a waiter tried to take somebody's unfinished beer at home, they would be clubbed for their efforts.

We said goodbye to Lysmar the next morning. He had been another brilliant host, in spite of the horrific hangovers he helped cause. We left his flat with a hand-drawn map of Belém and directions out of the city along raised cycle lanes that kept us away from the busy traffic. Our route was now taking us south-east, away from the Amazon and towards Brazil's harsh and hot interior. To make it back to Rio de Janeiro in time to meet our deadline we were taking a detour inland, rather than hugging the windy coastline. We were facing barren savannahs, soaring temperatures and long distances between towns, before we arrived at the coastal city of Salvador. It was time to say goodbye to the Amazon, a beautiful part of Brazil I was so glad we had visited.

19. Brazil: the interior

The bike lanes were a short-lived treat. Ten kilometres outside of Belém, we were spat out onto a busy, potholed road, where we competed with speeding buses for space. There had been a hike in temperature now that we were south of the Amazon, away from the rainforest and into the savannah, and by afternoon we had become attuned to finding the slightest bit of shade for a few minutes rest.

By the time we arrived in the agricultural town of Castanhal we were exhausted, and checked into a hotel and passed out. I woke several hours later with a banging headache – the result of too much heat and not enough water. It was an important lesson not be complacent about the sun. Going forward, we tried to stop regularly to take on cold fluids, and I wore a long sleeve cotton shirt to cover my skin.

Earlier, when we'd arrived in Castanhal, we were stopped by a friendly local who we met for dinner. Clayton ran a successful wholefood company, and in perfect English, he talked passionately about Brazil, including how he was depressed by the amount of corruption in the country. A longstanding problem in Brazilian politics and business, a 2010 study estimated the annual cost of corruption in the country at between 1.38 and 2.3 per cent of its GDP. That kind of money could have housed 2.9 million Brazilian families. The worst part, Clayton explained, was the politicians always seemed to get away with it.

The money could have helped repair some of roads in the area, which after Castanhal deteriorated significantly. There was heavy traffic and no hard shoulder, leaving us squashed against overgrown hedgerows while cars whooshed past. Bus drivers were the worst, weaving manically around anything slower than them, as if playing a computer game.

On one long hill, I got blown off the road twice as they whizzed past me with just centimetres to spare. It was only the middle of the afternoon but I was already fed up, and therefore, easily swayed by an ice-cream stall that beckoned me over with its list of tropical flavours. It turned out that the neighbouring stall, where a woman was clearing up the remains of lunch, was showing the Champions League Final on a small, fuzzy television. We bought cold sodas from her and, in the middle of a Brazilian market, sat down at a rickety wooden table to watch Chelsea unexpectedly beat Bayern Munich to become champions of Europe.

On the road the heat and crazy driving continued, added to which the terrain had grown hilly, rising and dipping incessantly. The distances between villages grew longer, removing the possibility of regular stops for cold drinks and, riding past endless fields of grass, there was little shade under which we could rest. We were completely exposed to the scorching sun.

It was lunchtime, there had been nothing along the road all day, and I was showing classic signs of heat exhaustion. I felt dizzy, my entire body was shaking and my thought process was unclear; I didn't want to continue, but I didn't want to stop either, I was incapable of making any coherent decision. We had pushed on for the last few hours in the hope that we must find a roadside stall soon, but nothing had appeared and I had grown increasingly dehydrated.

In the end, it was Paddy who made the decision that we should rest, and he ordered me to stop on the hard shoulder. There was nowhere to pull in from the road, but we were past caring. So, as traffic zoomed past, Paddy stood the two bikes up on their stands and threw the tarpaulin over the handlebars to create a crude shelter under which I could crawl. The shadow cast onto the tarmac was wide enough to shade the top half of my body – my legs still poked out the side, but it was blissful under there. While I lay recovering, Paddy brewed up a batch of noodles and stood guard as traffic barrelled downhill towards us until, after an hour, I felt well enough to continue.

A few hours later, we found a roadside settlement where we could at last buy a cold drink. Glugging thirstily, we slowly realised that a group of young children across the café were staring at us. This wasn't altogether unfamiliar, but it turned out they were working on their English homework and couldn't believe two strangers had walked in talking that very language. We invited them to bring over their text books so we could help fill in the answers – their teacher was in for a shock the next day at how much they had improved, but their English was already far better than our Portuguese.

Our terrible grasp of Portuguese was exposed again a few days later. The recent climbing had taken a heavy toll on our bums, and we had a bizarre conversation in a pharmacy trying to find a tub of petroleum jelly. Having failed to explain in Portuguese what we wanted, we tried hand signals, which involved lots of bum slapping. The bemused chemists offered us lubricant, followed by haemorrhoid cream before somebody who spoke English came to our rescue.

In our defence, we listened to language tapes daily, but our spoken Portuguese was very slow to improve. Our listening skills weren't much better either:

> ***Diary, 24 May 2012*** - *We stopped for a drink about halfway along today. It also happened to be our 18,000 kilometre point – we've come a long way! We got our photo taken by a woman in the shop we stopped in. She was lovely – quite short with beautiful brown skin, and she was super friendly, but we couldn't understand a word she was saying.*
>
> *She kept pointing at Paddy, and I was very confused as the only words I could make out were "Saddam Hussein". I thought I must have it wrong, but she kept doing this strange hand movement that could either have been 'beard' or 'decapitation'. Was she saying that Paddy looked like Saddam Hussein? Then she was definitely saying "Bin Laden" and "Osama". I was very confused.*

We took some consolation that in Belém, Lysmar had told us spoken Portuguese varied hugely around the country in terms of accent and variations of words. He also said Brazilians travelling to Portugal often communicated in English, because the language there was so different.

A few days later we found ourselves dodging traffic on the approach to Teresina, where we would be staying with our Couchsurfing host Luiz. Teresina was a great place for a break because, as Luiz said, there was nothing to see or do there. A hub for manufacturing, the city was reportedly the hottest in the country, and as a result nobody ventured outside during the day unless they had to. Instead, the streets came to life in the evening, where we joined the crowds crammed into outdoor bars and strolling along the riverfront.

It was hard to force ourselves back into the saddle after a few days off, but at least Paddy had identified a minor road we could leave by, thereby avoiding heavy traffic. The tarmac was beautifully smooth, plus it was practically deserted. We rode past scenic fields dotted with palm trees and cacti, while standing back from the road were *tepui* – tiny compared to those in Venezuela, but magnificent all the same. The area was like a small-scale *Gran Sabana*, but at 37 degrees Celsius, much hotter.

The locals were friendly and intrigued by us, flagging us down to ask questions about the trip. On one long hill we got overtaken by a pickup, only just moving faster than us. In the back was a class of school kids who waved and cheered hysterically at us, hanging over the sides to take photos on their phones. They made me laugh so much that I climbed even slower than normal.

Between towns and villages there was very little, and we often had the road to ourselves as we cycled along wide valleys covered in low trees and bordered by flat, ridged hills. It was a landscape of red earth, bushes in shades of green and brown, and a big blue sky. On one break, I looked over at Paddy who looked completely lost in thought, and I asked what he was thinking. "Nothing," he replied, "I'm just happy."

> ***Paddy**: I didn't really know how to answer Laura's question. It was extremely hot, our water had gone warm, and for the umpteenth time we were eating boring noodles for lunch by the side of the road. On paper, we shouldn't have been enjoying ourselves, but actually I was.*
>
> *The daily monotony of life in London was a long way away and I felt a sense of freedom. It was hard to know exactly what felt so good – perhaps it was the quietness of the road, the scenery or the playlist on my iPod. I felt lucky to be outdoors, lapping up new sights and sounds without any concerns in the world, and I loved the lack of restrictions travelling by bike allowed.*

We had cottoned on to the local trick of swapping large, empty soda bottles for ones full of ice whenever we stopped –

restaurant owners were more than happy to oblige. We would strap the bottles to our bikes, and the ice would slowly melt, keeping the water chilled long enough to get to the next stall. Sometimes, however, the distances were just too far.

One day, when our thermometer climbed to over 40 degrees, we found ourselves cycling through the middle of nowhere. The long road twisted through low, sandy bush-land, where the vegetation was tall enough to block our view of the horizon, but provided no shade. As the hours ticked on, our ice water melted, heated and diminished as we glugged thirstily at it. We pinned our hopes on finding something next to the radio mast we could see in the distance, so it was a crushing disappointment when we arrived two hours later and found just the mast.

Paddy, in particular, was suffering. He wasn't wearing his sun hat or shirt, leaving him exposed to the sun's rays, and by the time we finally found a busy roadside café after lunchtime, he was in a bad state, shaking and completely dazed. When the café owner came to take our order, Paddy couldn't understand him properly and shouted that he just wanted water. Fortunately, after some Coca-Cola and water, he gradually came around, but it was so unlike him to be rude, I was worried.

Our next stop off was in the town of Sao Raimundo Nonato, to explore the *Serra do Capivara* national park, home to cave paintings as old as 25,000 years. The people who drew them belonged to one of the oldest human communities in South America that lived in the area up to 50,000 years ago. We explored the steep cliffs, rock formations shaped by the wind, tall trees and gigantic cacti; and saw troops of monkeys, armadillos, and birds that hopped around the dry undergrowth. In the arid environment, the cave paintings were well-preserved, and we could clearly make out figures of people and animals that roamed the area thousands of years ago – a glimpse into life on the continent long before Europeans arrived.

From Sao Raimundo Nonato it was a long day of cycling along a rutted track to reach the lakeside town of Remanso, from where we hoped to find a boat across the gigantic Lago de Sobradinho. If that wasn't possible, we would have a huge detour around the edge of the lake on mainly unpaved roads. It would delay our arrival into Salvador significantly and jeopardise us arriving in Rio de Janeiro in time for our flight home, which was booked for 27 July, the day of the opening ceremony for the London 2012 Olympics.

The news from the port the next morning wasn't good. A group of fisherman packing up their nets, argued for a while whether a boat went from here to the town of Xique Xique or not, but they finally agreed that none did. Instead they suggested we go to the port of Passagem, 70 kilometres west, and see if there were any from there, but they didn't seem convinced. Faced with little other option, we prepared to leave for Passagem the next morning.

To combat the problem of carrying enough cold water, we bought a watermelon that I cut into quarters and tied to my bike straight from the freezer. Over the course of the day it kept us hydrated, but it also made me stop regularly for a pee; not the best thing when riding along a stretch of sandy road under repair by teams of workmen. On a particularly busy stretch of the road, I found a mound of sand behind which I could hide from view. I balanced successfully, but when I stood up the sand gave way and a stream of pee ran through my open-toe sandals. I returned to the bike cursing and trying to shake the wet, sandy mess out of my shoe, to Paddy's great amusement.

Soon after my toilet break we were back on tarmac and covered 70 kilometres by lunch, which we ate in the shady central square in the small town of Pilão Arcado. Nobody there had much idea about boats to Xique Xique either; it was starting to feel like we were on a wild goose chase, but with no other option, we set off to cover the extra 11 kilometres to the port. On the lonely stretch of tarmac we were stopped by an inquisitive motorcyclist who, when we arrived in Passagem, we found busily enquiring on our behalf about a boat. He had discovered one would leave the next morning to Piedras, a village 30 kilometres away from Xique Xique on the south of the lake. The place didn't appear on our map, but the locals seemed confident that a dirt road linked the two.

Passagem was chaotic. The quayside was a sandy slope leading down to shallow water surrounded by marshy grass. Wooden boats bobbed around, occasionally knocking each other. Black pigs with tiny piglets in tow rummaged through rubbish, and dogs trotted along the street scavenging for scraps discarded by fishermen. At the back of the sandy shore stood a tall ice factory where workers heaved heavy crates back and forth between the boats. People were busy but welcomed us, although nobody seemed to have a clue about which boats were coming and going.

There was nowhere to stay in Passagem, so we doubled back on ourselves to Piläo Arcado, getting up early to return to the port by eight am. However, when we arrived the news was that nothing would leave all day, and after sitting around for a few hours, we started to believe it. Disappointed, we headed back to our *pousada* in Piläo Arcado, in the process riding through the 19,000 kilometre mark, which we marked with beers in the sunny square.

We set off the next morning to catch an 11 am departure to Piedras, which our motorcyclist friend had arranged for us to travel on. Of course, when we turned up at nine that boat had already gone, but we found another literally just leaving. It was heading somewhere we had never heard of, but there was no time for discussion, the captain was already heaving our bikes through the dirty water.

> ***Diary, 9 June 2012*** *- The boat was banana-shaped – it curved higher at each end where there were small cabins, one where the captain steered from, and another the crew slept in. We were in the middle which was empty apart from the big freezer we sat on. The boat was about three metres wide, with v-shaped sides, and the floor was levelled out with planks.*
>
> *There were four crew members who were busy cleaning and three other passengers who were hitching a lift westwards. We came out of the large lake quickly and started travelling up the narrower Rio Säo Francisco. The other passengers got out along the river, in the middle of nowhere. All we could see were sand dunes and marshes. I have no idea where they were heading.*
>
> *For the first half of the journey, I tried to avoid watching one of the guys butchering the more unattractive parts of a cow. He was busy cleaning intestines and stomachs, and chopping the tongue and other bits from the four heads he had. At one point he put his knife down in a safe place, in the nose of a cow!*

The floor of the boat was covered in blood, and after each butchering they would scrub the parts clean and put them in the freezer. Any bits they didn't keep went overboard. The guy would grab the ears of the heads, empty of brain and tongue, and chuck them over the side. Rather an undignified end to the poor cows' lives, but I suppose the fish got a good feed. We couldn't work out what their cargo was. I wondered if they had carried the cows across alive, but I don't know.

It was dark by the time they dropped us off in a tiny village called Marracada – or something like that. They weren't stopping here themselves, but this was the only place on the north side of the river that they could leave us. We were on the boat for seven hours in total. It was a bit boring after a while and a little uncomfortable, but not too bad. The scenery was nice and the boat had good shade from the sun.

While we unloaded the bikes with the help of the crew, the captain went off to find somebody to drive us to Xique Xique, about 30 kilometres away. He was really nice; it was late, he must have been exhausted, and he wouldn't take money from us. In the end there was no car, but a guy invited us to stay in his house, which was a relief as the other option was camping on the uneven shore which was full of rubbish and pigs. I think Dinori could tell by my face that I didn't fancy that!

Dinori was 38 years old. He lived with his wife, Jaihon, and two of their three sons, the oldest of whom was 20. They were fishermen, but the older son was at college, a fact of which Dinori was very proud. Their house was a one-storey, two-bedroom, mud-brick structure, with a tidy lounge and dining room, plus a tiny kitchen on the back. It was simple, but they had mod-cons like a television, that blared out the popular Brazilian *telenova* soaps.

The villagers were all of indigenous appearance, apart from one blonde-haired little boy who kept running in and out of the lounge to stare at us, disbelieving he wasn't all that special anymore. In fact, we drew so much attention, with villagers crowding around the bare windows and doors of the house to get a peek that Dinori sent us on a walk with his sons so that people would leave. It was a small village, with about 100 houses and many welcoming people who all seemed to have heard about the visiting strangers. We went to bed about nine pm, the family insisting we take one of the bedrooms, while they crowded into the other together.

A loud cockerel woke us early and we ate breakfast with the family, *farinha de mandioca* – dried, cooked cassava which looked a little like couscous. Dinori was worried that we would get lost on the road to Xique Xique and insisted he and his youngest son, Daniel, accompany us by motorbike. It was lucky they did, as for much of the journey the road was a sandy track that split every few hundred metres during the two hours it took to reach town.

Alone again, we were now making a beeline for Salvador, over 600 kilometres away. The push was on to reach the Brazilian coast, but a miserable headwind had other ideas. We were reduced to a pathetic ten kilometres per hour as we fought the strong gusts, and managed just 40 more kilometres that afternoon to a petrol station *pousada* by the side of the road.

To avoid the same thing happening, the next morning we began a new routine. Our alarm clock would go off at five am, and we would be on the road 30 minutes before sunrise in an attempt to beat the worst of the heat and wind. It was also a ploy to finish early, so we could catch some of the Euros games which were being shown on television, seemingly to the general disinterest of Brazilians. We covered a wet and windy 70 kilometres in time to watch England earn a draw with France. By the signs of things we wouldn't be setting the competition on fire this year, but it was good entertainment while Paddy fixed a slow puncture that had been bugging us for days.

The next morning was another early start, but we needn't have worried about the sun as it never appeared. In fact, much to our amusement, the locals were wearing woolly hats. The reason for this became clear a few hours later, when we found ourselves crawling up some seriously steep slopes. By the time we had reached the town of *Morro do Chapeu,* the Hill's Hat, we were over 1,000 metres high and wearing fleecy tops.

The hilly terrain continued as we rode along the edge of the *Chapada Diamantina National Park*, an area of steep cliffs and valleys until, a week after leaving Xique Xique, we rolled down from the hills into the cobbled streets of Säo Felix. Across the Rio

Paraguaçu sat the old town of Cachoeira, now a popular tourist destination, serving expensive plates of *farinha de mandioca.* Today, however, the action was in Säo Felix where crowds of cowboys were arriving on horseback for a party outside the old Dannemann cigar factory. Horses stood roped to lamp posts and phone boxes, and as we rode out of town back into the hills, more were rushing to the party, their riders urging their mounts on.

The horses were far better suited to the hilly terrain than our heavy bikes as we followed the river towards the coast. After a few more days of menacing climbs and a good amount of pushing, we were finally rewarded with a view that I had dreamt of over the past few weeks; the outline of the Ihla de Itaparica, surrounded by the Atlantic Ocean.

The island was a popular escape for Brazilians, who came to enjoy the quiet beaches and leisure resorts, but for us it was an entry point to the city of Salvador. We rode along with big, wide smiles as we looked out at the Atlantic Ocean. Gone were the murky brown waters we had seen in the Guianas; here it sparkled blue, just as, almost a year earlier, we had left it further down the coast.

We had missed the last ferry across the bay for the day, so chose to celebrate reaching the Atlantic with *caipirinhas* in a restaurant overlooking the port. Three cocktails each was perhaps too many, as they were insanely strong and we quickly became very drunk. Dehydrated, pissed and with tired limbs, Paddy's legs started to cramp up halfway through the meal and he ended up flat on his back on the restaurant floor groaning, while I tried to stretch his muscles out at the same time as laughing hysterically. Fortunately, the staff found it as amusing as me.

This was it; we had made it around South America back to the Brazilian coast. Rio de Janeiro was now straightforward to navigate to, we just needed to keep the ocean on our left hand side, a fact that excited and terrified me in equal measure. It would be amazing to complete the journey, to make it all the way around, but at the same time, it would mean our journey would come to an end. I wasn't ready to resume a conventional life, but fortunately the next morning we would be in Salvador, a city that was anything but ordinary.

20. Brazil: the coast

The balaclava hid his face from view. Over his chest he wore a padded black vest and around his thighs were strapped holstered pistols, while he grasped a long black machine gun that pointed down the road, towards me. He was not alone. As I rounded the corner, more armed men came running forwards, sticking close to the wall to avoid detection.

Their hope to stay hidden was futile; the circus of cameramen and reporters following behind must surely have given the policemen away. The group's feet slapped heavily on the tarmac as they sprinted to a hole in the wall, through which they all climbed in search of their prey.

It felt as if we had arrived in a different Brazil. The day before, we had dodged a stray horse in a small village, now we were side-stepping armed policemen. We were back on the Brazilian coast, and already it seemed very different to the interior we had spent the past month cycling through.

Salvador de Bahia, with its outdoor festivities and carnival, was Brazil's 'capital of happiness', and the city was in party mood as we explored the old streets of the *Pelourinho* district with our Couchsurfing host, José. The three of us squeezed against a wall to pass a group of young drummers, smashing out rhythmic beats as they pounded the narrow cobbled streets.

We joined the thronging crowd towards the top of a wide flight of steps, looking down on a makeshift stage squeezed between buildings painted in pastel shades of yellow, green and pink. A single street lamp lit the crowd of gyrating hips and bouncing feet that moved to the samba beat of the band. It was hard not to be caught up in the atmosphere, invigorated by the lead singer dressed in a white robe and blue turban, a trumpet in one hand and a glass of red wine in the other.

It was a Tuesday, the best night for going out in Salvador, José's friends told us over dinner, because the place was packed with locals rather than tourists. José was Spanish, living and working in the city, and his friends were fellow-Spaniards, French, German, Portuguese and Brazilian, all conversing in English. The group next headed to a samba club, where a band played with effortless swagger and Brazilians danced with expertise. This was a place for the pros and we watched safely from the side-lines, enjoying our reintroduction to life on the Brazilian coast.

The party atmosphere was still going the next day, when we returned to view the sights by daylight. A group of young men and women, wearing white robes, were practising the complex moves of the *capoeira* in the main square. The dance was developed in Brazil by African slaves keen to practise defending themselves in case they should escape. As it was dangerous for a slave to be discovered practising aggressive moves, they were disguised as a dance performed to beat-filled music. With sweeps, low moves, cartwheels and high kicks, the dancing was mesmerising.

Slaves from across the Atlantic Ocean started arriving in Brazil in the 16th century, and were put to work on sugar cane plantations. By 1600 there may have been between 13,000 and 15,000 black slaves in the country, about 70 per cent of the labour force on the plantations. In the north-east, slaves made up half of the overall population, or two-thirds in sugar growing areas. The import of African slaves created a new demographic in the country, with inter-race relationships producing children of mixed ethnic heritage. The effects of this, coupled with the arrival of immigrants from around the globe, live on today in Brazil's diverse ethnic population.

Portuguese colonial influence shone through as we wandered around *Pelourinho,* where the main square was covered in colourful bunting that criss-crossed above the cobbles. Salvador was preparing for the annual São João festival, a tradition brought over by Portuguese settlers. In Europe the annual June celebrations marked midsummer, but the tradition had changed to celebrate the start of the Brazilian winter. The festivities were just gearing up; the actual São João day was 24 June, when the streets would be crammed with revellers.

We left the old streets to explore more of the city, heading down to the waterfront and a *Havaiana* store. Paddy had offered to treat me to a new pair of flip flops from the famous Brazilian store. Opened in the early 1960s by a Scotsman, the firm was the first to mass produce the sturdy sandals from rubber, and they were an instant hit in Brazil, where even poor people could afford them.

When the time came to leave, we gave José our hammocks, as we hadn't used them since the Amazon. In truth, we hadn't slept in the tent much recently, either. With the end in sight, and the realisation that our budget would last until Rio de Janeiro, we had become, not extravagant, but less careful than earlier in the trip. There would be time for counting the pennies when we were back earning in London.

We left Salvador not by road, but on a gigantic catamaran to the nearby island of Morro de São Paulo, where we spent a few days relaxing on white sandy beaches under the shade of palm trees. When we finally tore ourselves away, we headed back to the mainland and enjoyed a few days of easy cycling over flat terrain. On reaching the town of Camamu, however, the road got ridiculously steep, and our enthusiasm for being in the saddle rapidly diminished. Paddy's knee hurt and my back ached, which was all it took for us to agree to take another day off in the surfer town of Itacaré.

Packed with trendy *pousadas*, nice restaurants and bars, and with more palm tree-lined beaches, we quickly settled in. The motivation for getting moving again was slim. A Chilean cyclist we met who was heading north from Rio told us the hills got worse rather than better. Plus, we had less than 1,500 kilometres left to cycle. It was a simple fact that the sooner we got moving, the sooner the trip would end. By staying put, we could delay the inevitable.

In the end, when rain clouds settled over Itacaré's beaches, we could no longer justify staying. It was wet when we set off and the weather stayed much like that for several days.

> ***Diary, 29 June 2012*** - *A day of firsts – amazing that can still happen so far along. It was the first day it rained from us getting up to going to bed. There was no break in the weather at all. We had our full waterproofs on from start to finish. In that regard, it was one of the most miserable days of the entire trip. Grey sky and constant rain in the face. At lunch we bought*

pastels and watched people sheltering, waiting for it to end – they must still be there. We only stopped once on the road, to celebrate hitting 20,000 kilometres. Quite an achievement! It seems an incomprehensible number to us.

It was still raining when, in the dark, we finally pulled into the town of Canavieiras on the banks of the Rio Salsa. A woman opened the door of her *pousada* and kindly took us in even though we were dripping with water. I hurried to hang our clothes in the bathroom to dry, while Paddy locked the bikes in the back yard. Busy with our wet and muddy things, I paid little attention to what he was doing until I heard dogs barking and lots of shouting.

Paddy: *In my rush to get out of the wind and rain, I'd left our water bottles on the bike frames. I only realised when I got to the door of our room, and being tired, I decided rather than going all the way downstairs and through the garage, I would take a shortcut down the fire escape which came out into the yard.*

At the bottom of the stairs I climbed over the small gate that was locked. It was dark, the landlady must have turned the lights off when I headed upstairs, so I fumbled around trying to find the switch to see where I was going. It was at that point that I heard galloping legs, followed by two loud barks.

Instinctively, I dashed back to the fire escape and jumped over the gate just as the kitchen door opened and a voice shouted the dogs back. The landlady flicked the light on and from the top of the stairs I could see two black Rottweilers prowling around below. I was shaking in shock, and only then realised that one of them had taken a good nip at my Achilles. The teeth marks were visible but luckily no blood was drawn.

The only feasible way out of Canavieiras was by boat as the road took a huge diversion inland, weaving around mangrove swamps and rivers. Fortunately, it was a regular journey for locals, and we joined a small crowd down by the riverside, waiting for the daily departure of a convoy of wooden canoe-shaped boats. We set off at 8.40 am to catch the incoming tide. Our bikes were crammed into the nose of the boat with the handlebars hanging over the side, centimetres above the water level, while we sat in the middle, and the skipper at the back, steering the motor. We followed the river into a wide bay that opened to the Atlantic, but the boat swung into the mangrove forest before we reached the ocean.

When the driver slowed down to navigate the narrow channels, we could see deep into the forest. It looked like a magical world, with interlacing, knobbly roots creeping up from the murky brown water. The forests changed shape constantly, making navigation difficult, and at times we had to abandon the motor for a paddle as the water was so low. Our driver, however, knew the forest well and within two hours we pulled up in Belmonte and were back on our bikes continuing south.

The next afternoon, we rode into the resort of Porto Seguro. This whole strip of coastline was popular with Brazilian and Argentinian tourists. Parts of it were pretty, but we'd been spoilt with untouched beauty spots, and we rode quickly past the gigantic hotels dominating the coastline and a main street called *Passarela do Alcool*, or the *Alcohol Catwalk*.

From the quieter spot of Arrial d'Ajuda, it was an easy day climbing along the ridge of a fertile green valley. We managed only 70 kilometres, however, because of punctures in my back tyre. One was a total blow out when I was rolling downhill. It went flat fast and the bike starting tilting as if to fall over. If I applied the brakes it got worse, but I managed to bounce onto the verge, which brought the bike to a stop. The culprit was a big piece of metal that had buried into the tyre. Our Marathon Schwalbe tyres were the same ones we left Rio de Janeiro with, and after 20,000 kilometres they were thinning; we hoped they would last just a few more weeks to make it to the end.

Our route now took us away from the coast, south along the BR-101 highway, where we spotted our first road sign pointing towards Rio de Janeiro.

Diary, 3 July 2012 *- I think because returning to Rio has always been the target, it won't be that bad to arrive. It's being back in London that terrifies me. About a week after we get back we go to a leaving party, which is fancy dress. The effort of that seems bizarre from here. I don't want to get back into artificial fun – having to find things to do because everything else is dull.*

The BR-101 didn't start off too badly considering it was

Brazil's second busiest highway – it was the same road we had ridden along south out of Rio in the beginning. The stretch after Eunapolis was busy with traffic, but we had a hard shoulder to ourselves, friendly gradients and beautiful scenery to distract us. In the afternoon, we finally reached the odd-shaped mountains that had sat on the horizon for days. They looked like huge stones stood on their ends, with trees growing up to their peaks, almost like smaller version of Pão de Açúcar in Rio.

The next day the hard shoulder disappeared, leaving us fighting for the road. There was no space for drivers to overtake, but that didn't mean they slowed to pass, and several times I was pushed off the road by the whoosh of air from a passing car. It wasn't just me who hated it; at one point I turned around to see Paddy stood in the long grass, banging his handlebars in rage and despair. At lunch, we got chatting to a woman who said the road was notorious for accidents and that many truck drivers took drugs to stay awake. She reckoned they were so strung out that they probably didn't see us as they passed, which did nothing for my confidence. We had not come this far to be knocked off and killed now. The decision to take a bus the short distance to Linhares, where the quieter coastal road restarted, was one of the easiest of the entire trip.

Leaving Linhares, the only real traffic was Sunday cyclists out for a ride. One, Alessandro, hung back to cycle with us as we made our way towards the beachfront village of Regencia. A doctor, he spoke perfect English, and chatted to Paddy about all things bike related, while I pootled happily behind, taking in the view of forests and pastures that dominated the flat landscape.

Alessandro turned back when the tarmac ended, and we continued on, fighting into the wind as we turned south at the coast. At one point the trees in the fir forests were swaying so dramatically that I wondered if they might snap above our heads. We took it in turns to ride first, giving the other a little shelter from the wind, which persisted over the next few days as we crossed into the state of Rio de Janeiro.

We were riding along the coast on a single-lane road, quiet apart from trucks carrying sugar cane that wafted hot, sweet air as they passed. It was hilly and the scenery was reminiscent of

Normandy, with steep cliffs rising from the beach and rolling hills behind. The fields, however, were packed with spiky plants, on top of which grew plump pineapples. Around here, agriculture and industry ruled, meaning busy main roads with heavy vehicles and not the most entertaining scenery. So when the opportunity arose to take a short cut through a national park, we took it.

Several hours later, staring straight at the ocean, we began to think we might have taken a wrong turn. As we stood studying our map, a beach shack owner wandered over to us. Laughing heartily at our mistake, he told us we were 50 kilometres by road to Macaé, which was further than when we started. Alternatively, he said, it was possible to cycle along the beach, which was 18 kilometres.

Our heavy bikes would be a hindrance to cycling along the sand, but we were too lazy to retrace our steps along the road, and after downing bottles of cold soda, we set off pushing. We were following a narrow strip of sand between the ocean and an inland lake, and as the tide began to rise, I wondered if it would come in high enough to wash us away. I found it amusing we had got into the same situation as the day we arrived in Mencora in Peru, or at least I did until I realised this time there would be no pickup to rescue us.

Our average speed was a painstaking three kilometres per hour when moving, but we stopped regularly to catch our breath, meaning our progress was agonisingly slow. Pushing through thick, soft sand caused my calves and thighs to burn, so when we found a dirt trail heading inland from the beach, even though we had no idea where it headed, we decided to take it. It was mid-afternoon, we hadn't eaten, were short on water, and I was so exhausted that everything had become deliriously hilarious. When, after an hour of riding along the track, a huge Alsatian jumped out of a hedge, something inside me flipped, I shouted and waved my arms so wildly that the dog turned and fled. After composing myself, I looked ahead to see Paddy in the distance, knelt on the floor, hugging the ground; he had found tarmac.

At the main road, we discovered a restaurant still serving lunch. When the waiter told us that we were still 25 kilometres from Macaé, we burst into laughter. The entire morning's efforts had brought us almost no closer than when we set off hours earlier. During this time, however, we had passed through the 21,000 kilometre mark for the trip. It was our final thousand kilometre mark of our time in South America; we had less than 300 kilometres to ride to Rio de Janeiro.

The next day we reached Rio das Ostras to meet José, our final Warmshowers host. He had organised an interview with a local television station, which we did in the front garden while his bemused mum watched from the lounge. José had to explain the trip to the journalists, our Portuguese still wasn't up to a conversation, but we had mastered riding slowly while the cameraman got shots of our bikes.

After the reporters left, José showed us around town. The main highway ran one street back from the beachfront and was lined with stores that, even in the evening, were packed with people busy shopping for groceries, clothes and televisions. We had noticed many Brazilians seemed to have smart phones, tablets and huge television screens, but we couldn't work out how everybody afforded them. José explained most people couldn't; the country had a big problem with credit.

In the past decade more than 30 million Brazilians had escaped from poverty, creating an expanding middle class keen to spend on credit cards. In the late 2000s, however, the reality of buying on credit had hit as people struggled to pay off their debts. Many, like José, saw the country's experience as a reason to no longer buy on cards, but low unemployment and high wage growth meant that for many middle-class Brazilians, expensive consumer goods were increasingly more affordable anyway.

Rio was so close now that, over the next few days we took our time, stopping off at some of the final hotspots the coast had to offer. From the beachfront resorts, the road followed a thin strip of sand between the sea and a series of quiet lakes, and we stopped before the greater Rio de Janeiro area at a *pousada* next to the beach, ditching the bikes for a swim in the rough, cold Atlantic. As I sat on the beach, watching shellfish burying into the wet sand, I struggled to believe the next day would be our last full one on the road.

I felt a bit sick – the kind of queasy I used to feel before an exam.

It was the last morning we would set out not knowing where we would sleep that night. It was the last time we would spend the whole day in the saddle, experiencing new sights, smells and people; tomorrow, we would be back on old, familiar ground. If I didn't think about any of that, then I was fine, but it was hard to stop my mind drifting. "If I stop pedalling," I considered, "then we won't ever arrive in Rio."

The day started by us getting lost, again. So insistent were we to stick to the beach road that we didn't notice when it stopped running parallel to the main road. We ended up pushing through thick grass and under a barbed wire fence to correct ourselves. It was our final dirt road of the trip, by lunchtime we had picked up the main road we would follow all the way into Niteroi.

The outskirts of the city built up throughout the afternoon as we pedalled along the busy road, dirt thrown up by heavy traffic coating our sweaty skin. Before I realised it, the heart of the city was upon us, merging seamlessly with the suburbs. As the main road swept downhill gently towards the edge of the bay, we followed, knowing that across the other side sat Rio de Janeiro.

We stopped a few streets back from the water's edge, not quite prepared for our first view in 15 months of the city from where our trip began. Instead, we carried on as if this was just a normal day in the saddle, and set about finding somewhere to spend the night. Niteroi, it turned out, was an extremely expensive place to stay, and the only affordable place we could find was a grotty love motel, outside of which sat two burnt cars. As well as a bed, the first room we were shown had a masochistic chair in the shape of an octopus, and on the wall, a graphic poster of the ways couples could use it for their pleasure. Feeling slightly nauseous as the thought of how many bare buttocks might have sat on that seat, we opted for another room with a bog-standard bed.

There was little love in our room that night. We both felt differently about how we should spend the last day riding into Rio. I felt it was a private moment to share between the two of us, while Paddy was keen to be filmed by a national television crew. A family contact had put us in touch with the British Consulate in Rio, and the team there had organised media interviews on Ipanema Beach. It turned out the arrangements were so far along that it was too late to back out.

I was grumpy about having to go along with the plan, but my bad mood was only partially about that. My emotions were all over the place. Partly, I was excited about being at the end of the trip; it was a great achievement to have made it all the way around South American by bike. Yet, at the same time, I was still having fun and wasn't ready for it to end.

Paddy still hadn't learnt which bag we kept the cake in. We hadn't yet worked out how to explode the firecrackers we bought during the Säo Joäo festival, which we had planned to throw at chasing dogs. I still hadn't mastered how to light the stove, or managed to beat Paddy's best speed of the trip, 67 kilometres per hour. But it seemed time, and the road to Ipanema, had both run out.

After 15 amazing months on the road, we spent our final night on the road in a seedy love motel, barely talking. I sat on the edge of the plastic mattress, stirring the tomato sauce into our pasta, while Paddy updated our map of South America to show our progress over the past few weeks; a gigantic black loop now covered the chart. The door was barricaded by our bikes, off which hung the clothes I had hand-washed in the sink, in an attempt to remove the worst of the sweat and grime, ready for our TV appearance the next morning.

It was a restless sleep; we were kept awake by the banging of doors from the frequent arrivals and departures of courting couples. We were perhaps the only people in the entire establishment not having sex.

21. Ipanema Turtles

"Do you mind if I call you *Tartarugas de Ipanema*?" Tino asked. "Only I saw the picture of you with the giant turtle in French Guiana, and it occurred to me that you are like them. They travel a very long way and return to the beach where they started, just like you with Ipanema!"

Tino Marcos was a reporter for the evening news programme on the channel TV Globo – the show was the Brazilian equivalent of the BBC's 10 o'clock news. He attracted a big crowd as we stood chatting on the Ipanema promenade, and he kept popping off to sign autographs, while we rode along the beachfront for the cameras.

TV Globo was the second television company we had met that morning. The first, from SportTV – the equivalent of Sky Sports – had come to film us getting on the ferry in Niteroi. Their reporter, Rodrigo, had countless questions as we crossed the bay, which distracted me from the symbolism of the journey, and how, many months earlier I had worried that Paddy would insist on cycling across the bridge that spans the bay, connecting the two cities.

On the other side, in Rio, we were met by a driver at the ferry port, familiar from before. Rodrigo and the cameraman climbed into the back of the van, swinging the back doors open so they could film us on the move. For 20 minutes we found ourselves frantically pedalling along an oddly quiet highway, trying to keep up as they zoomed along at 30 kilometres an hour, the cameraman hanging out the back, Tour de France style.

When they'd got their shots, we moved onto the cycle lanes that hugged the sweeping bays and landscaped gardens, with the Cristo Redentor statue emerging above us as the early morning clouds burnt off. The road cut around the back of Pão de Açúcar, through a long, cool tunnel, and before long, we found ourselves on familiar red cycle lanes running the length of the packed Copacabana Beach.

In spite of my concerns about meeting the television crews,

the morning was turning out to be fun and a little surreal. We couldn't believe that national television channels had deemed us interesting enough to send camera crews along to film, and that they were taking the job seriously. I wondered if they had confused us with somebody important; we were just two Joe Bloggs who had decided to "play out on our bikes", in the words of my mum.

Away from the camera lens, it felt nice to have some time to ourselves as we cycled along Copacabana, wide smiles plastered across our faces. For the moment I wasn't thinking about the trip coming to an end, I was too caught up in the sense of achievement and excitement I felt. We rode past surfers braving the choppy waters and the stall where we had drunk cold coconuts on our first day in Rio, until we reached the end of the sand where the cycle lane ran out. From there we only had to ride around the headland onto the next crescent shaped beach: Ipanema.

We were met at the most easterly end of the beach by a group of British Consul officials, including the Consul-General, the TV Globo television team, and a few print journalists – Rodrigo and the SportTV team arrived a little after us, having got stuck in the Rio traffic. In our minds, our official start/finish point was the other end of the beach, close to the *favela* that we'd had to push our bikes past on the first day. We would head there after the interviews, which meant we could both do the media work and enjoy the final arrival together privately.

The Consul had brought T-shirts for us, emblazoned with the slogan 'Sport Is Great (Britain)', they looked much smarter than our dirty tops that we quickly covered up. A crowd of tourists gathered around as we posed for photographs, chatted to English-speaking reporters and rode along the beach with cameras strapped to our handlebars for footage for SportTV. We were slightly embarrassed by all the attention from the crowd; it wasn't as if we had broken any world records. So when the reporters started to pack up their gear and headed off to edit their footage, we got back into the saddle, Paddy held a clenched fist high and we rode off to lots of clapping. We had just four kilometres left of our journey around South America.

My thoughts turned to how I felt being back on the same cycle lane we had wobbled along on our very first day, unaccustomed then to the weight of the heavy bikes. The beach looked just as we had left it; a sandy white stretch lined with sunbathers, red parasols and volleyball nets. I recognised the stall where we drank the nerve reducing, but headache inducing, *caipirinhas* the night before we left Rio.

It was hard to place my emotions. I simply couldn't believe we had made it back to the start, it all seemed too surreal. I was proud of us, I knew that, and the smile spread across my face showed it. Inside, though, I felt a little numb. I had spent so long thinking about finishing, but now it was real. After 14 months and 12 days on the road, 13 countries and 21,299 kilometres, we pedalled up to the end of Ipanema Beach, where our wheels came to a final stop.

Paddy: *Balancing the bikes against each other, pointing towards the ocean, I wrapped our camera tripod around a lamp post and pressed record. This was a special moment and I wanted to capture how we looked – a bit shell-shocked, tired, excited and elated all at the same time.*

To celebrate the occasion, I pulled a bottle of Brazilian sparkling wine out of my pannier and started over-zealously spraying Laura Formula One-style much to the bemusement of passing walkers. Without a word, and after several gulps of cold bubbly, Laura did two things I have rarely seen her do; first, she ran; second, she jumped into the sea. I cracked up at the sight of her bobbing in the ocean – normally I have to throw her in because she has an irrational fear of sharks!

Surveying the scene across the beach, we didn't speak much to each other – it was hard to know what to say. In real terms, we had just stopped cycling at the end of a beach, in much the same way we had finished each day for the last 15 months. Aside from the fancy wine and spontaneous swimming, I didn't feel any different. On television over the following weeks, I saw victorious Olympic athletes have similar reactions, saying they couldn't quite believe what they had achieved. Everything they had done for the past few years had been gearing up to that moment and, when it finally happened, they were at a loss for words.

While I wouldn't rate our achievement anywhere near the scale of those of the Farahs, Ainslies or Trotts of this world, I like to think we shared the same feeling. It would take a long time to sink in that we had just ridden around the whole of South America. We might not have a gold medal, but we had a whole load of memories, new friends and strong leg muscles to show for it.

22. After the wheels stopped rolling

Our taxi driver was eyeing me quizzically in his rear-view mirror. We were heading to the airport for our flight home, and I was trying to explain in a mix of Portuguese and English what we had been doing in Brazil.

"Nós - todos da América do Sul de bicicleta," I said, rolling my hands in a pedalling motion to emphasise the "by bike" part.

Slowly, a look of recognition washed over his face, "You were on television," he said.

He wasn't the only person to recognise us after the footage of us arriving on Ipanema Beach was broadcast on national TV. Earlier that day, we were stopped on the metro by a couple who congratulated us on our achievement, and while walking along the street, a driver tooted and hung out of his window shouting excitedly, "ciclistas, ciclistas!" We really hadn't thought the news editors would deem us worthy to put on their programme, and expected the piece would be cut. Certainly, we didn't expect it to go out on national television to be watched by millions of Brazilians, and we had been out for dinner when it aired. Surprised by the attention, we responded to our 'fans' with fist pumps and wide smiles.

It wasn't just *Cariocas* who had seen us. We received emails from people we had met across Brazil, taken aback by our appearance on their national news programme. "You made it!" said the email from Fabio in Foz do Iguaçu, while our Brazilian friends as far away as Teresina, Belém and Salvador also got in contact.

Manfred, the German gardener we met on the very first day we left Rio, had spotted our television appearance too, and he invited us over for dinner to hear about the trip. It was strange to think back; moments like cycling through Argentina in the snow, or struggling at altitude in Bolivia felt like they had happened a lifetime ago already. 15 months was a long time to spend on the road and there were so many memories that it was hard to recall them all at once.

The image I'd had of South America before we set out was far removed from the place we discovered on the bikes. I remembered how paranoid I was in the beginning that we would be attacked by bandits or kidnapped by drug traffickers. I felt stupid now at how naive I had been, and how I had fallen for stereotypes and scare mongering about the continent.

Thanks to frequent warnings from locals in places like Venezuela, I never totally stopped worrying. However, my overriding memory is of all the strangers who went out of their way to help us on our journey. There were the truck drivers who threw us juicy oranges as we cycled through the Atacama Desert; the Brazilian family in the middle of nowhere who insisted on giving us their bedroom when we had nowhere to sleep; and the Colombian road cyclists who diverted their training ride to guide us through their city.

Some of the stereotypes about South Americans were undeniably true, like the women being gorgeous and, seemingly, everybody can dance. Yet, the most striking thing about the people we met as we made our way around on the continent, was that on the beaches of Rio, in the Andean mountains and the Guyanese jungle, we were all so similar. Like us they prioritised their families, worried about money and jobs, dreamt of visiting new places and enjoyed meeting new people. The language barrier didn't stop us conversing with people with whom we shared no common language – even in Suriname, where people spoke Dutch and Hindi, we communicated just fine with people, using a mixture of languages and hand gestures.

The continent was packed with rainforest and mountains, but we also discovered ancient civilisations, Jurassic lands, deserts and newly-created reservoirs where half submerged bus stops peaked out of the water. We saw snakes, spiders and wild sloths, but fortunately no jaguars. The highest temperature we cycled in was 40 degree Celsius, but actually South America can be cold, really cold, as we discovered when we got snowed-in climbing over the Andes.

South America is a crazy, passionate, beautiful continent. It is a place of extreme politics, history and culture, and of harsh, remote and breath-taking scenery. When we left Ipanema I genuinely couldn't imagine making it all the way around. Now, drinking cocktails on the sand, it didn't seem that big a deal to us that we had just ridden 21,299 kilometres around the continent that we had come to know and love. The idea of taking 15 months off from normal life to ride our bikes no longer felt so crazy either. Cycling through rainforests, running police checkpoints, hopping over to the Caribbean to get married, camping in the desert and sharing a room with a tarantula, all seemed pretty normal to me now.

The looks the England football manager, Roy Hodgson, and his three colleagues were giving me, suggested they disagreed about how normal it had all been. By now they had lowered their laptops and wanted to know why we stayed in the room with a poisonous spider rather than moving, or killing it. When I explained that the tarantula had lived there and that there was a 50 per cent chance it wouldn't have deadly venom, they looked at me as if I had lost the plot.

Fortunately, sat in the airport lounge, we were able to explain we'd been met at the end of the trip by the Consul-General. It so happened, that, as part of their scoping trip for places to stay for the 2014 Football World Cup, they had met with the same team from the Consulate. After mentioning a few familiar names they seemed to relax, realising that they weren't sat next to two nutcases.

We spent 30 minutes talking to them and sharing beers, as we waited to board our plane. They had a host of questions about where we had been, and as we talked, I began to think that perhaps the trip was more of an achievement than I was currently giving ourselves credit for.

"So, what's next?" asked Roy Hodgson as we stood up to leave. "Do you think you'll write a book?"

"Perhaps," I answered, "but I need to find a job first, unfortunately!"

"Well, good luck. If you wrote a book, I'd read it," he replied, before disappearing up to the front of the airplane, leaving us to sneak into the back where we could stop pretending to be cool.

"Roy Hodgson got me a beer!" screeched Paddy. It was a surreal end to a bonkers, fantastic and awesome 15 months.

Four weeks after returning to London, on a scorching hot August day, 100 of our friends and family joined us on an open-top boat cruise along the River Thames to celebrate our marriage. The boat was decorated in traditional white bunting, and scattered around were photographs from South America, while Paddy's contribution to the decorations was to position the bikes at the bow of the boat for everybody to admire. It was our wedding reception, welcome home party and celebration of the trip in one fantastic evening. Being home among friends and family was a great feeling.

As the boat made its way under Tower Bridge, the five Olympic rings hanging above the bridge's walkway cast a brief shadow onto the boat. We had watched the opening ceremony in Rio de Janeiro airport before we bumped into Roy Hodgson, and over the next few weeks visited the Olympic Park to watch some of the events taking place. We also ventured down to Richmond to cheer on Bradley Wiggins as he won a gold medal in the Olympic time trial, convincing ourselves that it was more important to show solidarity with a 'fellow cyclist' than to start looking for jobs.

Contrary to the concerns of our families, however, we were both back in employment within three months of arriving back in London, far faster than we had imagined. Paddy had been having fun spending his days laying out a mammoth photograph album from the trip, and, less enjoyably, scrubbing the bikes clean. Before his first day back in the City of London, he headed to the hairdressers to tame his wild locks, and with that the return to normal life was complete.

Readjusting hasn't been that bad though. Our time has been taken up meeting old friends and, in many cases, their new babies. The last two summers have passed in a blur of weddings, some as far away as Western Australia, which of course required a long holiday to explore, sometimes by bike. There have been family gatherings and new nieces, all of which we are glad to have been here for.

However, perhaps the return to normal life has been made easier by knowing that we already have plans for our next adventure. This time around we're planning something a little easier on the legs; a move to San Francisco, California, with Paddy's new job and a baby that we are excitedly looking forward to welcoming later this year.

It's an opportunity for both of us to take on new challenges in terms of our careers, to meet new people, make friends and discover a different part of the world. We're looking forward to having the beach and mountains close by, to sun in the summer and the opportunities that living on the west coast of the US will give us to explore northern and Central America. It's also an awful lot closer when we want to head back to South America to catch up with some of the great people we met there during our 15 months on the road.

After all, we're Ipanema Turtles, it's guaranteed that we'll be back. I know that now.

Picture selection

Top - Visiting the Rochina Favela, Rio de Janeiro. *Bottom* - Paddy after he lost his pannier in Paraguay, wearing a child's raincoat that made him look like this statue.

Top - Sharing red wine with Juan and Noemi who invited us to stay at their home in the north of Argentina. *Bottom* - Disagreeing with the Argentinians about who owns the Falklands Islands.

Top - Celebrating riding 5,000 kilometres from Rio de Janeiro, in the beautiful Uspallata Valley, Argentina. *Bottom* - Cycling up through the snow towards Chile. We didn't get much further before we discovered the road had been closed – we were so close to the border.

Top - A perfect campsite in the Atacama Desert, Chile.

Bottom - Paddy decided we should 'have an adventure' cycling across this salt plain, which ended with us having to ride along the railway line when the salt turned to mush.

Top - Riding across the bumpy surface of the Salar de Uyuni in Bolivia.

Bottom - With Lucho outside his *casa de ciclista* in Trujillo, Peru.

Top - Stuck in the sand on our way to Mancora, Peru. The track had completely disappeared and we were rescued by the pickup once Paddy had helped dig it out.

Bottom - Taking an impromptu part in a cycle demonstration in Pasaje, Ecuador.

Top - Paddy with the team he played goalkeeper for in Colombia, during a rain break.

Bottom - Clean and tidy for our wedding in Barbados.

Top - Paddy giving a radio interview underneath a poster of President Hugo Chávez in Aragua de Barcelona, Venezuela. *Bottom* - Stuck in the mud making our way along 'The Trail' from Linden to Lethem in Guyana.

Top - Exploring Paramaribo, Suriname. *Bottom* - We discovered this amazing giant leatherback turtle on a beach close to Cayenne, French Guiana. She was laying her eggs – an absolutely incredible thing to see.

Top - Struggling with the heat on the way to Teresina in northern Brazil. There was no shade on the road and we improvised with the tarp.
Bottom - Being cheered on by a group of school children as we made our way through the Brazilian interior.

Top - Paddy pushing his bike along the beach after our short cut went wrong. *Bottom* - We made it! Celebrating returning to Ipanema Beach where our trip had started 14 months and 12 days before. We had ridden 21,299 kilometres through 13 countries.

Acknowledgments

Thank you to everybody who read through the manuscript at various stages and offered feedback and comments – that's you guys: Brian, Christian, Grainne, Laura, Linda and Steph. I hope you like the finished product. Big thanks also go to Nicky for her fantastic work on the illustrations for the front cover, and to Matt for cleaning up my grammar. Thank you as well to Paddy's former employers Ark, particularly Ian and Nick, who sponsored our bikes for the trip – we named them 'Noah' and 'the Whale' after you. A special mention must go to everybody at home who supported us throughout the trip, especially our families who travelled to Barbados for our wedding.

Our trip around South America was made special by all the amazing people we met along the route. Thank you to all the brilliant Couchsurfers and Warmshowers hosts who welcomed us into their homes, even after they had seen the state of our dirty kit. As well, thanks to all those great people who we met along the road that spontaneously invited us to stay with them. Through you all, we learnt so much about your countries and your continent. Words can never express how grateful we are for your kindness, generosity and hospitality. You provided many of our favourite memories from South America.

But my biggest thanks has to be to Paddy, without whom I would never have attempted anything like this. I'm sorry I moaned about the cold, wind, hills and heat that I insisted would never end – you deserve a medal for putting up with me. Thank you for encouraging me over the mountains, looking after me when I got heat exhaustion and eating the vegetarian meals that I cooked, without complaint. Your navigation, planning and common sense got us all the way around South America in one piece. For that, and for many other reasons, I love you very much. Massive respect dude – you rock!

Author's Notes

Ipanema Turtles recounts the true, subjective experience of the 15 month cycle journey around South America that I made with my husband Patrick Mottram. The narrative is based on our diary accounts, blog posts and from personal memory, and is as accurate as personal bias and intellect allow. Real names have been used to describe people we met on route, unless we were asked not to name individuals. Descriptions of conversations have been paraphrased from memory.

We blog at **www.pedallingabout.com** about our various adventures by bike. You can read our blog posts from South America there and view photographs from the trip. You can also follows us on:

Facebook at **www.facebook.com/pedallingabout**

Twitter at **www.twitter.com/pedalling_about**

We really hope that you enjoyed reading this book.

If so, you can let everybody know by leaving a review at **www.amazon.co.uk** or **www.amazon.com**

You can read about our other adventures by bike at **www.pedallingabout.com**

Printed in Great Britain
by Amazon.co.uk, Ltd.,
Marston Gate.